THE STRENGTH TO CHANGE

PETER PUGH

THE STRENGTH TO CHANGE

TRANSFORMING A BUSINESS FOR THE 21ST CENTURY

PENGUIN BOOKS

PENGUIN BOOKS

Published by the Penguin Group
Penguin Books Ltd, 27 Wrights Lane, London W8 5TZ, England
Penguin Putnam Inc., 375 Hudson Street, New York, New York 10014, USA
Penguin Books Australia Ltd, Ringwood, Victoria, Australia
Penguin Books Canada Ltd, 10 Alcorn Avenue, Toronto, Ontario, Canada M4V 3B2
Penguin Books (NZ) Ltd, Private Bag 102902, NSMC, Auckland, New Zealand

Penguin Books Ltd, Registered Offices: Harmondsworth, Middlesex, England

First published in 1998
1 3 5 7 9 10 8 6 4 2

Printed in Great Britain by Clays Ltd, St Ives plc

A CIP catalogue record for this book is available from the British Library

ISBN 0–670–88049–3

Contents

	Foreword	7
	Introduction	9
	Dramatis Personae	11
1	They're going to publish	17
2	Among them were large-hearted and far-sighted men	37
3	Conversion is a high-risk strategy	56
4	We wanted to make it clear we didn't stand aloof	84
5	A unique opportunity	97
6	Stones were not left unturned	114
7	Unequivocal … the deal offered excellent value	128
8	One hurdle after another	138
9	Divide the work into manageable projects	155
10	A feeling of confidence in the new organisation	165
	Author's Note: Timetable	179
11	The sheer scale of it all	186
12	Something ought to be done!	205
13	The advisers	219
14	At the front	231
15	The great day is coming	236
16	A tidal wave of change	256
	Appendix	268
	Index	270

Foreword

Achieving successful change is a dominant management theme as the century ends. Even powerful external forces, like major marketplace shifts, often generate inadequate internal response, save in crisis. The Halifax Building Society faced no crisis. Yet its leadership acted decisively to enforce sweeping transformation by combining a large-scale merger with massive conversion from mutual status to quoted company.

The two went hand in hand. Mergers and conversion were already reshaping the building society sector and all financial services in a dynamic marketplace. The Halifax had absolutely no intention of being marooned in a sea of golden opportunities, of which merger with the Leeds was certainly one. To maintain its market leadership, moreover, the Halifax had to accept the challenge of conversion – on which, anyway, the Leeds insisted. But anybody who thinks that such decisions are easy, still less their implementation, will learn better from this enthralling, frank account.

The issues of merger and conversion were deeply pondered and debated over considerable time, with non-executive directors playing an important role, and the press (sometimes prescient, sometimes wildly off beam) acting as Greek chorus. Minds were changed and positions abandoned as analysis and intellect outweighed emotion. Nobody lost sight of the ultimate objective: to create a new organisation that could conquer the challenges of the new century.

Once the key decisions were taken, too, the Halifax rolled into action impressively to implement well-laid plans. As Peter Pugh tells so well, the organisation's 'can do' pragmatic prowess was demonstrated time and again as 'programme management' tackled merger and conversion – on the whole, brilliantly – by the modern method of breaking down formidable tasks into major components and manageable, discrete jobs, each entrusted to a team.

The Halifax's 'production led' culture differed materially from the somewhat freer and easier Leeds, with its well-exploited marketing awareness. The powers of '*Old Co.*' Halifax and Leeds proved highly complementary. The merged and quoted organisation, capitalised at £19 billion, is now seeking to draw on its combined talents to build a new century company. This valuable case study in effective transformation sets the stage for never-ending tests of the strength to change – and to win.

Robert Heller
26 May 1998

Introduction

By the early 1990s the building societies in Britain affected no less than 70 per cent of the population, and it was assumed that any move in interest rates and therefore mortgage interest rates affected everyone in the land. Therein lay the rub. Where was the future growth to come from? And how were the giants of the industry to keep others from encroaching and reducing their market share, or their margins, or both?

The answer was fresh fields, but this would require massive investment over a long period and only the very largest would be able to afford it. The Halifax Building Society was big – assets of £67 billion and profits approaching £900 million – but for this new game it was not big enough. The Halifax chairman, Jon Foulds, looked at the 1993 results of the Hong Kong and Shanghai Bank which showed profits of £2 billion and thought, 'supposing that muscle was turned on our industry?'.

It is not often that an author has the opportunity to observe a major change in the landscape of a country's economic environment and therefore to write a history as it happens. As the Halifax followed through on its strategy of growth, first by acquisition, and then by conversion to a public company, I enjoyed the privilege of talking to those who were making the huge transformation happen. And we should not be under any illusion about the size and significance of the change. The relatively cosy world of the building society movement was gone forever. By leaving its pond, where it was a very big fish and could do as it liked, and swimming out into the sea, where it was still sizeable but where there were plenty of others of similar stature, Halifax was making a giant dive into the unknown. Furthermore, it would have to live with the daily pressure of financial commentators questioning its every move or non-move.

One of the most impressive attributes of the Halifax is its realisation of the impact of its every action. With 20 million customers it knows that every move has to be thought through thoroughly. It has been very big for a long time and this stood it in good stead when it came to planning the logistics, first with the merger with the Leeds – the two societies have blended together more quickly than any other merger I have studied – and with the public flotation, in itself the biggest in history. As we shall see, the sheer size of the operation proved difficult for some advisers to grasp and lessons were learned in the area of robust contingency planning.

Fortunately, there were no disasters. The flotation was a great success and, as I write, the Halifax share price has moved to a new high, giving the company the ammunition for its next strategic move to prepare itself for the new century.

On a personal note, I would like to thank a number of people who have helped me research and write the book. I interviewed every Halifax and Leeds director, as well as most of the senior management, many of them several times. Without exception they all gave me as much time as I wanted, and this was during a period when they were all working seven days a week to complete the merger and prepare for flotation.

Jon Foulds was particularly keen that I should talk to everyone who he felt could make a contribution, thus making sure that a fair and rounded story was recorded.

My main conduit into the company was David Gilchrist, the company secretary and director of corporate affairs, and it's safe to say that the book would not have been completed or published without his contribution.

A company's advisers are never the best interviewees, perhaps because they fear offending a valued client. The exception was Andrew Peck of Linklaters who went beyond his duty of vetting the manuscript to eradicate defamation. He made many constructive suggestions.

Finally, I would like to thank Maureen Mortlock who word-processed six drafts of the book, Jeremy Cox who supervised the design and origination and who suggested the title, and Alastair Rolfe of Penguin, a sympathetic publisher.

Peter Pugh
29 May 1998

Dramatis Personae

Geoffrey Armitage was a non-executive director of Leeds from 1986 until 1995.

Judy Atchison was general manager, Market and Product Development at Leeds until August 1995, and was director of group marketing at Halifax. She left Halifax in March 1997.

Malcolm Barr was a non-executive director at Leeds from 1972 until 1995. He was president from 1979 until 1981 and president, then chairman from 1989 until 1995.

Mike Blackburn was chief executive of Leeds from 1987 and became chief executive of Halifax in August 1993.

Roger Boyes was finance director of Leeds and finance director and acting chief executive during 1994. Prior to the merger on 1 August 1995, he was appointed chief executive of Leeds and at the merger became group finance director of Halifax.

Howard Briggs was secretary at Leeds and is deputy company secretary at Halifax.

Lord Chadlington formerly Peter Gummer, has been a non-executive director at Halifax since 1994.

Chris Chadwick was commercial director at Leeds from 1989 until January 1995.

Roy Chapman has been a non-executive director of Halifax since 1994.

Tony Coleby has been a non-executive director of Halifax since 1994.

Nigel Colne has been a non-executive director of Halifax since 1992.

Derek Cook   was a non-executive director of Leeds from 1991 until 1995 and a non-executive director of Halifax from August 1995 until April 1998.

Mark Cornwall-Jones was a non-executive director of Halifax from 1980 until 1995.

James Crosby   joined Halifax in February 1994 as general manager of Halifax Financial Services and is now a main board director responsible for Financial Services and Insurance.

Valery Duggleby   was programme support manager in the Conversion Programme Office from September 1995 until August 1997.

Mike Ellis   was general manager, then managing director, Treasury and European Operations from 1994 until December 1996 and is now a main board director responsible for Banking & Savings, and Overseas Operations.

Duncan Ferguson   has been a non-executive director of Halifax since 1994.

Gren Folwell   was group finance director during 1994 and until July 1995. From August 1995 until December 1996 he was managing director, Building Society and is now deputy chief executive.

Jon Foulds   was appointed a non-executive director of Halifax in 1986 and became chairman in 1990.

David Gilchrist   was general manager then director of Corporate Affairs. He became group secretary in 1994. He is now company secretary and director of Corporate Affairs.

Ralph Hodge   was a non-executive director of Halifax from 1992 until April 1998.

Geoff Jackson   was general manager, Field Operations during 1994 and until August 1995 when he became director of Distribution. He is now managing director, HEAL.

David Jarratt was general manager, Human Resources at Leeds during 1994 and until August 1995 when he became head of Organisation and Redeployment at Halifax. He retired in November 1997.

Graham Johnston was group accountant, Financial Planning and Budgets until August 1995 when he became assistant general manager, Corporate Finance.

Chris Jowett was group solicitor during 1994 and currently has the same role.

John Kirkbright was controller, Group Market Development and Research during 1994 and until August 1995 when he became assistant general manager, Strategic Development and Research.

John King was a non-executive director at Leeds from 1991 until 1995.

Sir Timothy Kitson was a non-executive director of Leeds from 1983 until August 1995. At the merger he became a vice-chairman of Halifax Building Society until his retirement in June 1997.

Mike Lavender was an assistant general manager, Marketing Support Services during 1994 and is currently assistant general manager, Customer Communications.

David Lee was a non-executive director of Halifax from 1977 until 1994.

John Lee was general manager, Personnel during 1994 and was appointed to the main board that year. He is currently responsible for Group Personnel and Services.

Prue Leith was a non-executive director of Leeds from 1992 until 1995 and is currently a non-executive director of Halifax.

Gary Marsh has been assistant general manager, Group Corporate Affairs since 1994.

Paul Martin was general manager, Distribution at Leeds from September 1994 and until August 1995. At the merger he became general manager, Distribution. He is currently general manager, Group Strategy and Planning.

Donald McPherson has been an assistant secretary since 1994 and is currently responsible primarily for Shareholder Services.

John Miller was director of Information and Technology and executive director, Customer Operations at Leeds during 1994 and until August 1995 when he became Business Strategy and Operations director at Halifax. He is currently the main board director responsible for Housing and Technology.

John Morris was general manager, Finance at Leeds during 1994 and until August 1995 when he became general manager, Business Accounting at Halifax. He is currently general manager, Group Financial Management and Control.

Ann O'Brien was chief solicitor at Leeds during 1994 and until August 1995. She is currently deputy group solicitor at Halifax.

Joe Palmer was a non-executive director at Halifax from 1991 until 1993.

Ralph Pitman was executive information officer at Leeds during 1994 and until August 1995. He is currently head of Internal Communications at Halifax.

Philip Rogerson was a non-executive director of Leeds from 1994 until August 1995 when he became a non-executive director of Halifax.

Louis Sherwood has been a non-executive director of Halifax since 1997.

Dick Spelman was general manager, Marketing during 1994 and until August 1995 when he became director of Banking and Business Development. He is currently director of Distribution.

Bob Strachan   was a non-executive director of Leeds from 1986 until 1994.

Lord Swinton   was a non-executive director of Leeds from 1987 until 1994.

John Symons   was a non-executive director of Halifax from 1982 until 1995.

David Walkden   was assistant general manager, Commercial Lending during 1994. He became assistant general manager, Merger Programme Office (later, Conversion Programme Office) in December 1994 and is currently general manager, Mortgages.

Clive Whitaker   was manager, Corporate Project Office at Leeds during 1994 and became head of Group Planning in December 1994. He is currently head of Group Operational Risk at Halifax.

Sir James Whitaker was a non-executive director of Halifax from 1964 until 1994.

John Wood   has been a non-executive director of Halifax since 1986 and vice-chairman since 1991.

Charles Wycks   was head of Lending at Leeds during 1994 and until August 1995. At the merger he became responsible for mortgage products. He is currently head of Investor Relations at Halifax.

Arnold Ziff   was a non-executive director of Leeds from 1982 until 1995 and of Halifax from 1995 until 1997.

CHAPTER ONE

They're going to publish

All hell breaks loose
Being a plc will not alter our values
Yorkshire pudding
So far, so good
Opposition

All hell breaks loose

In the early evening of Thursday, 24 November 1994, David Gilchrist, group secretary at the Halifax Building Society, received a telephone call from John Willcock of *The Independent*.

Willcock told Gilchrist that he had received information from a 'reliable' source that the Halifax and Leeds building societies were going to merge and that the combined group would then abandon mutuality and convert to a plc. He was going to write the story. Did Mr Gilchrist have any comment?

Gilchrist did not have any comment except 'No comment' but he knew the game was up. Somehow, Willcock had got the story and that when it appeared in *The Independent* the next morning, 'No comment' would not be good enough.

There had been a number of speculative articles over the preceding months, though surprisingly few in view of the length and intensity of the negotiations and the number of meetings between the directors of the two societies. (It is a tribute to the integrity of all those in the know that there were not more leaks.) Neither board had been concerned about rumours of a merger. However, rumours of conversion were entirely different because the thought of societies floating on the stock

17

market could mean free share issues and so would bring rushes of speculative money into the societies.

Fortunately, a key group of the Halifax board members were in London for a dinner and were able to go into a huddle in the society's London flat in Jermyn Street. The conclusion was,

> '*The Independent* has got the story, they're going to publish, let's prepare ourselves for an announcement.'

Rachel Hirst, who had recently joined Shandwick specifically to handle the Halifax account, said later,

> 'Actually, it was a "no brain" sort of decision. We had to go live with this thing.'

The dinner took place at Boodles, where non-executive director, Mark Cornwall-Jones, who was a member, was hosting the evening which included some outside guests, Sir Geoffrey Mulcahy, executive chairman of Kingfisher, Sir Roger Gibbs, chairman of the Wellcome Trust and John Manser, group chief executive of Robert Fleming. It was a bizarre situation. The Halifax directors knew that this momentous announcement was about to be made, indeed was being printed in *The Independent* while they ate, and that they should be preparing themselves.

What they were having to do was make polite conversation and join in on a discussion about the future of financial services in Europe. Mulcahy was to say later, 'I wondered why Mike Blackburn said the same thing to me three times.' It must have been a great relief when the dinner was over and they could hurry back to Jermyn Street to make plans.

Meanwhile, the telephone lines from Jermyn Street had been busy. Gilchrist had stayed behind and had alerted all the key people in Halifax, in Leeds, at Shandwick, at Warburg and at Linklaters & Paines. Now the press announcement that everyone had agonised over for weeks had to be finalised and approved within hours. At 11 p.m., the first edition of the next day's newspapers were available and a purchase of *The Independent* at King's Cross confirmed that Willcock had not been bluffing. His opening paragraph said it all,

> 'Conversion of Halifax and Leeds Permanent building societies to Britain's third largest high street bank on the Abbey National model would result in a shares bonanza for the combined group's 18 million members.'

And it was not only John Willcock who was going to run the story. The whole financial section of *The Independent* was taking the deal as a *fait accompli* and was commenting on it. Hamish McRae, under the title, **Days of mutuality are numbered**, said,

> 'The planned merger of Halifax and Leeds together with the conversion to plc status will ... deliver two seismic shocks to Britain's financial system. The first is that it will consolidate South Yorkshire (sic) as a centre of financial power aside from London. The second is that the days of mutual ownership, certainly of building societies, perhaps also of mutual life assurance companies, may be drawing to a close.'

On another page, William Kay looked at the personalities of the chairman and chief executive of the Halifax in an article under the title, **Dynamic duo set to shake up sleepy industry**,

> 'Jon Foulds ... is rapidly emerging as one of the most powerful figures on the British financial scene. Tall and lean, with a passing resemblance to the actor Peter O'Toole, Foulds succeeded Tory MP Dick Hornby (as chairman) in 1990 with the determined remark, "There isn't such a thing as a non-executive chairman. You can say you are non-executive but, if something goes wrong, you are executive. The buck stops with the chairman" ... Foulds brushed aside the internal pretenders (to the position of chief executive when Sir James Birrell retired) and quietly started wooing Mike Blackburn ... The popular Mr Blackburn, 52, brought the whiff of private sector dynamism to the Leeds ... [H]is departure for the Halifax in August [he meant February] last year dealt the Leeds a blow from which it has not recovered. That is why he is now set to resume the helm there.'

And finally in *The Independent*'s 'View from City Road' under the heading, **Halifax should take on the big boys as a bank**, came the comment,

> 'In the Halifax and Leeds case, is merger the best way to tackle over-capacity? Perhaps, but there must be severe doubts, because it's hard to believe two mutual societies have got the grit and determination to carry out rationalisation on the scale necessary to make it work.

But, having done the deed, should a combined Halifax and Leeds group convert to a bank? The answer is almost certainly yes ... With or without a merger, Halifax would be sensible to convert to a bank as soon as possible if it wants to play with the big boys.'

The Halifax and Leeds directors did not know they were going to receive this barrage but it was perfectly clear that John Willcock had the facts and on good authority. Where did the leak come from?

Many speculated. Could it have been from the world of public relations, from Westminster or from the City? It did not really matter. What did matter was that both the Halifax and the Leeds directors and their PR, legal and financial advisers would need to be ready by early the following morning with their statements, and that the contingency planning should be in place to prevent a speculative rush of hot money into Halifax and Leeds accounts.

Rachel Hirst recalled the moment when she first heard of the leak,

'I remember it very well because my father had just had a hip operation and I was coming back from the hospital when my bleeper went. I didn't go home but went straight to the office and was there, apart from nipping home for the odd shower, all the way through to Saturday afternoon.'

Back in the Jermyn Street flat, plans were being finalised through the night and into Friday morning on what action to take once the whole world found out, either from their newspapers or from early news bulletins on radio and television. It was agreed that Mike Blackburn and Mike Ellis would go back to Halifax to reassure the Halifax staff and handle queries from the local media and the Halifax staff while Jon Foulds, Gren Folwell and David Gilchrist would stay in London and handle the regulators and the national media. After a telephone call to Roger Boyes in Leeds it was agreed that Boyes would handle the local media in Leeds while Blackburn handled the nationals in Halifax.

Telephone calls were flying all over the place until 12.45 a.m. on Friday. Robin Hepburn of Shandwick came in from Kent and, having bought all the early editions of the newspapers, worked with the Halifax team and the Warburg and Linklaters & Paines people at Warburg's office on the fine-tuning of a statement to be placed in all the national and relevant local newspapers. Meanwhile the Halifax-based team worked on an advertisement to be placed in Saturday's national and local newspapers. Gren Folwell said later,

> 'We had already reached draft X of the press release and the statement of our intention to merge and convert – including an outline of the share scheme. We had essentially got the authorities' agreement to proceed and were ready with plans to stop the opening of new share accounts to prevent carpet-bagging. In theory, everything was ready to pull the switch on 12 December. In practice, of course, an enormous effort had to be concentrated into a few hours. I had extensive final negotiations with the Building Societies Commission on the outline of the scheme. We were very conscious that the terms of the formal announcement would need to be mirrored in the Transfer Document – it was much more than a simple press release. And we had to explain things to Standard and Poor's and Moody's – our credit rating agencies. I cannot recall any other major financial transactions where the acquirer's rating was confirmed in such a short time scale.'

Foulds telephoned Warburg's office at 5.30 a.m. on the Friday and back-to-back interviews with radio, television and the press were arranged for the whole of the day, with Jon Foulds playing a major part in the press and TV interviews.

Being a plc will not alter our values

As Gren Folwell says, the leak had come less than three weeks before Halifax and Leeds were due to announce the merger and conversion plans anyway, and much of the material to be used on announcement was already prepared. Furthermore, contingency plans to cope with a leak had been laid.

Nevertheless, the situation as dawn broke on Friday, 25 November was not ideal, particularly in terms of getting the messages to the Leeds and Halifax staff. The directors and senior executives could not speak to everyone individually and it was inevitable that many employees would hear about the proposed merger either from the media or from third parties. In a damage limitation exercise Roger Boyes wrote to all Leeds staff,

'As I am sure you will realise, this was not the way we intended to inform staff, but press speculation has made it necessary to accelerate our plans.

I know that merger announcements can cause as much uncertainty as they do expectations. The Board and the Executive will do everything possible to remove any uncertainty. We will communicate with you on a regular and frequent basis, and ensure that communication on both sides is "matched". Also, we will ensure that any organisational issues are resolved as quickly as possible and manage this change properly. At the forefront of our thinking will be your needs and those of our customers.'

As we shall see, not all Leeds staff were reassured and it was vital that they should be. Even executives as senior as Judy Atchison at Leeds and Geoff Jackson at Halifax were surprised by the announcement.

Boyes himself felt the day went as smoothly as could be expected,

'The main thing was closing the shutters down rapidly to stop speculators. That was the key issue for us because that would have caused mayhem. It was all automatic, and all the contingency plans we'd put in place for managing mayhem in the branches worked. John Miller and his team had the capacity within the IT operation of Leeds to throw a switch to actually stop any new share accounts being opened.'

The pressure that the directors felt under can be gauged by the fact that they had planned dress rehearsals for the press conference on announcement. Lowe Bell had suggested 'joint rehearsals for the press conference probably lasting up to two hours with additional individual media training for those who so desired it'.

Mike Blackburn said it was 'vital to avoid a press leak before 12 December', as some projects were very complex, such as informing the branch staff, agencies and estate agencies. He reported that arrangements had been made to insert full page press advertisements from Day One, giving a 'hotline' 0800 number. This would provide up to 230 operators over a period of six months with the capacity to handle one million helpline calls. Staff would respond from a tightly predetermined script.

Mike Blackburn showed everyone a draft organisation structure but he doubted if it was necessary to go into such detail in the press release.

He was still making adjustments even at the highest level and was waiting for some key personnel data from Leeds. Nor did he know which executives might opt for early retirement.

As we know, those calm and relaxed plans for D-Day on 12 December were blown apart the next day by John Willcock's call to David Gilchrist.

Yorkshire pudding

Clearly neither the Halifax nor the Leeds boards wanted their staff to hear about the planned merger in this way. David Gilchrist was pretty sanguine about the media,

> 'Obviously there was a little frustration on the part of the press that it had broken in quite this way, but we explained it was a leak and very little we could do about that.'

However, he was much more concerned about the staff,

> 'Meanwhile, of course, there was the key problem of communication within the Halifax and Leeds. That was obviously a cause for real concern. During 1995, Halifax installed the Halifax television system so that head office could communicate instantly with all branches. Gilchrist said that they looked back and said, "If only we'd had that means of communication on Friday, 25 November." This was the biggest thing to hit the staff of the Leeds, and probably the Halifax, in their entire lives. If we'd had that medium we could have got the message across much more effectively.'

Up in Halifax that Friday morning the telephone calls from London were getting people out of bed. Dick Spelman, general manager, Marketing at the time, had gone to bed early having flown back from a board meeting in Jersey. He was woken by a call from Mike Ellis from the Halifax flat in Jermyn Street. Ellis put him in the picture about Willcock's article and they began a conversation along the lines of 'Do we need to activate the computer system change so that when we open for business in the morning we don't start opening accounts for people putting in large dollops of money?' Spelman said, 'I'll ring our computer systems general manager, get him out of bed and organise him to go in and fix the system.' He recalled,

'And that's what I did. I got hold of Richard Barrow, the general manager of IT, and told him we might want to fix the Halifax system but at any rate he should not go back to bed. Eventually, about 1.30 a.m. I think, Mike Ellis phoned back and said that they didn't want to interfere with the systems. All we should do was send out a brief statement on the computerised information system concerning media comment on a possible merger and saying that there would be a fuller statement from the board later in the morning. I let Richard Barrow go back to sleep, snatched a couple more hours myself and went into the office at 7 o'clock.'

Spelman had one or two more coded conversations with Ellis, by this time on his way back to Halifax on the train.

'When the guys did get back, all hell broke loose in terms of having to supplement that very brief message with the start of a flow of instructions as to what to do and not do as regards opening new accounts. During the day it got crazier and crazier. We were wheeling out messages to the network, working out how to print off overnight to them via the PC system, using the computer-based information system, then working out how to get copies of all the instructions by courier to all the agents who didn't have sophisticated computer equipment.
    While dealing with this control of money issue we had to prepare a press advertisement for the following day, have it agreed by all the legal and financial advisers of both Halifax and Leeds, and have it with the printers in time for the newspapers to have it by 7 o'clock that evening. At the same time we had to buy the space in all the newspapers.'

Once that was achieved everyone went home to change their clothes, but many went back to the office and worked through most of the Friday night until they saw the Saturday newspapers with the necessary announcements in place. They slept for a few hours in the office and then carried on through the week-end. As there was no central control room, Spelman created a make-shift one outside Ellis's office,

'I got BT and the engineering and supply people in, and we knocked down a whole row of secretaries' desks and pushed them down on to the third floor. During the course of Sunday afternoon we created

24

a complete control/master centre with five or six fax machines with direct links to the Leeds, merchant banks, accountants and lawyers. We also had to put in fax machines into the homes of key people who didn't already have them. On the Monday morning, Mike [Blackburn] came in and was confronted with this control room that had appeared from nowhere. It was an amazing 48 hours. Only recently Mike said, "For us that was the merger."'

Mike Ellis also felt the great excitement,

> 'Seeing the Halifax swing into action was exhilarating. It just shows what an awesome beast we can be at times. We did have contingency plans in place but we made the decision that all 1200 branches of the two societies would stop opening new accounts at lunch-time and that message had to be conveyed to all 1200.'

Conversations with bankers, lawyers, accountants and counterparts at Leeds continued all day and into the night – some, according to Ellis, becoming a little 'tetchy' as tiredness crept in.

> 'We waited, with cans of Boddingtons, until the papers became available at about 3 o'clock the next morning and we were very relieved that the press reaction was so good.'

One of the tasks was to prepare scripts for the helpline and it was decided that Judy Atchison, the Leeds marketing manager, should act as the calming voice. Ellis, who had not met her at that point, remembers that she was, 'very, very good at it. Sounded very good to me.'

Through all this excitement, Ellis was worrying about how he was going to face his Treasury boys, having told them only a few days earlier that their speculation about a merger with the Leeds was 'a load of rubbish'. In the event, he need not have worried,

> 'I felt I had to go over and apologise but when I went in they applauded. They were very upbeat about it all and were already allocating jobs among themselves and the Leeds guys, most of whom they knew through golf and football matches.'

Amidst all this excitement, were Halifax and Leeds successful in preventing carpet-baggers from speculating by opening Halifax accounts? (The expression, carpet-bagger, originated in the southern states of the USA during the reconstruction period, 1865–77, following the Civil War, and was used as a derogatory term by the defeated southerners for those northerners who came to the south, with little more than a carpet-bag, with, it was felt, the express intention of exploiting them.)

Both David Gilchrist and Mike Ellis were confident that they had been. Gilchrist said later,

> 'We have said consistently that there were no carpet-baggers with the Halifax. And I think that's a fact. Once we had made our announcement every other society obviously was going to suffer the attention of these "hot" money operators, the carpet-baggers. There were none with the Halifax nor with the Leeds.'

Ellis agreed,

> 'We looked to see if there'd been any abnormal activity that morning but there hadn't. There were no carpet-baggers.'

Meanwhile, down in Reading, where Ged Nicholls ran the office for the Independent Union for Halifax Staff, a BBC camera crew arrived at 10.30 a.m. to ask Nicholls' view on the merger. Nicholls had only arrived back from Stirling late the night before after a gruelling three weeks of

Cartoon by Thomas Nast, 1872
The Granger Collection

meetings with other union representatives, but he had been alerted at 7 a.m. He was ready for the merger but was taken by surprise by the planned conversion. He coped with the BBC, sent staff to the Sky studios at West Drayton and went himself to the ITV studios in London.

After all the interviews of Friday, 25 November the directors of both Halifax and Leeds awaited with interest, and perhaps some trepidation, the press' reaction. First into the frame was the London *Evening Standard*. It wrote under the headline, **Halifax-Leeds will wage war on banks**,

'The Halifax Building Society today declared war on Britain's high street banks ... Halifax has become increasingly concerned about the growing threat from low-cost operations such as Direct Line ... and from foreign banks.'

The *Evening Standard* had little time to carry out any research and put together an article of any depth. The reporter, Richard Wachman, rang a few analysts who gave off-the-cuff remarks. A spokesman at the stockbroker UBS said,

'I can't imagine why Halifax wants to float at a time when the home loans market is flat on its back. On the other hand, a listing would give it the opportunity to expand, perhaps via buying another bank.'

And the banking analyst at stockbroker Hoare Govett, Peter Tolman, said the move would allow the Halifax to retain its pre-eminent position as the industry's price setter.

But it was not the *Evening Standard*'s rapid reactions that the societies were interested in. How would the 'heavies' react over the week end? Needless to say, it was a big story and the coverage was enormous. The main reactions were as follows.

The *Financial Times* under the heading, **Inequality in society wedding**, could not see Leeds' motivation. It appreciated the problem of the management being cautious about closures and rationalisation but felt it would need to carry them through.

Most chairmen and chief executives care a great deal about what *Lex* on the back page of the *Financial Times* says about them. *Lex* enjoyed a reputation for being penetrating and analytical. The column also has a reputation for being acerbic and pretty sparing with words of praise.

What did *Lex* think of this deal? It did not like the fact that both Halifax and Leeds were playing down the scope for rationalisation and reminded its readers that a similar approach by the Nationwide and Anglia had meant years of poor return on assets when they merged in 1987. It did not think the loss of mutuality should bother members but concluded that, as shareholders, they should keep a tight watch on management.

'The last time societies were given greater freedom, they charged into estate agency with disastrous consequences. So the new shareholders will have to keep management on a tight rein.'

The Daily Telegraph (under City Comment) wrote in its article **Marriage certain to be fraught with trouble and strife**,

> ' … attempting a merger of such a size rapidly followed by flotation was … "asking for trouble".
>
> The short-term costs will decrease efficiency rather than raise it and the merger will work only if the management swings the axe on jobs. The guff yesterday about keeping head offices in Halifax and Leeds, just 18 miles apart, is ominous indeed, while talk of turning Leeds into a financial centre to rival Edinburgh smacks of hubris.'

That did not make very encouraging reading over the cornflakes on Saturday morning!

What was everyone else saying?

John Willcock, whose exclusive had forced everything into the open in the first place (he must have been delighted to be able to announce the deal when the City editors who had lunched with Foulds two days before did not extract anything) was much more positive. After interviewing Foulds, he said under the headline, **Bank would have edge on costs**,

> 'The proposed deal between the Halifax and Leeds building societies will produce a bank with a dramatically lower cost base than the traditional high street banks … Costs at both Halifax and Leeds amount to about 40 per cent of their earnings compared with a level of more than 60 per cent for most of the clearers.'

He quoted John Delahey, an analyst at Societé Générale who said,

> 'It will be an extremely well-capitalised institution, and will have a premium rating in world capital markets.'

Elsewhere in *The Independent*, Peter Rodgers was also complimentary,

> 'However much they play down the impact in public, the board of every large British bank and building society will have been shaken rigid by the announcement from the Halifax and Leeds building societies … The merger itself ranks rather low on the scale of seismic events in the financial services industry … What is really significant

– a veritable shift in the continental plates supporting the industry
... is the unexpected decision by the two societies to convert
themselves into a fully fledged bank, which will be the third largest
on Britain's high streets.'

Alex Brummer, the perceptive City editor of *The Guardian*, was anxious
not to let Halifax off the hook of its stated loyalty to mutuality without
some convincing explanation,

'If the flotation takes place, it will be the biggest in the UK, with the
new company having a market capitalisation of about £9 billion.
What is most startling about it, however, is that the Halifax – which
for five years has been extolling the virtues of mutuality – has taken
this plunge. Why the conversion?'

Brummer did not really need to ask the question; he could see why. It
was the regulatory framework which was fine for small societies and on
the whole did an excellent job. But it was cramping the style of the very
largest societies.

'Had the authorities been courageous enough to seek a root and
branch reform of financial supervision – bringing together banking
and building society scrutiny under one umbrella – then the valuable
concept of mutuality might have been preserved.
   As it is, the new Halifax plc has opted to join the world of full-
blooded capitalism. It brings one tremendous advantage to the party.
The north of England will now have its own world-class financial
institution in Halifax   linked with Leeds – boosting the cause of
finance away from the City of London.'

Jeff Randall, City editor of *The Sunday Times*, criticised the 'City know-
alls trying to pick holes in the mega-merger'. He, like others, thought
that the banks would not be relishing the prospect of a new force 'with
excellent consumer reputations and combined assets of £90 billion'.
   He continued (and those who saw one of the supposed benefits of
mutuality disappearing would have agreed with him),

'Every piece of research I have seen shows that building societies
are still held in far higher regard by customers than the banks. On
the whole, societies are trusted and are not regarded as rapacious or

bullying. The trick for the Halifax and Leeds will be keeping that image while competing head-on with banking's big boys.'

The *Financial Times* predicted that the psychological shock to the building society movement would be traumatic as it lost a third of its £280 billion of assets overnight. It did not feel that the retreat from mutuality was of great regret. A high level of home ownership had been achieved and, as the largest societies inevitably became financial services groups, mutuality was not necessarily appropriate.

This was the instant reaction to the merger and conversion proposals, which could perhaps be viewed as generally favourable, though almost inevitably with one or two objectors (*Financial Times* relatively mild; *The Daily Telegraph*, very strong).

Given a week to think about it (the Halifax and Leeds directors had originally chosen a Monday for the announcement in order to give the Sundays a week to think about the merger), how did the heavyweight and widely respected *Economist* view the merger proposal?

'The Halifax-Leeds deal is the most dramatic sign yet of the manoeuvres occurring in Britain's financial high street. The deal will have an important impact on banks and the dwindling band of building societies left on the high street. It will also shake insurers and, possibly, some fund managers too.'

Peter Simmonds, *The Economist* 23 June 1994

So far, so good

After so much preparation and so much secrecy it was perhaps a relief to have news of the merger out in the open. Nevertheless, the directors of the two societies were anxious to gauge reaction from their staff, their members and customers, and the media who could, of course, influence the attitudes of the first categories.

At the Leeds board meeting on Tuesday, 29 November, Piers Pottinger of the pubic relations firm, Lowe Bell, gave his reaction to the media coverage to date. He said that it was important to convey the Leeds message and particular attention should be paid to *The Daily Telegraph* and the *Financial Times* who had so far been 'more negative' than others. He felt it important that detailed market research among members and customers of the societies be used to give credibility to the merger in the face of a hostile media. In particular, close attention should be paid to disgruntled pressure groups and individuals. Job security had already emerged as a major issue and especially Leeds staff concerns would need to be allayed before wrong and damaging messages were conveyed to customers. It was decided to keep directors informed on a weekly basis in a circular which would track market research and press comment. Roger Boyes would remain the society's principal spokesperson but other directors, including the chairman, should become involved. William Nabarro, who ran the Leeds office of Hambros, could be particularly valuable in giving the media the merchant bank perspective. Attention should also be given to local Members of Parliament who could have a considerable influence. Finally, Pottinger urged a considered approach to the media rather than an instantaneous reaction to media comments.

On the same day at Permanent House in Leeds, Jon Foulds, John Wood and Mike Blackburn from Halifax met Sir Timothy Kitson, John King and Roger Boyes from Leeds. It was minuted that Jon Foulds and Roger Boyes,

> 'Each recounted the exciting and hectic events of Friday, 25 November. In the circumstances of the forced announcement, in which various parties had been obliged to react to situations and make instant decisions, it was felt that overall, events had passed off as well as could have been expected.'

In reviewing the press comment, Jon Foulds said that in retrospect it had been a mistake to presume that others would be as excited as the

31

executive at Halifax and Leeds were, but he felt that the press comment had become more favourable as the weekend had progressed. He was surprised that, in some ways, 'we had been so lightly let off, in particular escaping any accusation that we were decimating the building society industry'. However, he was now concerned that the banks and possibly building society competitors might, 'drip feed "poison" copy to the media'. He wanted to seize the initiative with a succession of positive stories and singled out the *Financial Times* as the key area in which to enlist support. He was concerned that the press releases did not explain sufficiently well the benefits of the merger, such as access to more branches. He was reassured by Mike Blackburn that the *Schedule 16* statement, which would be sent to all members before the Special General Meeting to vote on the merger, would spell out all these benefits clearly.

Over the following ten days, everyone was in overdrive, briefing staff, media and the great and the good, 'the movers and shakers'. At the next 'G8' meeting – the Group of Eight senior directors from Halifax and Leeds – at the Halifax London offices in Cornhill, Jon Foulds reported that he had 'breakfasted with the Prime Minister that morning and had managed to put across a number of relevant points. The PM's attitude had been friendly and, in a general way, supportive.'

Sir Timothy Kitson reported that Wilf Weeks of GJW, the parliamentary advisers to Halifax, was processing arrangements to hold briefing sessions for Yorkshire MPs. Roger Boyes and Mike Blackburn had met Jon Trickett, leader of Leeds City Council, Andrew Carter, leader of the Conservatives on the Council and Phil Smith, the chief officer. The meeting had been friendly and they were reassured by the group's commitment to Leeds emphasised by Halifax's separate negotiations to buy a building known as West Bank from Asda for use as offices for Halifax Direct. Mike Blackburn had met Michael Ellison, the chief executive officer of Calderdale Council, and others had met the Mayor of Calderdale and Sir Donald Thompson, the Conservative MP for Calder Valley.

John King was concerned whether the proper message was being conveyed to staff to counter the negative press reporting whereupon Mike Blackburn produced a draft copy of the first issue of *Converge*, a new weekly newsletter produced jointly by Halifax and Leeds especially for the staff and aimed at keeping them fully informed about the merger and subsequent conversion. In his review of staff attitudes, Roger Boyes said that exit polls taken at staff roadshows showed a positive attitude. The initial reticence, largely due to press comment, was giving way to the realisation that jobs would be safe even if the tasks involved changed. There was also a dawning realisation that staff would benefit financially from the share issue.

Opposition

The reaction of Members of Parliament was clearly going to be important as they could be influential both in terms of the public and indeed on such bodies as the Office of Fair Trading. Anthony Nelson, Economic Secretary to the Treasury, said he could not rule out referring the merger to the Monopolies and Mergers Commission. Speaking on BBC Radio's *The World at One* he said,

> 'It's not for me to comment on the merits or otherwise of this merger, or the conversion, especially as the Office of Fair Trading will no doubt wish to form a view on competition implications. Clearly this is a high society marriage in Yorkshire. It's an enormous deal and one that will change substantially the building societies landscape.'

Labour expressed its concern through its City spokesman, Alistair Darling, who said he would be raising the matter in the House of Commons. He had written to the Chancellor of the Exchequer asking him to examine the competition implications. The directors were therefore slightly alarmed that the Labour Member for Great Grimsby, Austin Mitchell, had tabled an early-day Motion which was highly critical. Initially the Motion bore only Mitchell's name as sponsor but care would be needed if others decided to join him. Mike Blackburn and Roger Boyes wrote a joint letter to every Member and they met Alice Mahon, the Labour Member for Halifax, and Derek Fatchett, the Labour Member for Leeds Central, on 12 December. Unfortunately, both had already asked Sir Bryan Carsberg, the director general of the Office of Fair Trading, to refer the proposal to the Monopolies and Mergers Commission. Blackburn and Boyes wrote to them following the meeting hoping that they might withdraw their request to Carsberg.

By 14 December, 27 MPs had added their names to Mitchell's early-day Motion but many Members were being supportive including the Labour Member for neighbouring Huddersfield, Barry Sheerman and the Labour Member for Leeds East, George Mudie. By Tuesday, 20 December, Mitchell's supporters had risen to 41 although it was felt that his campaign was running out of steam. Nevertheless, the Halifax and Leeds directors knew there would be some opponents of the proposed deal. What they did not know was the extent and from whom it would come. The Building Societies Members Association said the deal was 'born of greed for profits' and that 'thousands of people would be put out of work and many millions' worth of property would be thrown on the market'.

In spite of the fact that the Banking Insurance and Finance Union (BIFU) had no representation among Halifax staff, the negotiating officer, Joe Hoedemaker said, 'We have heard on the grapevine that thousands of jobs will go. Going for size does not necessarily give a better service and often means big job cuts.' He warned that he would be seeking a guarantee on compulsory redundancies such as BIFU had secured in the Northern Rock merger with North of England.

The Financial Services Staff Federation said,

'We believe it's quite wrong to combine the two societies if the end result is less customer choice, more boarded-up premises on our High Streets and more unemployment.'

Ged Nicholls, the general secretary of the Independent Union of Halifax Staff was broadly neutral,

'We were aware of the merger talks earlier this year. What surprised us was the intention to become a plc. We are concerned that 140 years of tradition as a mutual will disappear and that management will focus on the short-term share price rather than the long-term interests of customers.'

He felt that job losses were inevitable given that Halifax employed 3500 at head office and Leeds another 1500 only 16 miles away.

An early vociferous opponent was Serge Lourie, who was a Halifax member and a Liberal Democrat councillor in Richmond upon Thames in Surrey. Lourie was a veteran of the protest against the withdrawal of European Ferries' shareholder perks and he described himself as a firm believer in the mutual principle. He set about trying to organise an action group to demand accurate information on any choice the members would be called on to make. He told *The Guardian,*

'I am not accusing anyone of dishonesty. But the executives who drew up the plans have a vested interest in those plans succeeding. I am not sure that they are the best people to give us information about the future prospects for both societies, either separately, together, or as a plc ... This plan should not be allowed to go ahead without a great deal of consideration of not only what will be gained but what members might lose.

The Leeds and the Halifax are two fine institutions. Mutuality has served customers of both societies very well in the past, and it is not yet clear what we will gain from the deal – apart from a few shares. What we can be sure of, however, is that we will be lining the pockets of City institutions.'

Lourie had now called his group, the Halifax Action Group, and claimed he had received a 'large postbag' which provided evidence of 'considerable disquiet'. He pointed out that the Halifax, 'had been one of the most vociferous proponents of the mutual principle and opposed moving to plc status'. He went on to say that stakeholders in both societies should consider a number of issues.

'In principle, a mutual organisation, without having to pay dividends, should be able to charge lower rates to borrowers and offer higher rates to savers. Would making the already large Halifax and Leeds even larger benefit anyone other than directors and senior managers?

What would be the extent of rationalisation?

What benefit would there be to the Leeds in being swallowed by the Halifax where the chairman, vice-chairman and chief executive would all be from Halifax? [He was not quite correct. There were to be two vice-chairmen, one from each society.]

If the conversion was successful, what was to stop the management using excess funds to splash out on silly ventures as the TSB and some privatised utilities had done?

As senior staff will clearly benefit how could we gain objective recommendations?'

He concluded that the Halifax Action Group would monitor events closely and he hoped a similar group would be set up by the Leeds members and that the two could work closely together.

And Lourie soon found an ally in Halifax in Peter Judge, a Labour councillor on Calderdale Borough Council, the area of West Yorkshire centred on Halifax itself. Judge was planning to stand as an independent, anti-conversion candidate for election to Halifax's board in May. He was making the same point as Lourie,

> 'It is only the career directors who favour this move. Converting to a bank would not be in the interests of the ordinary Halifax member in the long run. If dividends have to be paid out to shareholders instead of being retained in the society, the cost of both mortgages and savings accounts will rise.'

To be eligible to stand for election, Judge would need nominations from at least 50 Halifax savers who had kept £100 in a share account for at least two years. The election was due to take place at the Halifax annual general meeting on 22 May. Judge was joined by Lourie in his quest to try for election to a place on the Halifax board and both successfully found the necessary 50 sponsors.

The other vociferous critic of the merger was the former chief executive of the Leeds, Leonard Hyde. He had been chief executive in the late 1970s and a board member until 1990. He said,

> ' ... if the current board of Leeds Permanent no longer feel able and capable to run the society as an independent and vibrant organisation they should have said so and not have so vehemently opposed the election of three people who sought to do so. If the Leeds Permanent and the Halifax have so much money to give away they should do so now by way of a bonus to investors and long-suffering borrowers and not indulge in a most expensive exercise which will ultimately destroy two very fine institutions.'

It was pretty strong stuff and we shall have to wait until the Special General Meetings called for 22 May 1995 for members to vote on the merger to see how many members agreed with Lourie, Judge and Hyde.

In spite of this opposition and the leaked announcement, the Halifax and Leeds directors could feel a certain sense of satisfaction at the general reaction to their proposal to merge and convert into a public company. Nevertheless, they were about to change the course of tradition and history, and we should now look at that history to see how the two societies had arrived in 1994 in such a strong position yet still felt a need to change.

CHAPTER TWO

Among them were large-hearted and far-sighted men

Wait for an accident and change the system
Why so large and important?
Changes in the early 1980s
Growth
Halifax – the biggest in the world
Leeds – also ambitious

Wait for an accident and change the system

The first known building society was established in Birmingham in 1775 and within 25 years up to 50 more were founded, mostly in the Midlands, Lancashire and Yorkshire. Building societies grew rapidly in industrial towns in the nineteenth century for several reasons. There was a natural desire for home ownership, and some skilled and white collar workers were in a position to achieve it. Mill-owners encouraged self-sufficiency in housing, which released them from the obligation of creating and managing their own estates of rented property (there was no public transport). The banks, mainly private, were not interested in lending on private property. Commercial lending was more profitable, and, in the bankers' view, safer. And finally, the Reform Act of 1832, which granted the vote to freeholders, meant that industrialists, many of whom harboured political ambitions, could further their cause by garnering the votes of their workers. For example, William Cobden, founder of the National Building Society (later to merge with the Abbey), was more concerned that his borrowers obtained the land, and hence the vote, than whether they actually had houses built on the land.

In the early nineteenth century a wider approach developed whereby societies moved towards becoming savings institutions. The pressure came from people wanting to speed up the process of house-building, and societies began to pay interest to those not wanting a house but willing to invest. To be able to pay this interest the societies had to charge interest to those borrowing. By the middle of the century the societies, though still tiny by today's standards, had grown in number to between 100 and 200, and were numerous enough to attract legislation in the form of the Regulation of Benefit Building Societies Act in 1836, which gave them official recognition.

In 1870, a Royal Commission on all friendly societies, including building societies, was established. This was followed by the first comprehensive Building Societies Act in 1874. The main feature of the Act was to limit building societies to building and owning land for the purposes of conducting their business. The law governing societies became progressively more restrictive as various collapses showed the need for tighter curbs. It has been likened to the development of the Victorian railway signalling system – wait for an accident to happen before changing the system in the light of the experience. In 1892, first the substantial Portsea Island Building Society, and then the Liberator Building Society, which was by far the largest in the country, collapsed. The Liberator failed primarily because it lent money on unsuitable properties. Such collapses only served to strengthen the traditional societies such as Halifax and Leeds, which had always lent money in a conservative way. In times of trouble people flee with their money to havens of security. As well as giving more power to the Registrar, the 1894 Act prohibited some of the societies' more dubious practices including second mortgages and the balloting for mortgages.

In the first half of the twentieth century, the period between the two world wars was one of rapid growth for the building society industry and by this time it could be described as an industry. There was very low, even negative, inflation and therefore low interest rates. Although the number of societies declined from 1336 in 1918 to 960 in 1939, a few through termination but most through merger, the number of shareholders rose from 625,000 to over two million and there were probably one and a half million borrowers by 1939 compared with about 500,000 in 1918. The total assets grew from £68 million in 1918 to £773 million in 1939 (£77 billion in today's money). In 1953, to celebrate the first 100 years of the Halifax Building Society, Oscar Hobson wrote a centenary book entitled *A Hundred Years of the Halifax*, in which he said of the inter-war years,

'These years were the golden age not only for our Society, but for the building society movement as a whole. They were the years of the greatest activity – up to the present – on the building of dwelling houses in this country, and the main and historic function of building societies is after all to assist in the building of *new* houses.

In 1937 the number of new houses completed in the United Kingdom reached the remarkable figure of 375,000, and a few months before war broke out in September 1939, the four millionth house to be built since the end of the 1914–18 war was completed. Of these four million, a little under three million were built by private enterprise and these were very largely financed by the building societies.'*

The 1940s was a quiet period, first because of the Second World War and subsequently because the Labour governments of 1945–51 concentrated on building houses for rent. However, a large increase in the number of houses built for owner-occupation in the 1950s brought a period of rapid expansion for the industry.

The next 25 years saw a further contraction in the number of societies from 726 in 1960 to only 190 in 1985, while at the same time the number of borrowers rose dramatically from 2.3 million in 1960 to 6.5 million in 1985. By 1992, the number of societies had fallen to 89 with total assets of £246 billion.

One by-product of the greater role of building societies was the increasing interest, shown by both government and the public in general, in rates of interest offered and charged. During the long period of Conservative governments from 1951 to 1964, much of the state interference in people's lives, erected out of necessity during the war, was dismantled.

However, Labour returned to power in 1964 and the more collectivist approach was once more adopted. Big business, indeed any profit-making organisation, was particularly suspect and in 1966 the Prices and Incomes Board was commissioned to investigate building society interest rates (during the 1964 General Election campaign the deputy leader of the Labour Party, George Brown, promised mortgages at an interest rate of 3 per cent!).

---

* Although the number of house completions has since exceeded the 1937 figure (1968 – 414,000) the number of owner-occupier completions has never since reached the 1937 figure.

During the 1970s the role of interest rates became even more significant, as both the world economy in general and Britain's in particular lurched from boom to bust under the influence of an upsurge in inflation, having been initially caused by the Vietnam War and given a final twist by the oil-producing nations (OPEC) quintupling the price of oil. This act at the end of 1973 halted a strong world boom in its tracks and turned it into a world recession. This economic instability led to much greater volatility in house prices and pushed building societies to the front of the political scene. House prices had risen steadily in the 1950s and 1960s but at the beginning of the 1970s they rose sharply as the rate of inflation rose and, more significantly, the availability of funds became greater as others besides building societies became lenders for house-purchase.*

The strong rise in prices, 37.4 per cent in 1972 followed by a further 32.1 per cent in 1973, could not continue, though of course as is usual at such times, many said that it would. A combination of a sharp increase in the mortgage rate from 8.5 per cent at the beginning of 1973 to 11 per cent by August and the OPEC oil price hikes in the autumn led to a rapid cooling in the market. Because retail price inflation was so high between 1974 and 1977, house prices did not decline on an annual basis in absolute terms, though in real terms they fell each year for those four years. This meant that there was no 'negative equity' as there was in the severe housing recession of the early 1990s. Those in debt were effectively baled out by inflation. In *real* terms, the 1973–6 recession in the housing market was worse than that of 1989–95 but, thanks to inflation, there were no serious arrears or repossessions.

There was much criticism of this boom/bust scenario and the building societies were blamed by some, first for fuelling the price rise, and then for stopping it. The possibility of direct controls on the societies was raised. However, after discussion between the government and the Building Societies Association, the Memorandum of Agreement on Building Society Mortgage Finance was drawn up in October 1973. As Mark Boleat said in his admirable book, *The Building Society Industry*, published by Allen & Unwin in 1986,

'The Memorandum implicitly assumed that house prices could be influenced by manipulation of lending policies and it should be noted that it was lending policies with regard to second-time buyers which

---

* See Appendix.

were felt to be particularly significant. This is in contrast to the analysis earlier in this chapter which suggests that it is the first-time buyer which is of significance. The difference is partially explained by the fact that the Memorandum of Agreement was a political document in which it was considered unacceptable to suggest that the housing market could be controlled by preventing people from becoming owner-occupiers.'

'Political' is the key word because house price inflation is not caused by the flow of mortgage finance. If it were, house prices would have been roaring ahead in the early 1990s as building societies and banks were only too eager to lend money.

Why so large and important?

The first reason that building societies in Britain have become so large and important is that Britain differs from most other industrial societies in that owner-occupation has grown to much higher levels.

The growth of owner-occupation in Great Britain, 1914–94

End year	Percentage of owner-occupied houses
1914	10.6
1950	29.5
1961	43.0
1965	46.6
1980	55.7
1985	60.5
1990	65.8
1994	66.7

In most other countries there is a reasonably healthy private rented sector. For example, in Switzerland and Germany most families rent throughout their lives rather than own. Most private landlords in Europe are small-scale and rely on mortgages from mortgage bankers and commercial banks. In Britain, until the First World War, about 90 per cent of houses were rented from private landlords. In 1914, rent control was introduced as a temporary measure but was never lifted. Indeed, successive Rent Acts meant that the provision of rented accommodation became increasingly unattractive to landlords. Owner-occupation was also encouraged by tax allowances such as relief on mortgage interest charges. (Until the 1990s the UK economy was, and was perceived to be, an inflation-prone economy where ownership of a house was considered a hedge against inflation.) This continuing move towards owner-occupation was given further encouragement by the Conservative Government's policy after 1979 of encouraging council tenants to buy their houses.

This decision to sell council houses, known as 'Right to Buy', was a significant factor in giving the housing market a boost in the 1980s. Between 1980 and 1990 owner-occupation grew by just over 10 per cent from 55.7 per cent to 65.8 per cent and about 80 per cent of that 10 per cent came from 'Right to Buy'. It was even more important for the building societies as the overwhelming proportion of 'Right to Buy' mortgages came from them. Furthermore, the Halifax enjoyed a market share of such purchases higher than its normal market share.

The second factor leading to the growth of building societies was the virtual monopoly of house purchase finance which they enjoyed. In other countries other types of financial institution, such as commercial and savings banks as well as specialist financial institutions, operated in the housing market in a significant way. In Britain, the building societies were dominant.

Another factor affecting the growth of building societies has been their willingness to lend a very high percentage of the value of a house, especially to first-time buyers. This trend has been accentuated by the major insurance companies' willingness to provide mortgage indemnity on the final 20–25 per cent of borrowing. By 1994, the total assets of the building societies were £301 billion, there were 44 million investors and 7.4 million borrowers with outstanding mortgages of £230 billion.

Changes in the early 1980s

The building societies had long operated under a Recommended Rate system, effectively a cartel, whereby the Building Societies Association at its monthly meeting recommended a rate, and all societies lent and borrowed at the same rate. The Prices and Incomes Board in its 1966 investigation reported that this practice,

> 'Tends to lead to the determination of margins between the invest-
> ment and mortgage rates that are sufficient to allow the least efficient

society to survive and, at the same time, to give generous margins to the more efficient societies. Theory would also suggest that competition would switch to non-price forms, but also that there would be attempts by more efficient societies to circumvent the constraints of the cartel.'

And indeed competition *did* switch to non-price forms such as branch development and societies *did* try to circumvent the cartel, eventually breaking it in the early 1980s.

For most of the 1970s the building societies' main competitors, the banks, were constrained in their freedom to lend – firstly, until 1971, by direct lending controls, and then by the 'Corset', which penalised lending by constraining asset growth. There was a period between 1971 and 1974 during the expansionary period of the Edward Heath Tory administration when the banks, especially the so-called secondary banks, became aggressive mortgage lenders. However, this period did not last long enough for the building societies to make any serious reassessment of their strategies.

It was the competition from the banks in the early 1980s that led to the formal ending of the Recommended Rate system in 1983. This was after the restrictions on their lending had been lifted by the ending of the 'Corset' following the abolition of foreign exchange controls by the Thatcher government of 1979. The governor of the Bank of England had already criticised the cartel in a speech to the Building Societies Association's annual conference in 1978 when he said,

> 'One would expect a recommended rate system to discourage efficiency and innovation and perhaps encourage competition of the wrong sort, for example, in unnecessary expenditure on outlets or branches … if societies could fix their own rates there might be scope for cutting costs and margins.'

For example, the Leeds expanded from 100 branches in 1974, to over 400 by the end of the decade during a period when the policy seemed to be: open branches at all cost.

The banks, having concentrated on businessmen in the past, suddenly seemed to discover that the personal customer was a potential money-earner rather than someone who occasionally caused irritation by exceeding his overdraft limit. As Mike Blackburn, chief executive of the Halifax put it,

'In the 1970s, to be a hero as a bank manager, you had to lend well to business accounts. The personal customer only featured when he became overdrawn.'

Suddenly, the banks were keen to increase their share of personal business and saw the mortgage market as a quick and easy way to achieve this objective. Their market penetration was quite dramatic. In 1980, bank net advances for house purchases were £593 million or 8 per cent of the market. In 1981 they were £2,447 million or 26 per cent and in 1982, £5,078 million or 36 per cent. The banks concentrated at the top end of the market where the building societies were least competitive. Because of the cartel, they had been able to charge higher rates of interest on large loans. And it was not only in lending that the banks were able to take market share from the building societies, it was also in attracting savings. The societies began to realise that the cartel might protect them from other societies but not from other financial institutions who were not subject to the cartel restrictions. The general effect of the cartel was to hold mortgage rates down, stifling the inflow of funds and the availability of mortgages. For a long time governments seemed happier with low mortgage rates but with mortgage rationing rather than a free market and no rationing.

For this and other reasons, many societies were already seeking ways to operate outside the cartel when the whole Recommended Rate system was thrown into disarray. In September 1983 the Abbey National Building Society, the second largest society in the country, announced its intention of withdrawing from the Interest Rates Undertaking. This marked the end of the cartel.

Growth

In his book, *The Building Society Industry in Transition*, published by Macmillan in 1989, Leigh Drake attributes the strong growth in mortgage lending to,

'Supply side factors associated with the deregulation of financial markets. As competition was introduced into the mortgage market in 1981 the mortgage rationing which had previously existed was gradually eliminated and borrowers were able to increase their capital gearing in the housing market following a period when it had been artificially depressed by a combination of mortgage rationing and high inflation.'

Also fuelling the demand, according to Drake, was the sharp rise in equity withdrawal or net cash withdrawal,

' ... facilitated by supply side financial innovation which led to the development of products which enabled individuals to take equity out of their properties.'

A third factor was the strong growth in real incomes once the recession of 1979–81 was over. While real personal disposable income grew at an average 2.2 per cent between 1973 and 1979, from 1983 to 1986 it grew at 3 per cent and this increased to 3.2 per cent in 1987. Demographic factors also played a part. The post-war baby boom produced another in the early 1960s with a knock-on effect on demand for housing in the early 1980s. Furthermore the demand of single people for houses increased sharply so that by 1986 almost 25 per cent of all households contained only one person, whereas in 1951 the proportion had been only 10 per cent.

A further boost was given by mortgage interest tax relief, still significant with full relief on the first £30,000 of the mortgage, and by the rise in house prices. Many people came to feel secure (wrongly, as it turned out) that house prices would go on rising and that the more they borrowed, the bigger capital gain (tax free) they would make.

Adding fuel to the fire was the increased lending by the banks to consumers. Not only were banks freed from the restraints of the 'Corset', the Bank of England changed the regulations governing the banks' capital base. This created a capital injection of no less than £8.4 billion into their ability to lend between 1980 and 1986.

Banks were not the only competitive threat to the building societies in the mortgage market. New, wholesale-funded lenders such as National Home Loans, Mortgage Corporation and Mortgage Express entered what they saw as a profitable, low-risk and fast-growing business.

This explosion in demand was satisfied by new and existing lenders, but what they did not recognise was that it constituted a one-off adjustment following the freezing of the previously controlled market. Once satisfied, the demand was not sustained, leaving too many lenders chasing too few borrowers and thus leading to the cut-throat competition among lenders in the early 1990s.

On the savings side, competition also intensified during the 1980s. As well as the banks' new-found interest in the personal customer, National Savings also provided competition. This attention from all sides brought a wave of new product development. Building societies were prompted to introduce a raft of new accounts offering interest premiums well above those on traditional share accounts.

The fierce competition was also reflected in the level of advertising. In 1980 the banks spent £8.6 million and the building societies £8.8 million on television advertising. In 1987 these figures had grown to £50.3 million and £41.1 million.

Halifax – the biggest in the world

The Halifax Permanent Benefit Building Society was founded in 1853 at a time of great social and industrial change. The town of Halifax in the north of England had benefited considerably from the changes brought about by the industrial revolution of the late eighteenth and early nineteenth centuries. For hundreds of years sheep farming, combined with cottage-based spinning and weaving, had been the main occupation of those who lived on the steep Pennine hills overlooking the valley of the River Calder. The industrial revolution brought about mechanisation, with textile machines replacing hand-crafts, and steam engines replacing waterwheels. Yorkshire iron, steel and coal fed the wool textile industry that grew up in the West Riding.

Halifax itself, on the banks of Hebble Brook, a tributary of the River Calder, had long been the centre of the region's 'piece trade', where local weavers sold their pieces of woollen and worsted cloth to wholesalers. Stealing cloth worth more than thirteen and a half pence could still be punished by beheading on a guillotine, which stood in Gibbet Street. No wonder thieves and vagrants chanted 'From Hell, Hull and Halifax, Good Lord deliver us'.

With the development of the large, steam-powered mills, the town grew rapidly from a population of about 11,000 in 1800 to 34,000 by 1853, the year the Halifax Building Society was founded in the Oak Room of the Old Cock Inn. One of the town's leading manufacturers was John Crossley who founded the famous Crossley carpet-making firm at Dean Clough Mill. Indeed, the town still bears all the hallmarks of this prosperous period – large mills, a parish church by Sir George Gilbert Scott who described it as, 'on the whole my best church', a town

46

hall by Sir Charles Barry and, to the south and west, the large houses of those who benefited most in this industrialisation. (Although not relevant to this period but to a later one, in the same year as the Halifax Building Society was founded, Henry Edmunds was born in Silver Street. Edmunds became an accomplished engineer and businessman but his place in history is assured as the man who introduced Henry Royce to the Honourable Charles Rolls in Manchester's Midland Hotel, in May 1904.)

The Earl of Halifax said in the *Foreword* to *A Hundred Years of the Halifax,* by Oscar Hobson,

> 'Building society foundations were laid at a time of social ferment, when the country's productive power had been enormously increased by industrial inventiveness. People moved into the towns, causing disequilibrium between the rural and urban populations which brought about serious overcrowding, especially in the northern area where the textile industry expanded rapidly. Nothing strains the inherent loyalty of the workers and threatens the established social order so much as the lack of good homes. It was fortunate indeed that at such a time, men of the calibre of the founders of the Halifax Society saw in the situation an opportunity to provide the remedy.
>
> Many harsh things have been said and written about the Victorian industrialists, but among them were large-hearted and far-sighted men who sought to employ their resources in ways that were socially useful … The fact that men of the eminence of Cobden and Bright were actively associated with the building society movement is sufficient evidence that it was animated by social ideals rather than by mere cupidity.'

The Halifax grew steadily through the 1860s and 1870s, and by 1881 its assets had reached £1,001,413 (as we have seen the total assets of the whole movement were £45 million in the 1890s). Progress in the 1880s and 1890s was slow and assets were still only just over £1 million in 1896. One of the contributing factors of Halifax's steady growth towards becoming the country's largest building society was the continuity of its leadership. One of its founders, and the secretary until he died in 1902, was Jonas Dearnley Taylor. At the 49th annual meeting of the society on 25 March 1902, the president, Alderman James Kilburn, paid a glowing tribute to Taylor. He said that he was really the founder of the society and it was thanks to his organising ability, persevering efforts, power of concentration and strict integrity that it had achieved its position. Taylor died in September that same year, but he was succeeded by the man who projected the Halifax on to the national stage, Enoch, eventually Sir Enoch, Hill. Born in 1865, the eldest son of a mill-worker in Leek, Staffordshire, Hill began work as a 'half-timer' at the age of eight for a shilling (5p in today's money but equivalent to about £7.50) a week. He showed himself to be a boy of exceptional ability and capacity for hard work and through exploitation of these qualities and a fortuitous marriage he eventually found himself running the administration of the Leek Building Society. When the post of secretary of the Halifax became vacant, Hill applied for the job, and was appointed at the age of 37 in 1903. The Society's assets were still only £1.4 million.

Hill began to make changes but progress was delayed by the First World War; in 1919, for example, the Halifax was still only substantially represented in Lancashire and Yorkshire, with a few agencies in Durham, Lincolnshire and Nottinghamshire and one or two in North Wales. However, in the 1920s the push south began. The first office in southern England was opened in Shaftesbury, Dorset in 1919. It was followed in the early 1920s by agencies in Bournemouth, Plymouth and Worthing. The first London office was opened at 124 Charing Cross Road in 1924.

In January 1928 the Halifax Permanent, by this time with assets of £33 million and already the largest society in the country, merged with its local competitor the Halifax Equitable, whose assets were £14 million. In the ten years since the end of the First World War, the Halifax had opened 100 new branches and agencies, doubling the number existing in 1918. Other building societies were expanding in the same way and Hill, managing director since 1917, said,

> 'The day of branches of building societies has arrived, and I am very glad to see that many of the important building societies are realising the advantages and benefits of branch offices and the opportunities thus secured of extending the benefits of their particular societies over greater areas, to the advantage of increased numbers.'

During the early 1930s, although it was the period of the Great Depression throughout the world, the merged Halifax societies doubled their assets, from £46,900,000 in 1928 to £92,600,000 in January 1934 and by 1939, on the eve of the outbreak of the Second World War, the assets had climbed to £128,200,000. The 1930s is always considered a decade of economic trauma, and for many it was. Nevertheless, as we have seen it was also a golden period for housebuilding and consequently, for building societies.

As part of this activity, the Halifax moved into Scotland, opening offices in Edinburgh and Glasgow in 1928. It also constructed Halifax House in the Strand in London. By the time Hill retired in 1938, the *Building Societies' Gazette* said that the Halifax,

> ' ... indisputably the greatest institution of its kind in the world, is the veritable creation of Enoch Hill, an expression of his genius and a measurement of his stature among men.'

The Second World War brought similar problems to those brought by the First World War, notably a slump in advances required and thereby a dramatic increase in liquidity. In 1919, 30 per cent of the society's assets of £5.9 million were in cash, or government or local government securities. In 1945 the percentage was 40 and by this time the assets were £132.8 million. For the remainder of the 1940s the problem was finding borrowers, thereby securing a better return. As Hobson pointed out in his book,

> 'This was due in the main to Government housing policy. The Government and the local authorities had after the First World War launched into house-building on a large scale but without imposing any restrictions on private building. After the Second World War, however, the Labour Government laid down that practically all houses should be built by the local authorities with Government assistance, for letting and not for sale. The proportion of all houses for which the local authorities were authorised to grant licenses to private builders was first set at one-fifth, then reduced to one-tenth and later raised to one-fifth again ... [T]he limitations imposed by the Minister of Health on private builders were far too severe. They not only militated against the full and most advantageous use of the country's building resources, thus unnecessarily raising the average cost of new houses, but they signally failed to satisfy the demand of that large section of the people which desired to own the houses it lived in.
>
> The financial effect of this housing policy was that the great bulk of the new houses was financed by Government advances from the Local Loans Fund and that very few of them were financed by building society mortgage. At the society's meeting in April 1950, for example, the president noted that, out of total advances granted

49

in the preceding years of £29,100,000, only £958,000 had been on the security of newly built houses.'

The restrictions imposed by the Labour governments between 1945 and 1951 were eased during the 1950s and, as we have already seen, the 1950s and 1960s were decades of strong expansion in the building society industry. The Halifax, as the largest society, played its full part in this expansion.

The early 1950s witnessed the one serious board-room row in the whole history of Halifax. The president was Algernon Denham who could be described as 'one of the old school'. The family ran a powerful family property business and Denham had joined the Halifax Permanent's board as long ago as 1922. By 1945, when he became president, he had already served for 23 years as a director. He pursued an extremely conservative policy, was very hands-on and was instrumental in the post-war decision of Halifax to lend only on the *pre-war* valuation of properties. Although the housing market was constrained in the immediate post-war years this policy undoubtedly lost Halifax some business.

The general manager was Fred Bentley, who had started working for Halifax in 1911 and had worked his way gradually to the top. Inevitably there were clashes with Denham as Bentley tried to exercise some independence and matters came to a head in 1956 in what became known as the 'Bentley Affair'.

In 1956, Bentley stood for, and was elected, chairman of the Building Societies Association. This was against the wishes of the Halifax board, who felt it might prove an embarrassment in view of recent differences of opinion between the society and the Association. John Spalding, chief general manager in the 1980s, recalled that the board had decided in principle on Enoch Hill's retirement that no Halifax employee should become chairman of the Building Societies Association.

Movements in the bank rate in late 1954 and early 1955 led to dis-agreement between Bentley and the Halifax board. The key contentious issue was the willingness of the majority of BSA members to attract large single investments or 'hot money' while the Halifax was much more conservative. The Building Societies Association therefore wanted higher rates to attract more funds so that lending could be increased, while the more cautious Halifax wanted to hold rates down.

At its meeting on 2 February 1955 the board decided to defer its decision on a move in interest rates, which resulted in an outburst from

Mr Bentley in the boardroom directed against the president and by inference against the rest of the board. This came as a complete surprise and shock to the board.

Disagreements about various building society matters, including the level of borrowing and lending rates and the 'hot money' issue, rumbled on between the society and the Association through 1955. At the beginning of 1956 the Halifax board learnt that Bentley was to be elected as chairman of the Association and resolved that the differences between the two should be settled as quickly and as amicably as possible to avoid further conflicts of interest. However, matters came to a head when Denham wrote to the Association. Bentley took strong exception to the letter, telling the board that unless it was withdrawn he would 'go into retirement from the service of the Society'.

Denham did not withdraw the letter and Bentley resigned, accusing the members of the board of treating him dishonourably. And Bentley did not go quietly. He made his own statement to the press and wrote to many of the managers and staff. Under the circumstances, Halifax had little choice but to resign from the Building Societies Association. This appeared to be a victory for Denham over Bentley, but Bentley stood for election to the board in 1957 and was duly elected.

Denham continued in office until 1961 to complete 39 years as a director and 16 as president – another, and very different example, of a very long-serving Halifax servant. He was succeeded by Ian Maclean, another man with a textile background, this time Crossley Carpets. Spalding recalled him as less ruthless than Denham but nevertheless as a determined chairman who expected to win arguments. 'His mind was set in concrete.' In spite of this he proved to be more of a chairman than his predecessor and set the scene for the modern division of responsibilities between chairman and chief executive. His early years as president were relatively calm though the later years of the 1960s and the early 1970s witnessed the effects of growing rates of inflation and a housing boom. He presided over some key developments, substantial branch growth and modernisation, a new head office and computerisation of investors' and borrowers' accounts. During his period of office his title was changed from president to chairman.

Maclean was succeeded in 1974 as chairman by Raymond, later Sir Raymond, Potter, a former general manager. He transferred to chairman well and worked closely with Albert Thayre through the rather difficult inflationary years of the late 1970s and early 1980s. Their path was eased by the continuing building society 'cartel' which effectively fixed borrowing and lending rates, an orderliness whose days were numbered.

Leeds – also ambitious

When the Halifax began life in 1853, the Leeds had already been operating for five years. The year 1848 is famous in European history for the many riots and minor revolutions that took place in many major cities, and in Britain there were many Chartist demonstrations. With these demonstrations many expressed the desire to live healthier, more secure, lives. Building societies were part of that expression. The Leeds built itself gradually and in a Royal Commission report on Friendly Societies, published in 1871, was commended as a model society. By the end of the 1870s and with assets of just over £1 million, the Leeds was similar in size to the Halifax.

Growth, as with the Halifax and all other societies, was hampered, first by the long recession from the mid-1870s to the mid-1890s and again by the First World War. At the end of that war, the assets of the Leeds were just over £2 million. During the 1920s and 1930s the Leeds expanded as the Halifax did, opening branches throughout Britain and also opening a large office in London. By 1930 the assets were £14 million (about the same size as the Halifax Equitable when it was absorbed by the Halifax in 1928) and by 1939, on the outbreak of war, almost £42 million.

In 1944, the Leeds almost merged with the Woolwich Equitable which would have produced a society with assets of £80 million, similar to those of the Abbey Road and National Building Societies who had recently merged to form the Abbey National. They would have vied for second place behind the Halifax whose assets at the time were just over £129 million. The Leeds/Woolwich merger would have worked well but it was not to be. As Les Grainger pointed out in his book, *A Personal Review of Leeds Permanent Building Society 1930–1980*,

> 'It was necessary before the merger could be effected that a resolution approving the amalgamation should be passed by a majority of three-quarters of the members actually present at a special meeting called for the purpose. The Registrar of Building Societies noted that even in peace time it was unlikely that more than a small minority of members would be likely to attend any such meeting and he

suggested that the views of those unable to be present should be ascertained on a reply card, notwithstanding that the result of a card vote could not be taken into account legally in ascertaining the required majority at the meeting itself. Perhaps he thought that if the result of such a vote, although of no legal effect, showed that the majority of members were against the amalgamation, the Directors would have second thoughts. But in the event, out of 21,252 completed cards returned, 19,908 were in favour of the amalgamation. On the strength of this the amalgamation seemed a certainty. The Woolwich members had already approved it. The new rule books for the British Building Society had been printed.

Then came the Special General Meeting of Leeds members which was held at 5.30 p.m. on 6 July 1944 in the Philosophical Hall, the scene of many important meetings in the life of the Society; 335 turned up to vote and only 195 of them approved the amalgamation. As the majority in favour of the proposal was less than three-quarters, the amalgamation could not go ahead. Thus it was that a minority of members present at a meeting could override the views of an overwhelming majority unable to attend.'

The progress of the Leeds after the war was similar to the building society industry as a whole, although by the mid-1960s it was growing faster than most. Indeed, Grainger was able to say in his book that,

' ... probably most gratifying was the fact that for the six-year period, 1964–69, the Society had led the assets growth table in the top five societies, as it did in the early 1970s.'

Howard Briggs, later to become secretary of Leeds and deputy secretary of new Halifax in August 1995, remembers that the society he joined in 1971 was extremely paternalistic and still small. Indeed the hundredth branch was opened in Wilmslow, Cheshire in that year. However, in 1972 the highly energetic Leonard Hyde, whom we have already met in chapter one, was appointed general manager and rapid branch expansion began. In 1973 alone, 53 new branches were opened and throughout most of the 1970s assets of the society expanded at 20 per cent a year. By 1980 the assets of the Leeds stood at £3 billion. Even allowing for inflation it was a long way from the £42 million of 1939.

Hyde remained general manager for five years before giving way to Stanley Walker. (Hyde remained on the board of Leeds until the late

1980s.) Walker was more of an intellectual and during his tenure it was generally recognised that Leeds head office and its systems failed to keep pace with the branch expansion. Walker was quickly succeeded by Peter Hemingway, an accountant who reined back the expansion and oversaw a period of consolidation in the first half of the 1980s. The major event of this period was the attempt to merge with the Leeds & Holbeck in 1985, which was agreed all the way down to the confirmation hearings of the Building Societies Commission (these can be quite serious and challenging events as we shall see later).

A combination of the husband of a member who said he had received a voting paper while his wife had not which made the society look incompetent, and allegations about 'fat cats' in the media embarrassed Leeds into withdrawing from the merger. Losing Leeds & Holbeck was not a great disaster. As the chairman of the time, Sir William Tweddle, pointed out, somewhat superciliously, 'They're only six weeks of our growth.'

Talks continued with other societies. The perennial favourite was the Woolwich. As we have already seen, the two boards had agreed on a merger as long ago as 1944. The extraordinary general meeting at the Woolwich agreed to the deal but that of the Leeds threw it out. The comment of one member summed up the general view, 'Tha knows it'll all go to they southerners.'

During the 1970s there had been brief talks with the National & Provincial, based in Bradford, quite serious talks with Britannia and, in the early 1980s, the Woolwich had approached them again. This time the Leeds board voted five to four in favour of the merger. However, Arnold Ziff, the founder and chairman of Town Centre Securities plc and chairman of Stylo plc, who had joined the Leeds in 1982, suggested to the chairman, Tom Harrington, that the four general managers should have a vote. In his view, the vote of the board, which consisted of eight non-executives and only one executive, Peter Hemingway, had been very close. As the new headquarters was going to be in Bexleyheath in Kent he felt that the general managers should have a say. Three of the four voted against.

'In that case', said Ziff, 'I'm changing my vote, so the board is now five to four against.' Once again a Leeds/Woolwich merger had fallen almost at the last fence.

In the meantime, the Leeds board wanted a new general manager and agreed that Hemingway should retire at 60 years of age. They asked Hemingway if there was a suitable internal candidate. 'No' was the answer. In that case, was there anyone suitable in the industry? The best two candidates seemed to be Andrew Longhurst of Cheltenham and Gloucester and Christopher Sharp of Northern Rock. Hemingway contacted Longhurst who turned him down. After several more months, Sharp came for an interview but also turned the offer down. Both would probably have been more interested if they could have brought their societies with them. However, the Leeds board turned this option down on the grounds that it would have looked like a 'reverse' takeover. Headhunters were appointed and produced an excellent prospect from Barclays who was interviewed and approved by the whole board. Unfortunately, he did not want to live in Leeds and turned down the offer as well. By this time Ziff was becoming impatient and, recalling a former deputy manager at the Park Row, Leeds, branch of Lloyds Bank (Ziff had been appointed to the northern board of Lloyds at about the same time as he joined the Leeds), he suggested they might like to talk to Mike Blackburn. Presumably he would have no problem returning to live in Leeds. Indeed he did not and he joined in July 1987 succeeding Peter Hemingway as chief executive in October.

CHAPTER THREE

Conversion is a high-risk strategy

£50 million is seven days' normal growth
Continue to review this question
The Building Societies Act 1986
This news caused a frisson
Is he bringing his society with him?
Short of best practice
I was so upset I couldn't sleep

£50 million is seven days' normal growth

While the changes outlined in chapter two were taking place in the building society industry, how was the Halifax viewing its future?

In July 1982, the chairman's committee instructed the executive to investigate and report on the feasibility of promoting a merger with another society in the top five societies, accepting approaches for a merger from other societies and expanding by accepting transfers of engagements.

By November 1983, the board was recording that there were a number of medium and small societies which might make good partners and that good relationships should be maintained with all potential partners.

It was felt that a merger with one of the top five societies would almost certainly bring a reference to the Monopolies and Mergers Commission.

On the other hand, there didn't seem much point in going through the costs and all the inevitable disruptions for the sake of buying small societies. At the board meeting of November 1983 it was reported that,

'Societies of less than £50 million have been excluded because of the heavy costs of such mergers in relation to the benefits achieved. £50 million is seven days' normal growth for the Halifax.'

(This was a slight exaggeration. In 1982–3 the assets of the Halifax increased from £11,913 million to £14,703 million, about £6 million a day; £50 million was therefore just over eight days' growth!) Irrespective of merger, the policy committee reported in March 1985 that,

'The major objectives of the Society probably relate to market share and to surplus. Given a market share objective, other objectives (type of lending, cost of borrowing, investors' products and services etc.) flow from this as strategies.'

And what was the market share the Halifax was aiming for? Defining market share as the proportion of all institutional lending for house purchase, the Society had enjoyed a share of 17–18 per cent in the late 1970s. This had fallen to 11.5 per cent in 1982 but recovered to 19.5 per cent in 1984. It would probably be 16–17 per cent in 1985 and the aim should be to sustain an 18–20 per cent share for the coming five years.

We cannot look at the approach of the Halifax to the challenges of the 1980s without considering its leaders. Richard, always known as Dick, Hornby succeeded Sir Raymond Potter as chairman of the Halifax in 1983. Born in 1922 in Lancashire, he had been educated at Winchester and, after serving in the King's Royal Rifle Corps during the war, won a scholarship to Trinity College, Oxford where he read PPE. After two and a half years of teaching at Eton he moved into commerce, first with a Unilever subsidiary, Hudson and Light (which operated from a warehouse in Wapping – a far cry from the cloisters of Winchester, Trinity and Eton!), and then with the advertising agency, J Walter Thompson, where he stayed, essentially as a copywriter, for 27 years. However, his real interest was in politics and after fighting a good battle in the 1955 General Election against former Prime Minister, Clement Atlee and a by-election against former Cabinet Minister, Herbert Morrison (Peter Mandelson's grandfather), he won the safe Tory seat of Tonbridge in a by-election in June 1956. He served as Tonbridge's Member until 1974 and as PPS to Duncan Sandys for a spell as well as Under Secretary for Commonwealth Relations between 1963 and 1964.

In 1974 he returned to J Walter Thompson on a full-time basis and, as he knew both the chairman of the Halifax, Raymond Potter, and the vice-chairman, Sir James Whitaker, he was an obvious choice to join the London board of the Halifax when the society felt the need both to strengthen its presence in London and to sharpen up its marketing. Two years later, Hornby joined the main board, became vice-chairman in 1981 and chairman in 1983. He was the first truly external chairman who was neither a local worthy nor an executive promoted from the ranks.

On reflection, he felt that the Halifax in the 1970s, while with every justification was proud of its history and reputation, nevertheless was a little staid and unsophisticated in marketing terms. It was in the mortgage and savings markets and nothing else. He hoped that he opened up the society a little and brought the board and the executive management closer together. Certainly he was chairman during a period of great change in the personal financial services industry.

Hornby's chief general manager for most of the 1980s was John Spalding (his title was changed to chief executive after three years). A solicitor by training, he had joined the society in 1962 after nine years as senior assistant solicitor at Hampshire County Council. He said of the move,

> 'It was something of a culture shock. I'd been working with two imaginatively managed local authorities. In Hampshire in the 1950s we used the very latest in technological equipment – Rank Xerox high-speed copiers and so forth. When I joined the world's biggest building society it had just one ancient wet-copying machine!'

Perhaps his greatest contribution to the Halifax was his own research into conversion – he went to the USA to study the conversion of the mutual Glendale Federal into a joint stock corporation – and the setting in motion of an exhaustive independent study into the whole concept of conversion. Certainly, his greatest contribution to the building society industry in general was his management of The Spalding Committee, set up in the early 1980s by the Conservative Government, to address the new situation in property lending following the removal of restrictions at the end of the 1970s and the collapse of the rates cartel. A new framework was necessary as the quota method of lending, with branch managers bidding for their quota, gave way to a free market where the banks were muscling in on the building societies' patch. Spalding himself realised that the Halifax was providing the banks with 'hot' leads by having a bank reference section on the society's mortgage application form. He made sure the section was deleted.

Gary Marsh, currently assistant general manager of Corporate Affairs, joined the Halifax as an economist from the textile group, Tootal in the early 1980s and was amazed to find that Halifax did not seem to have a budget system.

The textile industry was mired in recession and only those companies with tight financial controls survived. There may have been a recession in most of industry but the housing market had never really suffered. Even in the mid-1970s, although house prices fell in real terms, because of inflation they still rose in absolute terms and there were no waves of repossessions or negative equity. Marsh recalled,

> 'There was no budgetary system, no real system of control of expenditure, because there was no need to. People just spent what their managers thought was appropriate and there were informal controls right through to the very top.'

And Marsh found that administration was everything.

> 'It wasn't a marketing organisation because you had nothing to market. Your market was there, you didn't have to sell anything. Interest rates were set. All you needed to do was administer as efficiently as possible, that was it! As long as you ran a tight ship you could operate. That's how building societies were. But they were more paternalistic and – how can I put it? – more congenial places to work generally.'

Continue to review this question

In July 1985, the Halifax board was presented with the arguments for and against conversion. The arguments for could be summarised as follows.

- New, permanent capital – the Registrar had already indicated that he thought *substantial* increases in capital would be necessary.

- Company status would generate clearer operational targets and make it easier to adopt a 'profit centre' approach.

- Company status would allow a much wider range of activities.

- Building society legislation, existing and prospective, was emphasising membership participation. However laudable, this was expensive in costs and management time.

- Company status would facilitate acquisitions by the use of shares rather than cash.

- Fewer limits on the society's activities.

(It was also clear that the 1986 Act would be 'prescriptive' at a time when financial markets were moving quickly. The effect was to put Building Societies on the back foot in competitive terms.)

The main arguments against conversion were as follows.

- As a company vulnerable to take-over.

- If reserves distributed on conversion, a need for extra dividend on the reserves.

- Have to meet the Bank of England's criteria for capital adequacy and liquidity and vulnerable to any re-introduction of credit controls.

- Credit rating could be affected. Some wholesale funders might feel safer lending to a building society than a bank.

- External perception could change.

- Shareholder control would quickly pass to pension funds and insurance companies meaning less accountability to customer-members.

- Might be a loss of freedom to work with all sections of the community. Building societies are viewed as apolitical while large companies are viewed as part of 'big business'.

By May 1986, a board discussion paper pointed out that,

'If we choose to stay mutual we are, by implication, saying that the competitive period in mortgage lending will not last very long and will not push down margins very much. We are also assuming that diversification will not be rapid and will not be capital-intensive, or that capital ratios will be relaxed. Finally we are assuming that we can survive and prosper against competition from converted mutuals. These could be capital-rich, highly diversified and able – because of rapid growth – to pick up market share. This in turn could give them benefits of economies of scale and lower running costs.'

The paper concluded,

' … if current competitive trends continue, and the proposed legislation and supervisory structure remains in place, conversion to plc status may well become necessary. It is recommended that the Board should continue to review this question in the light of changing events.'

The Building Societies Act 1986

At the same time as the pressures were mounting on the interest rate cartel, other competitive pressures were leading the building societies to request changes in the law which would give them more freedom to compete with other financial institutions, most notably the clearing banks.

In mid-1981 the BSA established a committee chaired by John Spalding, the chief general manager of the Halifax, to review the constitution and powers of the societies and the laws governing them. A BSA paper was published in 1983 which invited public discussion and in 1984 final proposals were published. These proposals recommended that building societies, while retaining their basic character as mortgage providers, should be allowed to undertake a wider range of financial activities such as estate agency, conveyancing, personal and other loans and at the same time offer certain banking facilities such as cheque books, credit cards and cash dispensers. The proposals also included a recommendation that societies should be able to hold land for development and to operate in European Community countries. Most significantly, it was proposed that societies could convert from mutual status into corporate form – that is, become public limited companies.

In general the proposals found government support. This was the era of the Thatcher administrations at their most creative, sweeping away restrictive practices, whether on the shop-floor or in the operation of financial institutions. The Labour Party strongly opposed the conversion to plc aspects of the Bill that came before the House of Commons but on 25 July 1986, The Building Societies Act 1986 became law and it granted the societies most of what they had requested including the right to convert and, most importantly, the right to tap the wholesale money markets, initially for 20 per cent, and subsequently for 40 per cent, of their requirements. Specifically the Act permitted societies to provide the following services.

- Money transmission service.

- Foreign exchange services to individuals.

- Making or receiving payments as agents.

- Management, as agents, of mortgage investments.

- Arranging for the provision of services relating to the acquisition or disposal of investments (that is, as intermediaries, not as stock-brokers or investments advisers).

- Arranging for the provision of credit to individuals.

- Establishment and management of unit trust schemes for pensions (through a subsidiary).

- Establishment and, with regard to contributions and benefits, administration of pension schemes.

- Arranging for the provision of insurance of any description primarily to individuals.

- Giving advice on insurance of any description.

- Estate agency services (but only through a subsidiary – no employee involved in mortgage lending can act as an agent for the subsidiary).

- Surveys and valuations of land.

- Conveyancing (subject to rules to be laid before Parliament).

Some felt that the government was trying to force societies into conversion to public companies. However, the Green Paper of July 1984 which preceded the Act, stated clearly,

> 'A compulsory change to company status has been advocated by some in the past on the grounds that their mutual constitution insulates societies from the effects of competition, leaving too much scope for inefficiency and extravagance in their management ... The government does not accept that such a change is needed ...

However, it is wrong that a society cannot turn itself into a company if its members so wish … Although there are no signs that many societies will wish to become companies in the near future, this will provide greater flexibility … It will also provide a means by which a society which wished to diversify radically could acquire the necessary increase in its capital base reasonably quickly.'

Ian Stewart MP, the Economic Secretary to the Treasury and a former merchant banker, was given the task by the Chancellor of the Exchequer, Nigel, now Lord, Lawson, of piloting the Bill through the House of Commons. Stewart said that he did not want conversion to,

' … be an easy option … On the other hand, it seemed wrong to constrain the big societies from moving closer towards general banking if the managements and the members wanted this. So I was quite satisfied we needed a provision allowing societies to convert into plcs. Otherwise we would be imposing a potentially unnatural constraint on the large societies for a number of years.'

He did not want the conversion process to be unduly easy,

'My view was that it was a major step to become a plc and shouldn't be undertaken unless a society felt impelled to do it because it had a sense of being in a strait-jacket which it wanted to get out of.'

In assessing the advantage or otherwise of remaining a building society it is helpful to define the difference between a mutual form of business and that of a limited company. First the basis of member ownership differs radically. In a public limited company, in return for investing share capital, the owners of the capital expect to receive a return in the form of dividends and to benefit from any appreciation in the company's share price. Members of a building society receive interest on their investment but cannot benefit directly from the rise in the asset value of their institution. Another major difference is the ability of a plc to increase its capital through the issue of fresh equity. Building societies, until recently anyway, did not have access to an external capital market and had to rely on generating capital internally from surplus.

This restriction on building societies was lightened, but not completely removed, by the introduction of Permanent Interest Bearing Shares (PIBS) in 1991. PIBS are not true equity capital and market demand would always be limited. Nevertheless, for the Halifax they represented a toe in the water in its search for new sources of capital but they did not remove the 'access to new capital' argument which featured in the 1987–8 discussions on conversion.

This news caused a frisson

The debate about conversion within the Halifax did not die and discussions continued. In the autumn of 1987, the merchant bank, N M Rothschild, with other advisers, the stockbrokers, Cazenove & Co, the communications and marketing consultants, Dewe Rogerson, the legal firm, Linklaters & Paines and the accountants, Peat Marwick McLintock, had been commissioned to research thoroughly every aspect of conversion. In January 1988 the society announced publicly that it had decided to review its plc option. During the spring and early summer of 1988 the directors received a report from Rothschild, reports from Dewe Rogerson on market research among customers and intermediaries, and also written submissions by four members of the London board.

It is almost certain that when the Halifax appointed Rothschild to advise on whether to convert most people assumed that the true brief was on *how*, not *whether*. This belief is given credence by a comment by Margaret Reid in her book on Abbey National, *Conversion to PLC*,

> 'In the course of the Cliveden meeting directors heard that the Halifax ... were appointing Rothschild to advise it on matters to do with conversion. This news caused a frisson and perhaps provided yet more impetus towards reaching a decision.'

On 20 July 1988, the full board of the Halifax met to debate the issue. The executive management had already met in June for their discussions. Before the directors gave the chairman their views, the opinions of the management, especially those expressed at the recent strategy meeting at Middlethorpe Hall, near York, were put before the directors. Jim, later Sir James, Birrell, deputy chief executive, summarised the proceedings at the Middlethorpe Hall conference. He began with the philosophical point on whether members actually viewed themselves as members or merely as customers. The general view was that the distinction was no longer important. David Gilchrist, at the time general manager, Planning, felt that the society had to grow or change and that it needed the flexibility of powers and capital and the quality of bank regulation. This meant conversion, though ideally Gilchrist felt the society needed more time. Gren Folwell, then general manager, Finance, was in favour of conversion but did not feel that Rothschild had made an immediate case for additional capital – such as would be required, for instance, for the purchase of a life assurance company. Mike Whitehouse, operations director, accepted the ultimate inevitability of conversion but felt that for the time being the society should concentrate on growing internally. However, on balance the management was in favour of early conversion.

Certainly N M Rothschild was in favour of early conversion. It felt that conversion would be beneficial for staff employment and motivation providing the possibility of better incentives for senior executives and an SAYE option scheme for other employees. Rothschild also talked of an 'expansionist role', 'conversion telling the world the Halifax wants to move forward' and more controversially that 'popular perceptions (particularly among management) are that it is better to work for a bank than a building society'.

However, Rothschild's main conclusion was that Halifax's business plan, taken at its most ambitious, would require more capital and that flotation was the most effective and cheapest way of raising that capital.

(In the light of later developments it is fascinating to note that in its document presented to the board it talked of the business having a value of only £1.7 billion and of it raising a mere £1.5 billion from the flotation.)

On 2 June 1997 Halifax plc was valued on the stock market at £18 billion, a reflection of how it had grown in the previous nine years and also of how highly the banking sector was rated in the late 1990s compared with the late 1980s.

What did the directors think?

Sir James Whitaker, vice-chairman, favoured conversion, feeling that the days of friendly societies and building societies were numbered. The Abbey National had already decided to float and Sir James felt that there might be a loss of staff morale unless the Halifax floated as well. John Symons, a former director of BAT, on the other hand, wanted to retain mutual status. He saw no reason for raising extra capital, which would be more expensive, unless there was a clear idea of what the society would do with it. The conversion exercise would divert management and slow down development plans. He concluded,

'Conversion is a high-risk strategy based on one unlikely acquisition target and would be irreversible carrying the risk of being swallowed up.'

Alan Monckton, a chartered surveyor and landowner, also favoured conversion without delay. As the market had become mature with growth potential, limited acquisitions had become important whether in the UK or Europe and targets would be more willing to join a plc. Monckton made the point that under existing BSA legislation the society was prevented from raising the capital needed for expansion especially if it was to compete in the European Union. Richard Wheway, finance director, was against immediate conversion. In his view, a case on the grounds of either regulation or capital had not been made. It would be better to wait until the need was clearer and then to plan the exercise and its timing carefully. Mark Cornwall-Jones, a director of the investment management firm, John Govett, was in favour of conversion but not immediately. He had been impressed by the management view and felt that plc status was more appropriate for the types of business the Halifax was entering. Ronnie Archer, a director of Unilever, was still opposed to conversion, mainly on cost of capital grounds. David Lee, a director of Sheffield steelmaker Arthur Lee, was also against immediate conversion. Retention of mutual status would not inhibit the society's development. John Fforde, a former executive director of the Bank of England, could only see the benefit of conversion if the society planned to acquire a bank and an insurance company and create a group with assets of over £100 billion. If that were not the vision, the society should stay mutual. Eric Dodson, senior partner of Addleshaw, Sons & Latham, the Manchester solicitors, felt that those in favour of conversion had not proved their point. He felt the onus lay on those proposing conversion to demonstrate that change of the long-established status as a mutual was in the interests of the members. Jon Foulds was also against conversion, especially to raise capital for unspecified business. In his view, international capital markets were creative and flexible and mutual status should not prevent the society raising funds needed. John Wood, a company director and former chief executive of the printer, McCorquadale, was not so sure about the ease of raising capital and wondered whether the society might not regret converting now in two or three years' time. John Spalding was also against conversion immediately though he saw it as right for the future. He wanted to see careful planning to avoid the distraction that had occurred in the early 1970s when the new head office was being built.

The board were influenced by the calculations carried out by the economists Professor John Kay, and David Llewellyn, who was on the London board, on the increase in ROE which would be necessary to sustain realistic dividends and a safe capital base for a future plc.

It was appreciated that Rothschild would be heavily involved in the conversion process if it went ahead and the directors needed to take that into account when assessing Rothschild's strong arguments in favour of conversion. Due to the government's heavy privatisation programme and the possibility of a General Election in 1991 there was only one window of opportunity – and that was September 1989. To achieve that date with the 'long preparation' needed (Rothschild calculated it would take a year; in view of the time the conversion actually took in the 1990s, this was almost certainly an underestimate), the board would need to make a positive decision at their meeting on 20 July.

The chairman, Dick Hornby, summed up and also gave his own view. His conclusion was,

> 'I am reluctant to take an irreversible step in present conditions that might deprive members of an institution which has served them well and which is not under immediate threat.'

In the final analysis, the sense of the meeting was against immediate conversion while recognising that 'the door was not closed and that the decisions might well have to be reviewed in four to five years'. The general managers were recalled to the meeting and told of the decision. Michael Richardson and Simon Linnett of N M Rothschild were told shortly after the meeting, and a statement to the Halifax staff and the press was made within 24 hours.

Is he bringing his society with him?

After the boom years of the 1980s it was becoming clear in 1989 that the years ahead would be considerably more difficult in economic terms. The British government (and others elsewhere) had allowed its economies to grow too fast, and in an attempt to slow them down had raised interest rates sharply in 1988 and 1989. Sharply raising the cost of money is an effective way of dissuading people from borrowing it and, although consumers take some time to react, when they do so the effect can be dramatic. So it proved to be in Britain. The economy slowed a little in 1989, a little more in 1990 and then moved into recession in 1991. It stagnated in 1992 and only began to grow again when the government withdrew sterling from the European Exchange Rate Mechanism in September 1992 and reduced interest rates from 12 per cent to 6 per cent by January 1993. The effect on the housing market was traumatic. The year 1988 had provided the last hysterical months of the house price boom given a final fillip by Chancellor Lawson's budget measure in April to disallow dual mortgage interest rate relief from August. With interest rates rising the house price rise stalled and in 1989 prices began to fall, in some cases sharply. Many buyers, especially those who had bought recently, were caught in first one trap, higher interest payments, then a second, their houses were valued at a lower price than their borrowings and for some, a third, redundancy as the economy moved into recession.

For the building societies this was a very different market from that of only two years before. Repossessions soared (fortunately they were largely protected in that the insurance companies had covered potential losses with mortgage indemnity insurance). Housing transactions fell

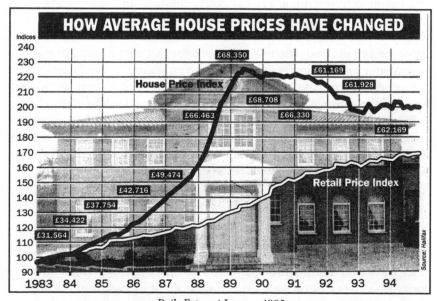

Daily Express 4 January 1995

dramatically. It was a new market and Halifax appointed a new chairman to cope with it.

The new chairman, Jon Foulds, was appointed in 1990. His father, a doctor, had known Dick Hornby's parents in the same town of Bury in Lancashire and Jon Foulds says, 'I can remember going there for tea.' Born there in 1932, Foulds had been put off the idea of becoming a general practitioner by doing the rounds with his father. Educated at the Quaker school, Bootham, in York, he joined his uncles' textile business after two years in the Fleet Air Arm. Within three years he helped them to close it down.

> 'We worked hard but we were getting nowhere and we were never going to get anywhere. We had much higher wage costs than our international competitors. It was the old Lancashire story.'

From textiles he moved to managing money, joining the Industrial and Commercial Finance Corporation (ICFC, now called 3i). He began in London in 1959 and loved it: 'It became my university, my passion and my hobby all rolled into one.' Seventeen years later he became chief executive, and ten years after that, in 1986, a non-executive director of the Halifax, which had been looking for someone with a financial background (though not a banker to avoid conflict of interest).

To Foulds, the Halifax was a completely new experience. 3i had become quite large but nothing like the size of the Halifax. In spite of its size the society did not talk of profits but of surpluses. He found it somewhat hierarchical and systems driven although the IT systems in place were very effective, if only in a narrow area. He was impressed by the openness, integrity and good humour of the board and management.

The chief executive who succeeded John Spalding in 1988 and who was therefore in place when Foulds became chairman was Jim Birrell, an accountant who had joined Halifax in 1968 after working for Price Waterhouse, Empire Stores in Bradford and finally as a director and company secretary at John Gladstone & Co. He had been heavily involved in the 1970s and 1980s in the computerisation of the society.

His main achievement in the late 1980s and early 1990s was to cope successfully with the burgeoning bad debt problem arising from the recession and sharp decline in house prices. (The society's bad debt provision rose from a paltry £2 million in 1985–6 to the horrendous figure of £373 million in 1992–3.) Jon Foulds described Birrell as,

'The last of the big-time building society chiefs who ran their empires in what was virtually a monopoly situation. He was a leading figure in the industry who took a proactive stance on issues and became chairman of the Council of Mortgage Lenders.'

Birrell led the mortgage-lending industry through an extremely difficult period with minimal adverse impact on borrowers or indeed lenders. He created the concept of *forbearance* policies, which gave borrowers as much time as possible to work themselves out of their problems while at the same time maintaining strict disciplines and strong balance sheets. It was for these services to the industry and for placing the Halifax in support of one or two rocky societies that he was knighted in 1993.

He was ably assisted by his operations director, Mike Whitehouse, a senior director who had masterminded the Halifax's IT development. Whitehouse was one of the first to spot the serious potential bad debt problem and to impose controls that ensured it never became a threatening situation for the society. As Dick Spelman, the then general manager, marketing, put it,

'It was a great opportunity for command and control, a situation for which Whitehouse was ideally suited.'

Some felt he was the obvious successor to Birrell. Gary Marsh said of him,

'He knew the business inside out. He was responsible for the development of our mainframe computer system and at that time it was the leading edge of building society systems. The front-office real-time and ATM systems that we had, more technologically advanced than the banks', were his baby.'

However, in the board's view he was not suitable and the society looked outside using the same headhunter, Michael Knight, who had been responsible for introducing Foulds to the Halifax in 1986. It was clearly a period of great change and the Halifax board wanted a man with a record of retailing, sound management and strong leadership. One man stood head and shoulders above all the competition. He was Mike Blackburn, chief executive of rival building society, the Leeds. The son of a retired County Treasurer, Blackburn had moved from being a bank manager with Lloyds in the early 1970s to running the bank's Business

Advisory Service, an operation employing 20 high flyers giving advice to small companies (small being defined as companies employing up to 200 employees with turnover up to £10 million). He was then asked to be Lloyds' representative to run the Access credit card operation from the retailing and processing point of view.

This was a big change in management terms as Access employed 5000 staff. He was also able to gain some international experience and contacts as he was appointed to the boards of Mastercard International and Eurocard International. When his four-year secondment at Access was at an end it was an easy decision to join the Leeds which also employed about 5000 staff and which was clearly, like all other building societies, going to become more like a bank.

Blackburn had quickly made a name for himself in the building society industry and, in December 1991, when the Government was forcing building societies and other mortgage lenders to agree its mortgage rescue scheme for people in arrears, it swore those involved in the negotiations to silence. Having done that, the Government then leaked its own story to the media to secure headlines such as 'Government takes lead in resolving mortgage crisis'. However, Blackburn decided to speak out and reminded the public that it was John Major who, as Chancellor of the Exchequer, had said of high interest rates, the source of the arrears problem, 'if they are not hurting, they are not working'. Then, he challenged the Government over retrospective legislation in the 1991 Budget describing it as the biggest building society robbery of all time. Peter Hemingway had already realised the size and importance of the issue and had begun the process necessary to try and reverse the decision. Leeds challenged the Treasury in the High Court over £57 million paid when the rules of taxation of interest on savings were changed. Woolwich had taken the Inland Revenue to the House of Lords and won a £70 million refund. In true Yorkshire fashion, the Leeds board had been happy for Woolwich to take the initiative and incur the legal costs, assuming that any favourable decision would equally benefit the Leeds. In this case they were wrong as the 1991 Budget blocked further claims. Leeds, at a cost of £500,000, wrote to its three million members alerting them to the battle with the Government. The battle was for another day but it brought Blackburn more favourable publicity.

Blackburn's time at the Leeds was considered an outstanding success. Adrian Coles, director general of the Building Societies Association, said,

'He really woke them up. The Leeds was the most conservative of societies but he rejuvenated it.'

Whitehouse's departure in October 1992 confirmed that it was more likely than not that Birrell's successor would be an external candidate, although one or two individual candidates did throw their hats into the ring. Senior Halifax management were told of Blackburn's appointment in early 1993 and a public announcement was made on 23 February. Blackburn was well known, liked and respected, and the appointment was welcomed. Inevitably there was a bit of, 'Why did we need expensive City headhunters to recruit someone 20 miles down the road?' and 'Is he bringing his society with him?'. However, the consensus was that the appointment was positive, exciting and a breath of fresh air. Blackburn joined the Halifax after a holiday and a little 'garden leave' at the beginning of June. He spent most of June and July making branch and departmental visits before taking over formally from Birrell in August 1993.

Following the Society's decision in 1988 not to pursue conversion in the foreseeable future, the Halifax had examined its strategy for the 1990s and at its annual strategy week-end in February 1989 agreed the following Mission Statement ...

'To become a leading retail financial services group, retaining our lead in the supply of UK housing finance and personal savings, and providing a range of financial products and services profitably and well so as to meet customer needs'

... and accepted these implications from that statement,

'the Society:

- must be widely perceived as a leading player in the market for personal sector financial services

- must offer a wide range, but probably not all, financial services demanded by the personal sector

- should be a leading supplier of mortgage finance and personal savings.'

The key strategic market implications would be that in housing finance the Halifax would be a market leader with its 15 per cent market share objectives maintained. There would be heavy emphasis on cross-selling through Halifax's estate agency outlets and other distribution channels. Money transmission, a prime financial relationship, would be important and with the society's strong customer position and technology could be developed internally making the acquisition of a bank unnecessary. In personal lending, emphasis would be placed on cross-selling to the existing customer base, with a gradual and limited extension of the product range. In insurance and assurance, the non-mortgage related product range would be significantly extended with possibly a joint venture or acquisition necessary to meet likely objectives. And finally, a proactive approach to product development and innovation would be taken in retail investments. The overall emphasis would be on housing finance but with a significant diversification into new markets.

The society was also open to making strategic acquisitions and given that it was a retailer of financial services and committed to remaining so, it could look in the fields of banking, consumer lending, insurance, other financial services and estate agency.

With regard to banking, the Society did not need to convert or acquire and was confident it could achieve the necessary changes in building society legislation. Current legislation only allowed the purchase of 15 per cent of an insurance company and the Society should perhaps consider the possibility of setting up a direct selling operation from scratch. Other financial services such as stockbroking, fund management and specialist mortgage lenders, were not key strategic markets and the best approach was probably joint ventures. In Estate Agency there was no real pressure for further extension into this field. The market was expected to be difficult in 1989 and 1990 and opportunities for further purchase would probably arise.

A year later, at the strategy meeting at Middlethorpe Hall in January 1990, it was agreed that there was 'no short-term reason to question our decision to retain mutual status', although in two to three years 'the, pros and cons would have to be reconsidered ... and we should ensure that no actions were taken which would remove our flexibility to consider conversion'.

Birrell, then chief executive, felt that mergers should be back on the agenda though he noted that they had led to difficulties elsewhere and wondered whether the Halifax would do any better. The general view was that a major merger would lead to, 'a significant diversion of resources and that we lacked the strength of management to undertake such an exercise'.

A similarly cautious approach was adopted towards acquisitions with the Society's recent experience, narrow range of skills, lack of spare management resources, risk averse mentality, limited project management ability and demands of the core business all pointing to 'a very cautious acquisitions policy'. Birrell pointed out later that the society's superior performance to its competitors, particularly the Abbey National, lessened the need of an acquisition.

Turning to the estate agency business Birrell referred to the original objectives of the venture, agreed by the board in February 1986, to,

'• improve the Halifax house-buying service and as a step towards the formation of an integrated housing service

• protect future mortgage origination for Class 1 new advances

• develop a new and profitable related business making an appropriate contribution to the Society's surplus.'

Birrell felt that the Society must concentrate on the first and (especially) the third objectives. There was no point in running an estate agency network for its own sake, it must be profitable.

At the strategy meeting in 1992, mutuality was again discussed. The conclusion was still in favour of retention.

'While few customers understood mutuality, there was a strong business case for its retention especially in terms of the cost of capital. Shareholders in companies had a stronger claim to the added value created by the success of the organisation than did members of societies, but it was not impossible for societies to distribute some or all of the profits to members.

A comparison between the Society (a mutual) and Marks and Spencer (a plc) pointed to more similarities than differences. Both were increasing their lead in their field, were not great innovators, were conservative, risk averse and had simple philosophies. Descriptions such as 'solid', 'safe' and 'dependable' all conveyed strength. That indicated that the image was based more on perception than on real differences and if that were the case the banks could make good the gap.

There was a feeling that there was more appreciation of mutuality than there had been in the 1980s, possibly as a result of the move towards customer orientation.

The Society wanted to have wider powers as a mutual, but with regulation of capital and resources rather then regulation by prescription.'

Birrell said later that the society was confident that with its good relations with Government agencies that wider powers as a mutual could be achieved. In his view the general feeling was that mutuality had helped the Halifax outperform the Abbey National and other competitors.

As we have seen, following the collapse of the Thatcher/Lawson boom of the mid-1980s the British, indeed the world, economy had suffered varying degrees of recession at the end of the 1980s and beginning of the 1990s. As interest rates rose, consumers' incomes were severely squeezed and, following the very sharp rises, from 1989 house prices fell not only in real terms but also, for the first time in living memory, in absolute terms. This left many households in a position of negative equity, which meant that their houses were worth less on the open market than the money borrowed to purchase them. Others found themselves unable to maintain their monthly interest payments and repossessions rose sharply. These factors led in 1990 and 1991 to the worst housing market that anyone could remember. But it's an ill wind and the Halifax 'was coming strongly through the worst housing market in memory and was therefore in a strong position to look for opportunities'. Also by early 1992, a major merger was back on the agenda and 'could expect to gain clearance from the Monopolies and Mergers Commission'.

Blackburn absorbed all this thinking of the previous five years and became convinced that the Halifax was not fulfilling its potential. On mergers the conclusion was that 'the choice lay between a large single merger to achieve a change in market share or several medium-sized mergers. For example, we might absorb a big society in three years but four smaller mergers, adding up to the size of one major society, might take ten years to absorb so that one big hit would be preferred.' The directors emphasised the difficulties that would be engendered by a hostile take-over.

At the board strategy meeting in February 1994, Blackburn's first, Jon Foulds, the chairman, told the group that the Society would need to focus on five items in the coming years.

'• Customer service – the key to gaining a competitive edge.

• Control of costs – paramount as it became harder to increase revenues.

- Managing risk on both sides of the balance sheet, especially Treasury and underwriting. Not to be risk-averse but to understand the risks.

- Staff issues – succession planning is not adequate for moving in to a higher gear. It will be hard to manage through the transition period.

- Management of change – an enormous change since 1986, which will continue. We must preserve the Halifax ethic through the changes.'

Mike Blackburn emphasised the main threads,

> '*Market leadership* – although operating in mature markets, the Halifax could maintain market leadership through organic growth. If growth by acquisition was deemed to be the way forward "we would have to fish with patience".'

> '*On low cost provision* – to consider the question of how the Halifax was to measure itself, against the Cheltenham and Gloucester with its 26 per cent cost/income ratio or against the Nat West/TSB with its 60 per cent plus.'

He concluded,

> 'We are becoming a different organisation and should consider our new peer group. We must benchmark and seek best practice in all areas; there must be a willingness and openness to share best practice within the organisation. External perspectives are important; we must become less insular.'

Blackburn wanted to see careful diversification, for example by increasing current account holders from 700,000 to 1.5 million by the year 2000. He wanted further expansion of the general insurance operation moving from just a broking base to taking more control of the product right through to handling customers' claims. Great care would be needed in any diversification in the areas of life, pensions and unit trusts and extreme care in any European initiative. In terms of mission and values, Blackburn wanted the Halifax, with its 13 million customers, to realise its 'enormous power and potential … Biggest goes without saying but best is important. We do want to maximise customer satisfaction and our credit ratings and capital strength should be at the top of the heap.'

On the question of mutuality versus plc, Jon Foulds was still in favour of retaining mutuality but with greater freedom: 'A mutual bank is preferable if achievable.' The new mission statement was agreed as, *To be the biggest and best personal finance business in the UK,* and it was suggested that this would be difficult to achieve without bank status.

Short of best practice

We have seen how the Halifax was planning to cope with the changes in the economic environment at the end of the 1980s. How did the Leeds see its future in 1988?

Mike Blackburn joined the Leeds in July 1987 and had taken over as chief executive in October 1987. He had found the Leeds 'warm and comfy' with many of its branches 'rather shabby with lots of paper around'. He found the people 'nice but a bit lacking in cutting edge'.

Blackburn quickly made some top management changes, in some cases bringing in fresh blood from outside. For example, Chris Chadwick was brought in from the retailing group, Burton, as commercial director and rapidly created a marketing function. Roger Boyes was brought in from the mining equipment manufacturer Fenner as finance director, and John Miller from director of operations at the 'Orange' mobile telephone company Microtel as IT director. He also recruited Judy Atchison from the manufacturing company Rank, Hovis, McDougall and, unusually for a woman in the building society world, she became a senior executive in Leeds. She remembers being utterly amazed that senior executives, even directors, went home for lunch, a bizarre concept for someone used to working in London.

In 1988 a cost-effectiveness programme was instituted and in September a strategic plan for the coming five years was published. It stated,

> 'Our overall objective over the period of this plan is to build a position for the Leeds as a successful specialist financial services institution, achieving a post-tax rate of return on capital of not less than 18 per cent.'

Within this overall objective the board of the Leeds planned to,

- provide a strongly differentiated house-buying service capable of forming the basis of lasting customer relationships

- deliver this service through an effective, efficient and attractive branch network, supported by first class information systems

- develop leading brands in each major product area that will combine to enhance the image and profitability of the Leeds

- become asset driven in terms of our balance-sheet management

- achieve cost-effective and flexible funding from the combination of the retail and wholesale markets, using on and off balance-sheet funding techniques

- achieve profitable growth via expansion of the mortgage business and diversification into new product areas, growing assets by 110 per cent and after-tax profits by 160 per cent over the period

- transform the Leeds into a cost-effective and flexible organisation via restructuring and improved communication and control systems to achieve a return on capital employed equal to or above the leaders in the financial services industry

- manage the business to ensure that conversion to plc status remains an option

- pursue alliances with other institutions as a route to becoming one of the major financial players of the 1990s

- create an enterprise culture linking rewards to individual and group achievements and performance against target, while ensuring that we continue to offer equal opportunities and a good working environment.

   'Through the attainment of these objectives we aim to revitalise the image of the Leeds in the eyes of staff, customers and other financial institutions.'

In Blackburn's view the operating efficiency fell 'short of best practice in the industry'. A number of initiatives were put in hand aimed at taking no less than £12 million out of the society's head office cost base. While the cost/income ratio was being reduced the society's marketing was beefed up mainly through the introduction of the *Home Arranger* service. He also felt there was poor communication between the three fields of product planning, the branches and finance, and steps were taken to address these problems.

Even with the growth that implementation of the board's plans would bring, the Leeds would still not be positioned 'as one of the major players in UK financial services'. It was felt that scale was likely to be an advantage in the financial environment of the 1990s, especially when it came to retail and wholesale funding.

> 'We therefore believe that over the term of this plan (1988–93) we should aim for one or several alliances with other financial institutions of significant size.'

The most attractive possibilities seemed to be other building societies or UK insurance companies. Foreign banks were also seen as a possibility but not as attractive.

A move in the very near future, before the internal 'vital changes' had been implemented, was probably not ideal, although, ' ... we cannot allow competitors to pre-empt us in mergers that would damage our long-term ability to build a strong position'. The result of this dichotomy was a two-part plan. In the short term, it intended to identify potentially attractive merger candidates, establish priorities for merger and a clear ranking of attractive candidates, begin preliminary discussions while assessing competitor activity but nevertheless avoid active pursuit of a merger unless either the candidate was willing to be acquired or it becomes a tactical necessity. The second part of the plan was to pursue actively merger possibilities with the attractive candidates. One likely development, which could ultimately lead to merger, was the pursuit of joint ventures.

On the subject of conversion, the Leeds had already commissioned Hambros Bank to conduct a feasibility study. Hambros had reported that conversion was a 'feasible option' but had highlighted the enormity of the task and the need for intensive management commitment and effort. In August 1988 (a month after the Halifax came to the same decision) conversion was ruled out for the immediate future but 'it must remain a live issue for us'. The envisaged growth would almost certainly require substantial additional capital and could, at the very least, involve alliances with non-mutual organisations. The Leeds intended to realise maximum value if conversion became inevitable and to this end intended to maximise its financial performance, especially in the areas used by the City to evaluate financial institutions. It also intended to present its results in a manner that would lead to the most favourable interpretation of its performance as well as 'engage in marketing activity to improve our corporate image'.

Finally, the Strategic Plan of 1988 stated that the key strategic objective was to generate more profit by increasing the Leeds' share of the total mortgage volume.

While these plans were being formulated Blackburn brought in the Boston Consulting Group to analyse the society and give strategic advice. Its conclusion was that the Leeds was, 'too big to be small and too small to be big', and also that it was 'price taker rather than price maker', waiting on the decisions of the Halifax or the Abbey National on rates. In Blackburn's view it would have to be bigger, almost certainly much bigger. As a first step the Leeds absorbed the Southdown Building Society at the beginning of 1992 and regarded the exercise as a blueprint for future mergers.

At the same time the drive for efficiency continued and, in spite of some anguish and hostile questions at the Annual General Meeting, 10 per cent of the branch network was closed. At the beginning of the 1990s a new general ledger system, which gave a better 'handle on costs', was installed. Blackburn remembers that managers from the Halifax came over to Leeds to see how it had been done.

New marketing initiatives were promoted with four new savings accounts launched – *Liquid Gold, Solid Gold, Bonus Gold* and *Tessa Gold*. A very strong advertising campaign featuring actor George Cole, which had been initiated by Peter Hemingway, achieved great success. At the same time a Leeds credit card was also introduced. While all this was happening the Leeds also built a new headquarters, which was clearly needed for efficient operations, in the city. At the same time, a number of new non-executive directors were appointed. When Blackburn had arrived in 1987, the board was made up exclusively of Yorkshire residents from the world of business and the professions. The chairman, Malcolm Barr, saw the need to look outside the county and the Building Societies Regulator had also made some comment about parochialism. As a consequence, Prue Leith (the restaurateur and author), John King (formerly of British Telecom) and Derek Cook (the managing director of Pilkington) were invited to join the board.

I was so upset I couldn't sleep

When the five years ended in 1993, two major events had occurred that would colour the board's drawing up of their next *Five-Year Plan*. At the beginning of 1993 the chief executive, Mike Blackburn, left the Leeds to become chief executive of the Halifax. The Leeds was extremely unhappy to lose him but as the chairman, Malcolm Barr, said,

> 'I was not surprised. We thought he was superb. Others would think so too. We had no alternative but to congratulate him.'

Sir Timothy Kitson, the deputy chairman of Leeds at the time, claimed that he knew it was going to happen the previous autumn. Arnold Ziff, influential in the original appointment, admits he was furious. 'I was so upset I couldn't sleep but at four o'clock in the morning I realised what a good career move it was for him and I forgave him.'

The second factor affecting the formulation of the next plan was the announcement of talks with the Bradford-based National & Provincial Building Society with a view to merger. In view of the eventual collapse of the merger plan and the fact that almost every senior Leeds executive seems to have been vehemently opposed to it, it is difficult to imagine how the merger idea can have been formulated in the first place. The main reason seems to have been the Leeds' desire to find a suitable chief executive to fill the vacuum created by the departure of Mike Blackburn.

Through the spring and summer of 1993 the Leeds board used the services of headhunters to find a suitable external candidate. One of these was David O'Brien, chief executive of the National & Provincial. At his interview O'Brien suggested the merger and the Leeds directors, Malcolm Barr, John King and Bob Strachan expressed their enthusiasm on the grounds that it would kill two birds with one stone. It would fill the chief executive slot and give Leeds greater size and presence in the mortgage market.

O'Brien certainly talked a good book in promoting his unorthodox business strategy and enjoyed, for a time and in some circles, a high reputation. In August 1993, it was announced that the Leeds and National & Provincial were to merge, and discussions on procedure and future plans continued during the year. However, it soon became clear to the executive members of the Leeds board and to the Leeds' senior management that the cultures of the two societies were completely different and, as one of the conditions of the merger was O'Brien becoming chief executive of the new group, they were very unhappy about the prospect. For example, Judy Atchison made it clear that she would leave if the merger with National & Provincial went through. O'Brien's management theories, which he called the *understanding process*, were at odds with common practice. National & Provincial executives were given some very strange titles such as director of customer engagement, process facilitator, manager of the understanding process, and staff meetings were referred to as *understanding events*.

John Miller, the systems director at Leeds, had been recruited by Mike Blackburn in April 1992 and brought a fresh approach to the society's view of itself and the industry. His background was large manufacturing companies with an emphasis on electronics and communications. His most recent appointments had been national sales director at Otis Elevator, managing director of the public telecommunications switching and systems division of Thorn Ericsson and operations director of Microtel Communications, a start-up company created by British Aerospace to exploit the licence for establishing a personal communications network.

The first thing he did when he arrived at Leeds was to put together a review of the whole building society industry. It showed the importance of critical mass so, in theory, Miller was not opposed to merger or acquisition. But he was opposed to merger with National & Provincial because, leaving aside the emotional opposition within Leeds, in his view such a merger was not viable financially given his opinion that the National & Provincial mortgage book and bad debt provisions were not up to Leeds standards.

In an attempt to produce an argument against merger with National & Provincial, a document was put forward as an addendum to the new *Five-Year Plan* called *Merger Considerations*. It propounded various reasons that could be used for rejecting *any* merger. However, it was National & Provincial that everyone wanted to avoid and after some of the Leeds senior management had resigned and the best of the rest had made their views very clear to the chairman the merger was abandoned.

Roger Boyes was to say later,

'Their agenda was quite clear, a cuckoo laying its eggs in the Leeds Permanent's nest and the Leeds becoming part of an experiment in management. That was not what the Leeds was there for. Mike Blackburn left a well-managed, efficient operation with highly motivated people. All his work over several years would have been destroyed within six months. At the end of the day, somebody had to say "No".'

What should the Leeds do now? It had lost its chief executive and failed to replace him, and it had now entered publicly into merger talks with another very substantial building society and been forced to abandon them. We would have to say that if the Leeds had already converted to plc status it would have been extremely vulnerable to take-over. However, not all was doom and gloom. The financial results to 30 September 1993 showed continued growth. Operating profits rose 23 per cent to £317.3 million and pre-tax profits rose 22 per cent to £189 million. As the City investment house, UBS, pointed out,

'Leeds Permanent's long- and short-term ratings were raised by IBCA on 23 February, from A+/A1 to AA-/A1+. This recognition of the Leeds' improved strength seems surprising as it comes (1) after the abandonment of the merger with N & P and (2) during the continued absence of a chief executive. However, both factors seem to have had no discernible effect on the Society's financial performance. This has continued to improve recently, and IBCA quoted good profitability, strong capital ratios, improving asset quality and a stable funding situation as grounds for the upgrade, alongside the general improvement in the UK housing market.'

This was all very well but Leeds directors knew in their heart of hearts that they *were* vulnerable, and that they needed a viable plan for the future and that that plan would almost certainly involve a merger or acquisition.

CHAPTER FOUR

We wanted to make it clear we didn't stand aloof

Too small to be big, too big to be small

I've never known such uncertainty

Project Aviary

Too small to be big, too big to be small

With the collapse of the proposed merger with the National & Provincial at the end of 1993, the senior executives at the Leeds realised that a new strategy would need to be formulated. To assist them they turned to the management consultants Arthur D Little.

ADL worked closely with the marketing team at the Leeds through the spring of 1994 with a view to presenting a strategy paper at the Leeds Board Conference due to be held at Wood Hall, Linton on 27 and 28 June 1994.

By this time, of course, talks with Halifax had been under way for over two months. ADL was aware of them and its report was bound to be coloured by this knowledge. Similarly its report was bound to have an influence on the Leeds directors' attitudes to the talks.

On 27 June ADL duly presented its findings and proposals under the heading, 'Directing the Leeds for the year 2000'. These showed that the financial services industry was in turmoil. Until recently the industry had been dominated by three main categories of player, each with a distinct traditional product focus. Building societies had concentrated on mortgages and savings, insurance companies on insurance, life policies and pensions, and banks on loans, unsecured or secured and current accounts. However, the lines were now becoming blurred and all the players were moving into each other's markets. Furthermore, building societies were seeking safety through merger – for example, North of England with Northern Rock, Heart of England with Cheltenham & Gloucester, and Haywards Heath with Yorkshire. Banks had been buying insurance companies: Lloyds had bought a majority stake in Abbey Life; Abbey National had bought Scottish Mutual; and National Westminster created NatWest Life. At the same time building societies had begun to set up life and investment companies. And banks were not satisfied with acquiring insurance companies, they wanted building societies too. Lloyds had bid for Cheltenham & Gloucester, and both the Royal Bank of Scotland and the TSB had expressed an interest in acquiring a society.

The regulatory and financial environment was also changing. The recent legislation requiring the disclosure of agents' commissions was bringing pressure on prices while increased regulation was resulting in heavier compliance costs. For building societies the precarious nature of their mutuality and independence was highlighted by the Lloyds offer ranging from £500 to as much as £10,500 to each Cheltenham & Gloucester member.

Faced with this turmoil, where should the Leeds go? In ADL's view it could go one of three ways – organic growth, merger or acquisition. If it chose organic growth, should it aim for more or less regional focus, a wider or narrower product line, wider or narrower target customer segments, more or less in-house manufacture of non-core products, its current or different structure of cost? If it chose merger, should it be with another building society, a bank or an insurance company? Or, should the Leeds consider converting into a public company?

ADL demonstrated to the Leeds directors that growth in the mortgage and savings market was slowing down, as indeed it was in the associated markets of life and pensions, unsecured lending, insurance premiums and current accounts. Customers were becoming increasingly price sensitive, with direct selling competing on price and the competition in all areas, mortgages, savings, insurance, pensions and investments, emphasising price. Finding and sustaining a competitive edge – whether in service, convenience or price – was becoming increasingly difficult. The number of building societies had already fallen from 273 in 1980 to less than 100 and would continue to fall further. By the year 2000, ADL predicted that the industry would be more concentrated and technology based and there would be only six to ten major players who would all be broadly based and strong in all product segments with national coverage exploiting *all* means of distribution. The only other successful players would be in niches, either product or regional or in method of distribution. Anyone left in the middle ground would be struggling.

Having made that point, ADL's next statement was, 'The Leeds today is positioned in the middle ground', Barclays, National Westminster, Lloyds and Midland were in the strongest position with complete national coverage offering full personal financial services. Bank of Scotland, Royal Bank of Scotland and TSB offered all services but were less strong nationally, especially Bank of Scotland which was only regional. The Halifax and Abbey National were strong nationally but not quite up with the banks on the full services. At the other end, Prudential and Standard Life were strong nationally but had so far concentrated on core products. The Cheltenham & Gloucester and Friends Provident were also restricted in their products and were not nationally strong. Bang in the middle was the Leeds with a rating of weak national with some cross-selling.

The Leeds distribution was neither truly national nor dominant locally. There were a large number of branches in Scotland, along the M62 corridor and in London but nowhere did the society enjoy a 15 per cent share of the market in terms of branches, although in many regions it was more than 5 per cent. Furthermore, many of the branches were small and generating low volumes and the Leeds lacked a direct selling operation. With regard to products, the Leeds was strong in its core market of mortgages and savings, where it enjoyed around a 4.5 per cent market share, but very small in other areas of financial services. Involvement in life, pensions, lending and investments was only just beginning. In all cases its market share was less than 0.5 per cent.

Worse, even within its core area – mortgages and savings – Leeds sales had been declining for the last four years in an already slowing market and income from other sources – valuation, mortgage fees, general insurance commission and life and investment commission – had been flat at around £100 million. On the other hand, management expenses had been growing faster than the rate of inflation and were up from just over £160 million in 1990 to nearly £240 million in 1994 while profits had grown scarcely faster than inflation over the same period.

Given this situation ADL concluded that organic growth was not a sensible option. The Leeds *would* survive but would not be a major player and would find life increasingly difficult as it was squeezed on all sides. The other option was merger but ADL, to the dismay of some

Leeds directors, suggested that the society should strongly consider merging with another larger society (in other words, in all but name, be taken over).

It showed that there were seven classes of stakeholder – members, employees, the community, intermediaries, non-member customers (depositors), money and capital market lenders, and suppliers. Of these, by far the most important were the members, and their needs and expectations were changing. Whereas in the past members had accepted building society mergers with small financial rewards, the recent offer by Lloyds Bank to Cheltenham & Gloucester members had alerted every building society member to the value locked up in his or her society.

As Stephen Lawrence put it, 'The genie was out of the bottle and no one could put it back.'

As part of the exercise ADL put forward a profile of likely partners, whether by merger or acquisition. It began with the leading building societies – Halifax, Nationwide, Woolwich, Alliance & Leicester, Bradford & Bingley, and Britannia – and profiled in depth the societies with assets greater than £5 billion.

It then looked at: the banks – Abbey National, Bank of Scotland, Barclays, Hong Kong and Shanghai, Lloyds, National Westminster, Royal Bank of Scotland and TSB; the insurance companies – Commercial Union, General Accident, Prudential, Standard Life and Sun Alliance, the conglomerate BAT; and finally some foreign financial institutions – Allied Irish Bank, Bank of Ireland, Deutsche Bank, Fortis, International Nederlanden Group and National Australia Bank.

In consultation with ADL, Leeds directors decided that they had four options once they had concluded that in the financial services environment of the 1990s they were too large to be a niche player but too small to compete with the large multi-national financial services institutions.

The first option was to downsize to become a niche player but this was really impractical. The second was to merge with smaller societies but this would mean a continuous and wearing process of mergers before critical mass was achieved. The third was to be acquired by a large UK or European financial services company but this could again be a long process and would not meet one of the Leeds' requirements, its commitment to a West Yorkshire base. The fourth option, and the only one acceptable, was a merger with a larger UK building society. Of the societies highlighted by ADL, merger with the Alliance & Leicester or Woolwich, both of which had attractions, would still not bring the Leeds to a size capable of competing with the biggest. The Nationwide would satisfy the size criterion but not the West Yorkshire base requirement. Furthermore, the Nationwide's recent performance had been erratic. As the summer of 1994 progressed ADL advised the Leeds board that a merger with the Halifax, followed by conversion to plc status, would release most value to the members.

At the board meeting on 28 June it was reported that a number of approaches of varying degrees of intensity and formality had been received in the last year. It was resolved,

> ' ... not to remain independent by following a strategy of natural growth, but to seek union with a partner or partners that would make the society one of the ten biggest operators in the financial services market.'

Accordingly it was agreed that there were three possible options for achieving this objective.

1 Seek a merger with the Halifax, provided full value could be released to members and accept any consequent loss of the society's identity.

2 Achieve growth in size by a multi-merger route, by following negotiations with the another building society and mutual life assurer, but not both organisations simultaneously and with a preference for the building society merger to come first.

3 Seek a major bank to take over the society.

All, except the chairman Malcolm Barr, agreed that priority should be given to seeking a merger with the Halifax. Barr said that this would give the Halifax growth but not the Leeds which, 'would cease to have its own identity or ability to give its members any choice'. He could see no need to rush into any merger because 'the Society was financially sound and had major policies for sustained future growth'. He requested that his dissent be noted.

I've never known such uncertainty

The Halifax had already established its strategy for the years through to 2000 and this strategy was built around its Mission Statement which proclaimed that it wanted to be *the biggest and the best personal finance business in the UK*. To fulfil this Mission it would have to achieve certain objectives. The first was to be market leader in the core business of lending and short-term savings, with 'market leader' meaning a 25 per cent share of the mortgage market. The second was to develop aggressively the life insurance, pensions and investment business by offering value for money through outstanding performance and fair pricing, with the objective of being in the top ten of all life insurance businesses by the year 2000 and progressing on to be in the top five. The third objective was to become an influential force in providing protection for the home and family via the development or acquisition of a general insurance business. The fourth was to become an influential force in providing protection against the cost of medical services obtained from the private sector by the development or acquisition of a health insurance business. The fifth was to focus on obtaining the primary financial relationship with customers by stronger growth in transaction-related business, in current accounts. The sixth was to develop aggressively the personal lending business. The seventh was to concentrate on building financial strength by prudent balance sheet management and to position the society to become a triple A rated business and, finally, the eighth was to develop and implement a set of values that the society believed in and would live by.

In the annual Halifax press conference in 1994, held on 23 March, Jon Foulds welcomed publication of the *Treasury Review of the Building Societies Act* pointing out that mutuality had dominated the housing finance sector for well over a hundred years. It had been of profit benefit to savers and borrowers but there would need to be changes in the future and outdated legislation might prevent building societies from being as helpful to their members as they had in the past. Foulds called for, 'wider banking powers to be offered to building societies. Injecting some competition from mutuals into the wider banking scene would undoubtedly be a healthy and welcome move.' He hoped the Government would take the same view.

He reiterated his views on the *Treasury Review* at the Annual General Meeting on 23 May,

'We will need wider access to world banking markets to enable us to meet forecast customer needs.'

He stated that the Halifax board were still in favour of mutuality but foresaw further rationalisation in the mortgage industry and felt Halifax should be involved,

'This could include a merger with another society.'

The media quickly picked up on these remarks and on 24 May, under the headline, **Halifax seeks merger to make biggest society bigger**, Sara McConnell said in *The Times,*

> 'The announcement marks a significant shift in Halifax strategy. Its top position appears unassailable. A quarter of all building society mortgages are from the Halifax and it has not needed to consider taking over another society, analysts say. However, like all societies, it faces fierce competition in the mortgage market, particularly from banks, which have unfettered access to wholesale money to lend as fixed-rate loans. Mr Foulds made clear that the Halifax was more interested in strengthening its position as a mutual organisation than becoming a public company in the short term. However, if the Treasury refuses to lift restrictions on building societies' access to wholesale markets, conversion may be the only option, Mr Foulds hinted. At present, societies can fund only 40 per cent of their loans from wholesale markets.
>
> Mr Foulds' remarks are certain to intensify debate over the future of building societies, particularly as they come on the eve of a court hearing on whether the proposed take-over of the Cheltenham & Gloucester Building Society by Lloyds Bank is lawful. The deal, if permitted, would be the first take-over of a building society by a bank. Societies, fearful of losing their mutual status, are urging the Treasury to tighten the Building Societies Act to prevent more such deals.
>
> David Gilchrist, the Halifax's general manager, said: "There is slight concern that the current rules for mergers would make mergers unattractive compared with deals like the C & G and Lloyds." ...
> "The Halifax is keen to approach, and be approached by, societies that may otherwise face a bank take-over and loss of mutual status," Mr Gilchrist said. "We wanted to make it clear that we didn't stand aloof ... There are 85 building societies now and there will be nothing like that number by the end of the century." John Wrigglesworth, building societies analyst with UBS, said that middle-sized societies with strong reserves and good management were the likeliest targets for the Halifax. These include the Coventry, the Birmingham Midshires, the Yorkshire, the Derbyshire and the Northern Rock, which is merging with the North of England.'

And *The Guardian* on the same day quoted Mike Blackburn,

> "'During my time in the building society movement I've never known such uncertainty, but a High Court ruling which endorsed the Lloyds take-over could encourage different groupings within the industry and change the pecking order. Our industry is well-known for its merger activity and we will look positively on any merger which we think would benefit the members and staff of both parties.'"

According to *The Guardian*,

> 'Mr Blackburn says he has no plans to take over his old society, Leeds Permanent, which has been without a chief executive since his departure.'

Project Aviary

At the strategy conference of the Halifax Board at Stapleford Park in February 1994 the possibility of a merger or mergers with other building societies had been discussed and the conclusion reached that a single large merger was infinitely preferable to several smaller ones over a protracted period. The society had set the goal in its Mission Statement of being the biggest and the best personal financial services business in the United Kingdom. It was the number one mortgage lender but its position as number one in the retail savings market had recently come under threat from National Savings.

However, the board recognised that rationalisation elsewhere in the industry could threaten its position and it should probably aim for a share of 25 per cent of the net lending market to secure its dominant position. Through the spring and early summer of 1994 the board continued to consider and debate the merits of organic growth and merger for fulfilling the Mission Statement and came to the conclusion that the merger route was significantly more financially attractive.

Having come to the conclusion that merger with another society was the best option, Halifax ran its eye over the possibilities among the next ten societies graded by size after themselves.

As long ago as 1990 Group Market Research and Development, under former banker John Kirkbright, had conducted a detailed survey of the other societies code-named *Project Aviary* in which each society had been given the name of a bird. Most were immediately dismissed as too small, but four were analysed in detail and reports outlining the advantages and disadvantages of merger/acquisition were presented. Before looking specifically at the four, *Project Aviary* considered the case for and against merger strategy. The case for was summarised as follows.

- Merger with another substantial society would increase the Society's share of the UK mortgage market and would make it virtually unassailable by other lenders.

- A merger would be a 'stick to the knitting' strategy. Recent diversification had achieved limited success.

- The right merger would strengthen the branch network by spreading into areas where Halifax was relatively weak, notably London and the South East.

- Again the right merger would enlarge the customer base as well as improve its composition by adding higher social groupings. Mergers were a relatively cheap and easy means of acquiring assets and capital. (As we shall see, this was to change during 1994.)

A merger would bring:

- economies of scale

- enlargement of capital base

- protection against take-over

- elimination of excess capacity in industry

- strengthening of management and direct entry into areas where they had no presence.

The arguments against merger were as follows.

- Halifax was already exposed to and dependent on the UK mortgage market, itself likely to be more difficult in the 1990s than in the 1980s.

- A merger would concentrate the risk.

- Management's eye could be taken off the ball and developments already in hand could suffer.

- There would be considerable rationalisation costs. Nationwide Anglia had experienced severe difficulties in pursuing rationalisation and controlling costs, partly linked to agreements made to secure the merger.

- There could be an adverse effect on staff.

Most important was what was described as 'The Catch 22 difficulty'. To make the merger work considerable rationalisation would be necessary. But to gain the agreement of the targeted society it could be difficult to reach acquiescence with such a programme. A policy of shared pain could lead to problems with Halifax staff. Finally, there would probably be a loss of some customers who would want to spread their investments and/or commitments.

The team focused on the Woolwich, code-named *Blackbird,* National & Provincial (*Starling*), Nationwide (*Thrush*) and Leeds Permanent (*Sparrow*). The team concluded that a swoop on *Blackbird* or *Starling* would increase the dependency on the UK mortgage and savings market and reduce Halifax's focus on its new developments. The feeling was that *Blackbird* would not favour a merger with the Halifax but would be much more likely to favour *Sparrow,* which would be a meeting of equals. An approach to *Starling* would probably be more successful but the business was not seen to be attractive.

Group Market Development and Research was not convinced that merger was the best way forward anyway and concluded its report, with the comment,

> 'We are not convinced about both the ability of the Society to manage such a merger alongside its present range of challenging management tasks within the process of further diversification, nor are we convinced about the specific benefits of a larger asset base.
>
> Our view is that if we are committed to being a leading financial services provider we should concentrate resources on developing the insurance side of our business and this is where our greatest market opportunity lies in the next ten years.'

The 1994 decision to open discussions with the Leeds was unconnected with *Project Aviary* of 1990, but in view of later events, it is interesting to see what it said about the management of *Sparrow* (Leeds) in December 1990.

'*Sparrow* has undergone fundamental changes in structure, systems and corporate culture in recent years following the appointment of Mike Blackburn as chief executive in October 1987. Blackburn took over at a time *Sparrow* was facing painful questions about its future survival.

A number of key initiatives attributed to Blackburn include:

- The recruitment of key senior executives from outside the traditional industry to introduce the latest ideas in commercial development, research and product planning.

- The development and implementation of the strategic plan with a strong focus on the traditional core mortgage business.

- Cost cutting programmes to reduce management expenses. Cuts equivalent to savings of £15 million a year were introduced.

- Restructure of the branch network from 25 areas to 8 regions which stripped out a layer of management. The closure of 60 branches which did not offer potential for future mortgage business.

- The removal of the "old guard" with over 100 managerial staff being removed.

Sparrow has undergone a significant cultural change brought about by the influx of new people and a clear sense of direction.'

The report said of Mike Blackburn,

'Personal ambitions are thought to include managing a much larger society/financial institution and if this cannot be achieved with *Sparrow* then he might move in two or three years time. A major consideration is the future development and survival of *Sparrow* and other similar sized societies. Previously a senior executive of Lloyds Bank, it is likely that Blackburn has considered a number of strategic options, including merger and backing *Sparrow* into a larger financial institution, in the event of a "not so friendly/hostile approach". The new senior management recognised *Sparrow* is too big for specialist regional or local markets, but not large enough to compete fully in retail financial services markets with the major banks and building societies.

The society has developed a highly focused strategy to concentrate on the housing finance market and pulled back from diversifying into the traditional banking products area. The only exception is the credit card which was pushed forward by the chief executive. It is unlikely that such a product would be considered within the current strategic plan.

The strong northern bias of the society has protected it somewhat from the extremes of the recession in the housing market in the south of the country. The major concentration is on bottom line profit and *Sparrow* is prepared to sacrifice volume and market share to preserve margins. Market share in itself is not a strategic objective but rather the profitable growth of the balance sheet.

The problem of size and critical mass may be an issue in two or three years. *Sparrow* is thought to have looked at and discounted a possible merger with *Starling*. *Sparrow* may be looking at a merger with a similar sized society where there is a good fit. *Blackbird* is a possible candidate although a major stumbling block may be the share out of top jobs.'

When the question of mergers was picked up in 1994 all the birds had migrated and the code-names were much more mundane. By this time Nationwide had lost some of its attraction for the Halifax in spite of its size. It was still coping with the merger with Anglia and there would clearly be a need for heavy joint rationalisation if Halifax acquired them. Finally, the Office of Fair Trading would look at any such deal very carefully.

Woolwich was seen as a solid rather than good performer, but its recent merger with Town & Country appeared to have been handled well. It was considered reasonably innovative and had diversified into insurance and Europe. It would be a good merger prospect bringing improved geographical distribution. However, it was believed to value its independence and would expect to be the dominant partner in any merger.

The Alliance & Leicester had benefited from the acquisition of Girobank and, believing it had put its house in order, had adopted a more aggressive stance in the marketplace. It was thought it would prefer a conversion/acquisition more than a traditional merger.

The Cheltenham & Gloucester was being acquired by Lloyds Bank.

Bradford & Bingley was a strong believer in mutuality and was interested in merging with other societies. It could be a good fit except for the overlap of branches and the fact that it valued its independence.

The National & Provincial had a culture all its own, the main reason for its failed merger with the Leeds. The chief executive (the original reason for the Leeds interest) had recently been replaced by the finance director. Many of its branches were small and overlapped with those of the Halifax.

Compared with these others, Leeds stood out as the best prospect. With assets of £19,493 million it was placed between Alliance & Leicester with assets of £21,086 million and Cheltenham & Gloucester with assets of £17,687 million. It was felt to be 'a relatively good performer with a culture similar to that of Halifax'. The recent failure of the proposed merger with National & Provincial, and the delay in appointing a new chief executive, had led to speculation about its future. It was believed to be considering various strategic options including merger, acquisition and conversion. Apart from the branch overlap, Leeds would be a good fit for a merger.

CHAPTER FIVE

A unique opportunity

There was an element of wooing
Shadows and mirrors
A joint response would run to 100 pages
Negotiations should cease forthwith

There was an element of wooing

There have been many different stories on how talks between the Halifax and Leeds began and indeed we should wonder, in all seriousness, what actually constitutes talks beginning? Does a conversation between Sir Timothy Kitson, deputy chairman of the Leeds, and Mike Blackburn, former chief executive of the Leeds and now chief executive of the Halifax, constitute the beginning of talks if nothing is followed up? Do other conversations on the Wakefield to London train, used by both Leeds and Halifax directors, count as the opening of talks?

One event is certain. Mike Blackburn, chief executive of Halifax, and John Miller, an executive director of Leeds, were both invited by Olivetti to the England vs. Wales rugby international at Twickenham on 19 March 1994. (England won the game but, somewhat bizarrely, Wales were then presented with a new cup which was presented to the winner of the Five Nations championship.) Blackburn offered Miller a lift back to Yorkshire after the match and during that journey conversation turned, as it does, first to business, then to building society business, and finally to Halifax and Leeds business.

Was Blackburn, former chief executive of Leeds, indulging in some wooing? He said later,

'My own view was that the Halifax wasn't big enough and I didn't want to preside personally over the slide of the Halifax from a number one position. I obviously knew that a merger with the Leeds would be a jolly good thing for the Halifax. In that sense there was an element of wooing. That car journey was an opportunity for me to share both the thinking of the Halifax and encourage the Leeds along the same lines.'

The two agreed that the financial services industry was going through a period of great change and that large conglomerates in the bank financial

"The time has come," the Walrus said ...
Chris White, *Banking World* January 1995

services field, now being referred to as *bancassurance,* would emerge. Whereas Halifax were number one in the present building society field and Leeds number five, in the new world they would only be number six and number fifteen respectively. That was not acceptable to either of them. The Halifax board had already endorsed the society's mission statement which effectively said that only number one was acceptable. As Gren Folwell, Halifax's group finance director, said,

'We'd produced what I refer to as "The Blue Book", our mission and strategy to the year 2000. That book said ... We need to merge with a major building society because it's too expensive to grow organically in the mortgage area.'

For Leeds the question was – do we want to be independent at number fifteen or part of number one?

This conversation, perhaps unlike some others, was sufficiently serious for Miller to send by fax a hand-written agenda to Blackburn's house the next day. The code-names *East* and *West* had already been established and the three-page fax laid out,

> Objective – To determine if agreement can be reached on the principles required to ensure an orderly and beneficial merger of *East* and *West.*
>
> • Does it make business sense?
> • Can it be 'sold' internally?
> • Can it be 'sold' externally?

It went on to suggest a one-day workshop to determine whether the objective could be achieved and gave an agenda – outlined below – to cover the key issues, which were:

- executive and non-executive management

- business and brand names

- strategy and direction

- brand management

- business units – mortgages, savings etc.

- future development plans

- review of support functions

- distribution policy

- external issues such as merger process, conversion to plc etc.

- internal issues such as downsizing, gaining of board and staff acceptance.

This conversation and fax were followed by the first of a series of clandestine meetings between key Halifax and Leeds directors. From

Halifax came Blackburn, Gren Folwell (the group finance director) and Mike Ellis (a general manager in the Treasury department) who had been asked by Blackburn the previous autumn to look at the strategic possibility of a merger and suggest possible candidates. From the Leeds came Roger Boyes (finance director and acting chief executive), John Miller and Chris Chadwick (commercial director). The first meeting took place secretly at Roger Boyes' home on a Saturday morning.

According to Miller there was general recognition that here was a unique opportunity. Apart from the expenses associated with the merger, there would be no cost and they could make a quantum leap in size in a marketplace where size would count. And the merged operation would be *big*.

The assets of Halifax were £67 billion and its profits £866 million, Leeds assets were £19.5 billion and profits £186 million. Combined, the assets would be £86.5 billion with profits of £1.05 billion. This would dwarf their nearest rival, Nationwide, whose assets were only £35 billion. In terms of customers and borrowers, Halifax had 1.86 million borrowers and around 6 million investing members. With Leeds' 500,000 borrowers and around 2 million investing members the combined total, before eliminating duplicates, would be 2.3 million borrowers and 8 million investing members.

The number of people 'in the know' was extremely restricted but one person who was told at an early stage was David Gilchrist, Halifax's group secretary. Was he surprised?

'In one way I was surprised because we had talked about the idea of going for a sizeable merger and there had been endless analysis work and discussion, papers and lengthy documents on potential targets with matrices on who was a good merger target and who not. It all seemed to end in "paralysis by analysis". We'd been doing it for many years and never got anywhere. It was surprising and stimulating to find that someone had actually started to talk to a potential partner and received what appeared to be a favourable response.'

And did Gilchrist think it would happen?

'I could see there was a distinct possibility but I could foresee snags. The Halifax had been for a long time rather a process driven organisation. Those in charge of the internal processes and systems had them very well worked out. You could press a button and the Halifax would run "by the book". I suppose, to an extent, it applied to the personnel side also. The Halifax had its own culture, its own rather paternalistic attitude to staff and it would be known that in terms of administration and computer systems in particular, as well as personnel, how this sort of exercise could be disruptive. So I saw the probability of some internal resistance from the Halifax and I also saw the possibility of hostile bidders for the Leeds.'

Gilchrist's view of the Halifax was more than endorsed by John Lee, personnel director, who had joined the society in 1993 after many years' experience with ICI. He found,

' ... an organisation incredibly centrally controlled, an organisation very structured, very hierarchical with very clear chains of command and a very rigid control of decision making.'

On Monday, 9 May, John Miller gave to Roger Boyes a 24-page *Merger Dossier East and West*, which was marked 'Secret'. In it he outlined details about Halifax and included the benefits of a merger. In terms of strategic positioning,

'*West*'s financial strength and resources are unassailable. It is the largest UK building society and all key performance indicators have moved positively during the period under review, despite the recession in the housing market, including continued business investment, and continued product diversification programmes. Its Treasury Department is renowned and, together with asset quality, has enabled *West* to enjoy the highest credit-rating in the sector.'

He made the point that the Leeds would be backing a known winner and would be able to participate in the shaping of future events. The alternative could be unpleasant because if the Halifax decided to convert to plc status it would come under the jurisdiction of the Bank of England with a possible downgrading of the remaining building society sector.

If the two, once merged, decided to float, the market capitalisation achieved would probably be higher thanks to the rationalisation and cost reduction achieved. This would act as a deterrent to a would-be predator for the Leeds and also as an inducement to members to approve the deal. He showed that the scope for branch rationalisation was considerable. Leeds had 455 branches and Halifax 706, to give a combined total of 1161. Using the four-digit postcode, 400 overlapped.

Miller highlighted the benefits to each in various aspects. In size, Halifax would achieve cost-effective asset growth and Leeds, critical mass. In product synergy, Halifax would welcome Leeds' strong branded products, *Liquid Gold, Solid Gold* and *Home Arranger*. In return Leeds would gain a cheque book operation facilitating the development of customer relationships. Halifax would obtain an increased customer base with cross-sell potential while Leeds would have a broader range of products. Both had set up *Life* operations recently and Leeds would benefit from a bigger customer base. Two head offices, potentially a problem, would be used to provide additional capacity for Halifax expansion and would therefore not require a Leeds closure with the ensuing embarrassment. For both, rationalisation of an increased branch network would bring benefits. On the estate agency front, Halifax would gain additional distribution and Leeds would achieve critical mass as well as the enhanced potential for mortgage cross-selling. For employees, Halifax would gain access to more resources and Leeds would be able to offer greater career opportunities. As for the members, they should benefit from an improved quality of access to branches, a wider range of products and services, and there would be the potential for a merger bonus as well as a windfall distribution if the merged group converted to a plc.

The two sides agreed that they would need a firm policy on employment prospects following the merger. They were not public companies with large numbers of shareholders, most of them institutional, and they were not asking for any money. There was, therefore, no necessity to demonstrate huge immediate savings by declaring that millions would be cut from costs by making thousands redundant. Such statements seemed to be necessary when other financial institutions that were public companies announced mergers and take-overs.

With the Halifax and the Leeds an opposite pressure was in play. Each member, irrespective of the size of his/her investment, had one vote and a large proportion of the members lived in the Halifax and Leeds areas. It would not help the vote on the merger plan if a large number of employees were experiencing dissatisfaction through fear of losing their jobs.

The policy would be that any displacement of personnel would be managed by early retirement, voluntary redundancy, natural wastage and a natural growth strategy. If compulsory redundancy proved necessary it would only be as a last resort.

Looking at the branch network there seemed to be a significant overlap of 400 branches but this should not necessarily mean that 400 would be closed. If the growth strategy worked many could probably be used in other financial service areas. The stated policy on employment would apply.

> 'If the outcome of a future review recommends certain closures the policy with regard to employment still prevails. Branch staff are among our most highly trained people; their skills should not be wasted.'

With regard to life insurance, pensions and unit trusts, both societies were pursuing virtually identical strategies and the issue would be which ones used to retain and which platform to use. The whole idea of a merger looked very attractive.

Nevertheless, those assembled must have been aware of the obstacles to be overcome, however logical a merger might be. Not only would there be internal opponents, but also, at the highest level, outside regulatory authorities such as the Monopolies and Mergers Commission, which might not be wholly enthusiastic. But that was for the future. Were the key players in favour? If they were not, there was no point in pursuing the talks. If they were, then the key issues could be tackled one by one and when all was agreed they could consider how to tackle likely opponents. According to Mike Ellis, it was clear from an early stage that 'the Leeds executive directors wanted to come aboard'. However, it was also clear that part of the package was that a merger should be followed by conversion into a public company. Without that and the promise of free shares, the Leeds board knew they would not be able to sell the deal to their members. As we have seen, the Lloyds offer to Cheltenham & Gloucester members had opened the eyes of everyone to the value locked up in building societies. A strategic merger would not suffice. This was likely to be a serious sticking point for the Halifax with their recent expressions of preference for remaining a mutual.

After the initial meetings in April, Mike Ellis, asked by Mike Blackburn to provide a great deal of detailed information on the two societies, requested a better defined 'brief'. He knew that to complete the research successfully he would need to put a team together. This raised the question of confidentiality and in a memo to Blackburn he summarised the situation as he saw it. In the light of subsequent events it makes interesting reading.

As we have seen, *Project Aviary* had given Leeds the code-name, *Sparrow*. This use of *Sparrow* did not last and all other documentation right up to the public announcement uses the code-names *East* for Leeds and *West* for Halifax. It is easy to see why *Sparrow* was not going to be used in communications with the Leeds. If they were *Sparrow* what was the Halifax going to be? *Vulture*, perhaps? There were going to be problems enough making the deal look like a genuine merger rather than a take-over without people comparing the sizes and temperaments of birds.

Of more importance, Ellis defined the Leeds' predicament, which he saw exactly as Arthur D Little had defined it – 'too small to compete in the current market but too large to relegate itself to being a niche player'. He could see that merger with someone was inevitable and that they were also vulnerable to take-over: 'They would be an ideal target for the Abbey National but *East*'s national network and brand image could attract a much broader interest.'

The branch overlap was clearly going to be a problem but before they could begin to resolve it they would need to decide what they were going to sell through the network. Would the merged company have a combined sales force? Would there be separate branches for financial services?

One of the attractions of *East* for Ellis was the fact that its business was 'uncluttered'. There was no money transmission although there was a Visa card operation. He knew that they had invested heavily in recent years in new technology, and had heard that they were having some problems integrating their mortgage and savings systems which were operated in two different types of mainframe. He saw an advantage in the fact that *East* was located nearby though he acknowledged this was not a justifiable business reason in itself.

Nevertheless, there was sufficient agreement for secret talks to continue. The two chairmen, Jon Foulds of the Halifax and Malcolm Barr of the Leeds, were informed. Foulds was perhaps the more enthusiastic although he was faced with the problem that if conversion to a public limited company was part of the agenda, he was on record recently as being strongly in favour of the Halifax remaining a mutual. He recalled later that he realised in looking at the 1993 results for the Hong Kong and Shanghai Bank, which showed profits of £2 billion, that size would be necessary to meet the competition if that muscle was used through Hong Kong and Shanghai's recently acquired subsidiary, Midland Bank. As for his 'conversion to conversion' he said later,

'At the time I said it [preference for mutuality] I believed it. Abbey National was paying hundreds of millions in dividends while we were strengthening our capital base. I think it paid out £750 million in its first five years as a public company. I changed my mind for two reasons. First, after the passing of the 1986 Building Societies Act which broadened the services we could offer we took advantage of most of the possibilities, for example credit cards, insurance and estate agency – especially estate agency. We believed it important to be in at the first stage of the house purchase transaction. We spent £200 million on about 90 businesses. These diversifications had nothing to do with mutuality. We were building another category of customers who were not members of the society and the fastest increase was coming from non-members. It was leading to an unstable situation. Separation of ownership from the customer relationship was increasingly desirable.

Second, one thing that building societies offered was security for savings. We were drawing on the reserves which supported that promise and using them as risk capital. I think that even if we had not merged with the Leeds, within 12 months we would have made the commitment to convert.'

As we have seen, Malcolm Barr was initially opposed to a merger with the Halifax. Nevertheless, on Monday, 16 May 1994, Roger Boyes telephoned Mike Blackburn to tell him that Barr was happy for talks to continue.

Shadows and mirrors

And proceed they did. Blackburn's diary shows that there was a meeting at Roger Boyes' house during the evening of Tuesday, 31 May, another at John Miller's house on Thursday, 9 June, and another two days later, also at Miller's house. This was followed by further meetings at the Leeds flat on Friday, 17 June, and at Boyes' house on Thursday, 30 June, with two further meetings on Thursday, 7 July, in York and Saturday, 9 July. Secrecy was paramount. As Mike Ellis said,

'The early meetings were all off-site. We never used any corporate premises other than corporate flats. For example, we met at Mike Blackburn's house, Roger Boyes' house, John Miller's home and

Gren Folwell's flat. Everything was clouded in secrecy, cloak and dagger stuff. And the lengths we went to … I was due down in London for two days so I was staying overnight and I took my bags down as I was going with Richard Schofield from Treasury. I went to the meeting with my bags and then caught the train back to go to a meeting at Roger's house before returning to London. Sure enough, as I was catching the train back to London, Schofield appeared so I had to duck behind a wall … Treasury are always a suspicious lot in any event. They used to put me through these guessing games regularly.'

At times the secrecy could lead to moments of farce. Graham Johnston, who visited the Leeds head office regularly, agreed with Chris Chadwick that he was from a (fictitious) consultancy company called Windsor Research. At the second meeting, one of Chadwick's colleagues got into the lift with them and Chadwick felt obliged to introduce him. He said: 'Can I introduce you to Graham Johnston of … ' then stopped because he couldn't remember the mythical name. Johnston said 'Windsor Research' and at the same time Chadwick said 'KPMG'.

During these meetings agreement was quickly reached that the corporate name would be Halifax but that the Leeds' brand names using 'Gold', such as *Liquid Gold*, would be retained. They also agreed on the retention of the recently completed Leeds head office as a major operational centre.

Additionally, it became clear that the two executive teams at the highest level could be brought together without the shedding of much blood. Mike Ellis remembers,

'There were no problems, an immediate rapport. We were all different people and individuals but it gelled.'

It was really too early to be considering executive positions in detail but the key players needed to feel comfortable about their futures and it was easy to see how the two top teams would weld together. Halifax had not replaced Whitehouse, its formidable operations director, and Leeds had still not appointed a new chief executive after the departure of Blackburn in February 1993.

By the end of May the two sides had reached agreement on most major issues. As well as the corporate name and brand names, the strategy and direction were agreed as, 'to be the biggest and best personal finance business in the UK'. On competitive strategy it was agreed that the new group would aim to,

> ' ... dominate in the core business of lending, continue to develop intermediary business through coverage and product, develop *Life*, pensions and investment business, develop general insurance business and also health insurance. The business structure was agreed as a financial services organisation offering a full range of retail financial services and products with a balanced business on the assets and liabilities side of the balance sheet, a national distribution capability, intent on building long-term, enduring customer relationships while developing alternative distribution channels for improving customer service and enhancing their competitive position. The new head office would be at the Halifax present head office but a significant presence would be maintained at the Leeds head office. The new chairman would be Halifax's present chairman, Jon Foulds, and the chief executive, Halifax's chief executive, Mike Blackburn. The non-executive board would be considered by an appropriate committee.'

On the executive team, the minutes of the meeting held at Roger Boyes' house on 31 May, said,

> '*West*'s chief executive officer to be given the current structure/names of *East*'s Executive team. *West*'s chief executive officer to consider the organisation design most appropriate to the merged business.
>
> Objectives: efficiency, best fit for role, and attempt, within the bounds of common sense, to align executives from both organisations against meaningful roles. Ensure, prior to merger announcement, that all executives know what part they will play in the merged organisation. Avoid uncertainty.'

With regard to due diligence it was agreed that an exchange of auditors' files would suffice in view of the quality and standing of the two organisations.

As far as the operational framework was concerned, the date for the announcements was originally set for November 1994, but as both societies had key events in that month it was agreed that the announcements should be brought forward to mid-October. The immediate timetable was agreed with the respective chairmen's committees being briefed no later than 14 June and, subject to the outcome, the respective boards being made aware of the discussions during June with a business proposition being put forward at the July board meetings, 'with the objective of obtaining approval for the merger/ flotation process to commence'.

A joint response would run to 100 pages

By the end of June, matters had progressed far enough for Jon Foulds, Mike Blackburn and Mike Ellis to have a meeting with Sir David Scholey, Anthony Brooke and Anthony Hotson of the merchant bank, S G Warburg.

After telling the Warburg Group that the Halifax was considering a merger with another building society, Foulds requested an undertaking from Warburg that when he revealed the name they would not act for the society or anyone else interested in acquiring or merging with that society. Scholey said that if he had guessed correctly the identity of the society the bank had acted on an issue in the past but it was now closed and if the Halifax was happy about that he would give the undertaking. When the society was revealed as Leeds, it turned out that Scholey had guessed correctly.

Foulds requested a fee proposal and stressed the need for objective advice. Conversion was an option but there were advantages in being a mutual which were not to be given up lightly. The two issues of merger and conversion were separate and it was only on the merger issue that Halifax was currently seeking advice.

Although both sets of executives were in agreement on virtually all the major issues, the involvement of legal and corporate finance advisers soon began to highlight some of the differences, and on 15 July 1994 Mike Ellis wrote a 'strictly private and confidential' memorandum to Mike Blackburn and Gren Folwell headed *The Search for Compromise*. He stated the problem in the opening two sentences,

> 'As you are aware, the first signs are that it is going to be difficult to agree a joint legal/corporate finance view. *East*'s advisers appear to have a brief to make it work, whilst our advisers are concentrating on the severe difficulties in any linkage.'

The main area of possible contention was Leeds board's determination to realise shareholder value. Under these circumstances they would probably favour a take-over, thereby yielding more cash for their members. However, the acquirers would probably not offer the same advantages as a merger with Halifax. On previous agreed building society mergers, bonuses amounting from 0.5 per cent to 1 per cent of savings balances had been the order of the day, usually paid to members of the smaller society and often justified on the basis of equalisation of reserve ratios. If a society with a reserve ratio of 5 per cent had merged with a society with a 5.5 per cent reserve ratio, a 0.5 per cent bonus had been justified on the basis of reserve ratio equalisation. It had therefore meant small pay-outs to members – £5 to £10 on a £1000 balance. The ball was in Halifax's court. As Ellis put it,

> 'If it is announced that *East* are strongly attracted by merger with ourselves, but wish to secure some confidence concerning the future realisation of shareholder value, the onus is on us to determine what can be said in this respect.'

Ellis went on to say that he thought conversion, with or without a merger, was inevitable in the 'very near future' because of the financial pressures building up and the need to acquire or merge with other societies to fulfil the Mission Statement. In the end the key would be, ' … how far our board will go to meet *East*'s desires'.

At 11.20 a.m. on 19 July, Roger Boyes, with his two advisers from the legal firm, Allen & Overy, and two from Hambros Bank, met Gren Folwell and Mike Ellis, with their two advisers from the legal firm, Linklaters & Paines, and two from the merchant bank, S G Warburg. The two sets of advisers had been talking since 10 a.m. but Halifax's advisers told Folwell and Ellis that they ' … thought it was impossible to agree joint advice. The questions were phrased in such a way that a joint response would run to 100 pages and still provide little in the way of illumination.'

At 2.10 p.m. Gren Folwell and Mike Ellis got together with Roger Boyes. Boyes made it clear that there was little point in discussing the option of merger with the possibility of conversion because the Leeds was most unlikely to accept a proposal without a definite statement on conversion. At 2.30 p.m. the advisers were brought in but little progress was made. At 3.45 p.m. the two sides broke up to confer separately with their own advisers. The Halifax team were disappointed that, '*East*'s advisers had a specific remit to address and were not particularly interested in discussing alternatives'.

At 4.20 p.m. both sides, including advisers, met again. Boyes asked William Nabarro of Hambros Bank on the action that would have to be taken if Leeds were to consider merger without a firm commitment to conversion. Nabarro said that if there was no guarantee of conversion, consideration would have to be given to the amount of bonus paid, 'For example, looking at Lloyds/C & G and twice value, it may be appropriate for a bonus of up to *East*'s reserves being paid with the possibility of conversion (but no guarantee) representing a potential goodwill element.'

This idea of paying about 5 per cent to Leeds members and nothing to Halifax members was clearly a non-starter. The Halifax members would never approve it. It would also weaken the combined reserves.

Gren Folwell was being very polite when he said that he could not make any immediate response to this suggestion as there were many new issues involved, not least the fiduciary duty of Halifax to act in the best interests of its members. Boyes and Nabarro fully understood this.

Finally, at 4.45 p.m., in discussion with its advisers, the Halifax pair agreed that the final suggestion of Nabarro was not really 'in the spirit of the discussions so far held'. It had been a long day!

That same evening the Halifax board met over supper and discussed the merger/conversion conundrum. They knew that they would have problems with their own members if the Leeds members were to receive a larger bonus. Perhaps conversion/acquisition was the way forward rather than merger/conversion.

Halifax felt it had to respond to this latest proposal, but the very fact that it had been made after three months of intensive discussion highlighted the strategic dilemma the Leeds board faced. Did they want a merger with the best possible partner or did they want to sell to the highest bidder? So far, the negotiations had all been conducted on a basis of partners seeking to merge with proportionate shares in the management of the business and proportionate pain from any necessary rationalisation. If Halifax was going to pay Leeds members a sum equivalent to the net worth of Leeds, then this was really a take-over. There were arguments for the Leeds idea but most of the benefits went to Leeds members and there were arguments against, mainly the obvious dissatisfaction of Halifax members who would see their counterparts at Leeds receiving a higher bonus. Halifax would put it to Leeds,

'Do you want to merge with the best possible partner or do you want to sell yourselves at the highest possible price?'

Negotiations should cease forthwith

In the meantime, the Leeds board were becoming more concerned. Once it was learned that the Halifax was reluctant to commit to conversion the Leeds chairman, Malcolm Barr, felt that 'negotiations should cease forthwith'.

On Friday, 22 July, the big guns from the two societies came together again to meet on neutral ground in York. From the Halifax came the chairman, Jon Foulds, the vice-chairman, John Wood, the chief executive, Mike Blackburn and the finance director, Gren Folwell. From the Leeds came the chairman, Malcolm Barr, the two vice-chairmen, Sir Timothy Kitson and John King and the finance director, Roger Boyes.

All were agreed that, after months of negotiation carried out in a spirit of goodwill, there was commercial logic in a merger between the two societies. However, there was still a fundamental issue to be resolved and this was encapsulated in a memorandum put forward by Linklaters & Paines in response to a series of questions put jointly by the respective chairman's committees of the two societies. Linklaters & Paines had proposed two options and called them *Option D* and *Option E*. (*Options A*, *B* and *C* had been rejected as 'merger only' options.) In simple terms, *Option D* contained a commitment to review the constitution of the new business (plc or mutual) at an appropriate time after merger, while *Option E* contained a clear commitment (subject to conditions of a technical nature) to change the constitution of the new business at an appropriate time after merger. As far as the Leeds board were concerned, *Option D* would present a problem as they would be agreeing to cede control for what appeared to be an uncertain outcome. Could the assembled company therefore debate *Option E* first?

Jon Foulds replied and reminded everyone that the Halifax had looked at the possibility of becoming a public company in great detail in 1988. It had decided to remain mutual, but he accepted the decision had been a close one. The Halifax was not 'philosophically' against conversion, but the change would have to be for the right strategic reasons. Times had changed since 1988 and Halifax now had a different mix of people on its board, some of whom felt that the issue should be considered again. Foulds himself felt that 'overwhelming pressure' would arise from Halifax's limited ability to access the national and international capital and money markets in its current mutual building society form. In other words, Halifax was starting to outgrow its sector.

Furthermore, if a merger with the Leeds did take place, this would make the group 30 per cent larger and would only exacerbate the problem. The authorities would also probably think that mutuality was unsuitable for a group with £90 billion of assets. Taking all this into consideration, Foulds believed that a change of constitution would come about for sound business reasons. However, ' ... all the evidence is suggesting that the Halifax could not openly commit in a public document to change its constitution from being a mutual building society to a publicly quoted bank'.

Foulds suggested to the Leeds representatives that the Leeds board could gain more from the merged group which would be 'a dominant player in European personal financial services' than from a 'cash on the table' offer. The two businesses, placed together, would create a business which, when floated, valued greater than the sum of the two separate parts. They would gain value from each other.

The Lloyds/C & G deal was one that had to be taken into account. It had changed people's perception of the value of building societies and members' stakes in them. Foulds suggested they wait for the final outcome of the High Court hearing on the Lloyds/C & G proposals before any further steps were taken.

All agreed that they should try to find a further option, perhaps *Option D+*, which would be somewhere between *Option D* and *Option E.*

A further meeting took place two days later between Boyes and his advisers, and Folwell, Ellis and theirs. Again the main topic was conversion, with the Leeds side insisting that they must not lay themselves open to the accusation of not realising member value. The Halifax would have to convince them that conversion was 'more likely than not'.

The next day Boyes met Folwell and Ellis again and, with a feeling that the conversion issue was bringing everything to a halt, discussed how they could break the log jam and proceed. It was felt that the Halifax board meeting would discuss conversion irrespective of the Leeds merger and that they should meet again at the end of August after both boards had considered their position. It was agreed at this meeting that any press speculation would be met with the comment, 'We do not comment on rumour or speculation'.

This was necessary as *The Observer* had published an article by the personal finance editor, Maria Scott, under the headline **Leeds and Halifax in merger talks**. This article had advanced several logical reasons why a Halifax/Leeds merger would make sense to both parties including the following.

- Combined assets of £80 billion and more than 16 million customers.

- Blackburn's desire to increase the society's share of the mortgage market and, at its annual meeting in May, chairman Jon Foulds said Halifax was interested in mergers as a way to achieve this.

- Leeds had been without a chief executive for more than a year.

The business editor, Michael Smith, on another page under the heading, **Giants get the urge to merge** assumed that Halifax and Leeds were already in discussion and had virtually reached agreement, saying,

> ' ... Halifax's decision to link with a society the size of Leeds Permanent will also raise a few eyebrows.'

This attention from the media soon brought a letter from the Office of Fair trading.

It explained that under the Fair Trading Act of 1973, the Director General of Fair Trading had a duty to keep himself informed about transactions to which the Act might apply. In certain circumstances a reference to the Monopolies and Mergers Commission might be made. These were,

> 'Where two or more enterprises (at least one of which must be carried on in the UK) cease to be distinct and, as a result, a share of 25 per cent held by one enterprise in the supply or acquisition of goods or services of a particular description in the UK, or a substantial part of the UK, is created or enhanced and/or the total assets of the acquired enterprise exceed £70 million.'

At a meeting four days later between Blackburn and Folwell from the Halifax, and Barr and Boyes from the Leeds, Barr and Boyes confirmed that all but one of their board were in favour of the deal provided it released value to their members.

CHAPTER SIX

Stones were not left unturned

Where will your money best be placed?
In truth, the members did not
understand mutuality
It was a low point
Taking ourselves over a cliff

Where will your money best be placed?

As we have seen in the previous chapter, the key issue that would block a Halifax/Leeds merger was conversion. The Leeds directors wanted a merger, indeed were probably more keen on it than the Halifax directors, but they knew that they could not present the deal to their members without a substantial reward. As we have also seen, the Lloyds Bank offer for Cheltenham & Gloucester had made it much less likely that any future large building society merger or acquisition would be countenanced without a substantial payment to the members.

The original deal agreed between Lloyds Bank and Cheltenham & Gloucester Building Society stipulated that voting investors would receive an average of £1200 and borrowers £500. This offer was seen as generous by many. After all, why should short-term borrowers and investors receive a bonus? It also led to great speculation as to which building society would be next and opened up a completely different approach to investing money in a building society.

Traditionally, such investment had been seen as ultra safe, but dull. Indeed, in the inflationary 1970s it had been worse than dull because the performance of most other investments had been protected against inflation, whereas the capital plus interest in a building society savings account did not keep pace with the annual inflation rates of 10 per cent and more, which were common in the 1970s. In the 1980s they appeared dull against a booming stock market. The advertisements for unit trusts never tired of pointing out how an investment with them had vastly outperformed one in a building society savings account. Now a 'safe' investment in a building society could also bring the prospect of a large capital gain. Financial advisers and the personal finance sections of the press began to try to spot the next victims. The 'Weekend Money' section of *The Times* on Saturday, 28 May 1994, said,

> 'So where will your money be best placed? These are the possibles:
>
> **Yorkshire**. The 12th largest and this week touted as the best possible take-over target for the Halifax. It reports a rush of activity since the C & G announcement, as hopeful investors open accounts.
>
> **Coventry**. The 15th largest society has also seen an increase in new accounts in the past three weeks. Like the Yorkshire, it has strong reserves and good management.
>
> **Birmingham Midshires**. Another possible Halifax target. It is far enough away from Halifax's northern power base to prevent too many branch closures and job losses. It reported an inflow of £40 million in the first four months of this year but has not identified any of this specifically as "take-over" money.
>
> **Northern Rock** announced a merger with the smaller North of England a few weeks ago, making it one of the top ten. North of England investors can only expect a small bonus for the merger but could be in luck (and in line for another payout) if the Northern Rock in turn merges with the Halifax.'

In June 1994 there was a setback to the Lloyds bid for Cheltenham & Gloucester. Vice-chancellor Sir David Nicholls upheld in the High Court the Building Societies Commission's view that terms of the deal contravened the Building Societies Act. The Commission's main objection was that the deal would give cash bonuses to investors of less than two years' standing. The Court held that the relevant section of the Act was intended to prevent speculative investment in building societies. The director general of the Building Societies Association, Adrian Coles, said,

> 'The decision is consistent with how most people interpret the law, and it is what most building societies wished. There was a fear that

societies would fall victim to waves of speculative cash chasing the latest take-over tip, which was what the original act had sought to avoid.'

Lloyds was forced to amend its offer and in early August 1994 announced that it had reached agreement with the Cheltenham & Gloucester whereby it would still pay £1.8 billion, but this would now be paid only to investing members of two years' standing and depositors, and not to borrowers and that, at 13.54 per cent of the balance of the qualifying accounts, would be higher than originally envisaged. The average windfall would be £2200 but those with only £100 in their account would still receive £513.54. Those with £1000 would receive £635.44, those with £10,000, £1854 and those with £100,000, £14,044.

These payouts increased the pressure on the Leeds board to make certain that whatever they decided, merger or acquisition, they would have to ensure a certain and relatively speedy cash return for their members.

In truth, the members did not understand mutuality

As we have seen, the Halifax board and indeed senior management, carried out thorough research and a full debate on the possibility of conversion from a mutual building society into a public limited company in 1988. In the end, although the executive management were in favour of conversion, the board decided against.

During the research period the Treasury agreed to widen building society powers removing one of the society's objections to restrictions placed on them. This weakened the case for conversion and the business plan put forward by the executive management did not make a convincing case for raising substantial new capital, which might only have been possible as a plc. For working capital the costs of operating as a plc were considerably higher.

Since 1988 there had been a number of developments. The Abbey National converted successfully in 1989, and there was much talk of other conversions and the acquisition of small building societies by banks. Nothing much actually happened for a number of years, perhaps due to the severe recession in the housing market which forced most societies to concentrate in crisis management as bad debts mounted. The recession also made many societies less attractive. With regard to conversion perhaps some took the lead from Halifax who enjoyed a reputation for 'getting it right'.

By 1994, the housing market was emerging from recession and the prospects were a stable but low-growth market for the foreseeable future. A number of societies, including Halifax, wanted to broaden their range of activities to cover the whole of the personal financial services market. The emphasis was likely to be in the savings area and this would bring the societies into direct competition with the banks. It would seem clear that there would be room only for a very limited number of major players offering a coherent range of full services. Lloyds Bank understood this and moved quickly to acquire a major and innovative society, Cheltenham & Gloucester. As we have recounted, this acquisition was seen by many as signalling the end of 'cosy' society mergers and would in future mean big handouts to society members. For Halifax it could bring pressure from members to convert and the society could be forced into conversion at a time not of the board's choosing.

The key issues before the directors in considering conversion were,

> 'The Mission. This was defined as "to be the biggest and best personal finance business in the UK" and agreed by the directors in February 1994. If the society planned to remain in the personal sector conversion would not be necessary, though it might be desirable, but if there were plans to move into the corporate sector, conversion would be essential. Remaining mutual would not seem to be a barrier to achieving the mission but plc status might provide the society with the flexibility to respond if it lost its number one position through rationalisation elsewhere in the industry.

> On the issue of capital, Halifax did not currently need extra capital but this could mean that the timing for conversion was ideal in that the market would not expect the society to return to the market within a short period with a demand for further capital. Indeed, the society would have to plan carefully what to do if the capital was raised at the time of flotation. The experience of the TSB was not an entirely happy precedent.

> On powers, building societies were at a disadvantage to banks in that banks were free of prescriptive regulation whereas societies were not. After much negotiation the society had obtained most of the powers it sought but during long periods of negotiation with the Treasury and the Building Societies Commission it had found itself at a competitive disadvantage.

The next issue was Halifax's new businesses, *Halifax Life* and *Halifax Personal Banking*. It was conceivable that *Halifax Life* could grow to a size that within a generation could rival the society itself. If so, it would be inappropriate for it to be controlled by a mutual building society with capital and powers constraints inhibiting growth.

On funding, it would seem essential the society achieve bank status in order to fund the £40 billion non-retail liabilities envisaged by the end of the decade. The society had sought other routes to achieve bank status but conversion seemed to be the simplest and quickest.

On the concept of mutuality, the directors had to decide how important was the generally warm feeling engendered by the concept of mutuality – surpluses rather than profits, secure and friendly image (no society member had lost money since the war), diversity in the financial services sector and a strong employment and decision-making base outside London. In truth, the members themselves did not really understand mutuality. Research carried out in 1992 showed that only 3 per cent of a sample of Halifax members were aware of their ownership rights and a survey of 500 members taken after the Lloyds/Cheltenham & Gloucester announcement, showed that 75 per cent could not attempt to explain what mutuality meant in the context of a building society, 50 per cent could not say what the difference would be if a society became a plc and 28 per cent said there would be no difference.'

However, if the members might not know how to define a mutual, they would surely know that if being a member of the Cheltenham & Gloucester building society meant a substantial cash hand-out from Lloyds Bank, being a member of the mighty Halifax could be one way of giving the members those benefits if the society were to decide to become a plc.

In considering all these arguments the directors knew that in the summer of 1994 conditions were very different from the last time, in 1988, when they had considered conversion in great detail. Now, merger loomed large in the equation. All knew that negotiations with Leeds had been going on for several months and that all major points had been agreed except the critical one as far as the Leeds board was concerned – they felt they could not merge with Halifax unless they could offer their members a large bonus, almost certainly impractical, or they could guarantee that the merged societies would convert in the foreseeable future thereby releasing value to their members. In simple terms, if Halifax directors said no to conversion, they could almost certainly say goodbye to Leeds and, as David Gilchrist pointed out in his background notes for their discussion, they could almost certainly say goodbye to *any* building society merger because, post Lloyds/Cheltenham & Gloucester, all the society boards would have the same problem.

One problem of Leeds insisting on conversion was the danger of putting itself in play if it became public knowledge that it was prepared to abandon mutuality. In a memo to Mike Blackburn on 5 July, Mike Ellis emphasised the value of decoupling the issues of merger and conversion,

> 'The Boards of both *East* and *West* would have to be convinced of the case for conversion. To satisfy prudential requirements this would take a considerable period, probably delaying any announcement to say December 1994. It would be difficult, to say the least, to maintain confidentiality during this period.
>
> The attitude of the Commission to any linked announcement is unknown but it is reasonable to assume that satisfying the Commission will extend still further the timing of any announcement.
>
> In addition to the above, I believe that there are practical and commercial reasons for decoupling the issues. The merger should be bedded down before conversion. On a practical level we need the business to be fully integrated and systems in place which will satisfy the Bank of England. From a commercial viewpoint, we are likely to maximise value by securing economies of scale and more fully developing new businesses such as *Life*, in the period post merger. This need not be a long period during which we should, for prudential reasons, ensure that systems are in place to support any conversion.
>
> The Board of *East* are clearly concerned regarding the issue of realising shareholder value but they may accept that such value will be considerably enhanced post merger.'

The attitude of Halifax to demutualistion and conversion by early July was summed up in a briefing document to the chairman's committee on 5 July.

> 'The final recommendation on this complex and far-reaching issue had yet to be debated by the Board, simply because there has not been a need to do so.

119

However, the executives have stated that they expect the business to convert to a public limited company in the foreseeable future. The future is defined as 1997. The issues that have led them to this conclusion are [as follows].

- Operational funding requirements, money and capital markets – e.g. counter party limits/sector exposure etc.

- The possibility that future legislation or public pressure could force mutuals to distribute a greater proportion of their profits which are in excess of capital adequacy requirements.

- Their strategy demands substantial horizontal growth (general insurance, health insurance etc.). It could be that this can only be satisfactorily funded via the equity markets.

- The rather more complex question of accountability.'

If the decision to convert was taken by both societies, a public statement would have to be carefully planned as,

'A simple unqualified statement of intention to demutualise could seriously disrupt the money markets. Both businesses could attract huge speculative money flows.'

At this stage, July 1994, the timetable stretched three years ahead with three months preparing for the statement to merge and convert, the merger programme then being completed by about June 1995 with the conversion process taking eighteen months to two years after that. This proved to be an extremely accurate prediction of how events would unfold.

It was a low point

The debate over conversion was beginning to cause serious problems in the merger discussions. While the two sides were stuck between what became known as *Option D* (effectively a merger with no guarantee of conversion) and *Option E* (merger and guarantee of conversion) and then considered William Nabarro's *Option D+* (merger with bonus to Leeds members), a further option emerged during August and this was referred to as *Option D++* (*Options A, B* and *C* had all been ruled out on the basis that they did not include conversion). At the Leeds board meeting of 29 August, John King said that the way forward may be *Option D++*, which envisaged a commitment by Halifax, on announcement of the merger, 'to conversion appearing inevitable, but timing dependent on regulatory approval, commercial development and state of the equity market'. It was an attempt to move as close as possible to *Option E* without the necessity of giving an absolute guarantee of commitment to conversion. The Leeds board thought the wording could be improved to portray a more positive approach.

On Thursday, 25 August, John King met Jon Foulds and told him that a number of factors, most notably the Lloyds payments to the Cheltenham & Gloucester members, had made the Leeds board realise that they must look at every option to ensure they fulfilled their fiduciary duty. This entailed a great deal of desk research which could not be completed in time for the Leeds board meeting of 30 August and a decision would have to be deferred until the 27 September board meeting.

Foulds was concerned about a slippage in the timetable for several reasons. First, it increased the possibility of leaks and he showed King a letter he had received from Patrick Weever of *The Sunday Telegraph* which indicated he sensed something was afoot. Second, a delayed announcement would bring it close to the Lloyds/Cheltenham & Gloucester payout, scheduled for February 1995, inviting comparisons that might not necessarily be favourable. Third, both Halifax and Leeds had planned management conferences for early November and it was important that management be properly briefed. Finally, Halifax was holding open several senior management positions in anticipation of the deal. As King acknowledged, the final point applied even more seriously to Leeds as its chief executive position had now been vacant for 18 months.

Graham Johnston felt at the time that a real crisis point had been reached,

> 'At that point, to jump to the stage that John King was wanting us to move to, though we felt it an inevitable position eventually, would be a great leap of faith without Halifax board approval. We had great problems with this. Jon Foulds had gone on holiday as had Gren Folwell. It was Friday, 2nd September. Mike Ellis and I were in the office, Mike Blackburn was away on business. We spent the whole day on the 'phone to Gren at his home in North Yorkshire and to Roger Boyes and his advisers. We couldn't get hold of Mike

Blackburn. It was a low point, certainly my low point. That was the one day when I felt the merger was actually getting away from us. But Gren fought very hard for it, he did a super job.'

David Gilchrist felt that the Leeds board were in a potentially very difficult situation,

> 'I imagine they said to themselves, with advice from their merchant bank, "We've been through difficult times, lost our chief executive, failed to merge with N & P and have been operating without a chief executive for a considerable time. The last thing we can afford to do is announce a merger with the Halifax only to have a hostile bidder appear over the horizon and take that away from us." It would have been a tremendous loss of face and I think it was probably one of the reasons why they insisted on merger plus conversion.'

For his part King felt that Halifax was moving towards an announcement on the commitment to convert. In support, he showed a letter dated the day after his meeting with Foulds. The letter was from Gren Folwell but was written on behalf of Foulds who had gone on holiday. It confirmed that the deliberations of the Halifax board with respect to conversion had now reached the stage where 'the pressure for change from this source (ability to raise capital to grow the business) seems inexorable and particularly so in the context of a merger'. The whole Leeds board felt that this letter was a major step forward and strongly reinforced their determination to press for *Option E.*

Taking ourselves over a cliff

The moment of truth had arrived. If the merger was to proceed, the Halifax board had to agree on conversion as part of the package. Intense discussion and consultation took place throughout September and October. Andrew Peck of Linklaters & Paines was to say later that this was a very tricky period for the whole project. He felt that Leeds had a better sense of its future than Halifax. It had been forced to face its stark choices and had done so systematically. Halifax, in its position as number one, could take a more measured view of its development. On 7 September, at an informal meeting of the Halifax board in London, the directors asked themselves again – should they give up mutual status and was this the right moment to do so? Most directors would have preferred the decision to come through in an evolutionary rather than a forced way, but accepted that this was now probably no longer possible. David Gilchrist said later,

> 'The difficulty from our point of view was that we had so recently and publicly said in the Report and Accounts that we saw our future as a mutual. The change of direction necessary, merger and conversion, meant that the Halifax board wanted more time to think about it, go over all the familiar arguments again and look at conversion in isolation rather than be pushed into it by the interests of the Leeds.'

And concern was expressed about the finality of the decision – the phrase 'taking ourselves over a cliff' was used – and also about the danger of bad execution if merger and conversion were tackled at the same time.

The next Halifax board meeting was on Wednesday, 21 September, and the directors met informally the evening before to consider David Gilchrist's paper laying out the conversion pros and cons. The main points raised were queries on the profitability of non-core activities, the necessity of bank status for better wholesale funding and the flexibility, even to the point of looking at other acquisitions rather than Leeds, which conversion would bring. The chairman, Jon Foulds, was a little worried that Halifax could be left standing in a flurry of deals following the Lloyds/Cheltenham & Gloucester deal and thus the merger with Leeds was attractive.

At the formal board meeting the next day, the directors considered two papers from their advisers. The first was, *Duties of Directors Considering Conversion*. In this the advisers said it was not the duty of directors to find a 'right' answer but, 'to weigh up all the factors and exercise their judgement as directors reasonably to reach a conclusion which, if it turns out to be in favour of conversion, they believe can be properly put to members'. The main thrust of the paper was that the directors' duty was to present members with a fair balance of arguments and a reasoned recommendation.

The second paper was *Control of Investment Flows and Cash Payments to Members on Conversion*. This was advice on how to deal with hot money flowing into the society in the hope of quick gains through conversion. The recommendation was to relate benefits to the size of a member's balance with a clear out-off date, the date of public announcement.

At the end of the meeting, the chairman set out the timetable. A special board would be held on 11 October which would firm up the merger proposal. At the board on 19 October both issues, merger and conversion, would be decided.

On 11 October the board met without advisers. In the morning Mike Ellis presented the case for the merger without conversion outlining the points that had been agreed with the Leeds. These were:

- retention of Halifax mission and name

- retention of most of Leeds product brands

- retention of corporate headquarters in Halifax

- retention of Leeds head office for key operations.

Key positions would include:

- new chairman   Jon Foulds (Halifax)

- new vice-chairmen   John Wood (Halifax) and a Leeds director

- new chief executive   Mike Blackburn (Halifax).

Additionally:

- employment reductions would be through natural wastage, voluntary redundancy and early retirement, and

- between 350 and 400 branches would overlap, but some could survive for delivery of other financial services.

The directors were concerned about opposition to network rationalisation and the costs and time involved in systems integration and on employment issues. They were reminded of the negative impact on the Leeds/National & Provincial merger by the announcement that there would be 3000 redundancies. On financial forecasts the directors wanted to be very conservative, feeling that the synergistic benefits, always so loudly trumpeted on such occasions, would come through only slowly. It was thought possible that the deal would be referred to the Monopolies and Mergers Commission but this was not felt to be disastrous. Indeed, it could 'be advantageous in securing high-level political support for our move in terms of creating a powerful non-metropolitan counter-weight to the banks'.

In the afternoon the Board considered a paper *Conversion to plc.* The discussion covered capital-raising on conversion (there was no case for conversion in order to raise additional new capital), diversification, the difficulty for a mutual in defining clear objectives and the inexorable general move towards plc status (mutuality probably only sustainable for two to five years). Size was important – mutuality implied a niche position. In overall public favourability, some plcs (Marks and Spencer, Sainsbury's) were a long way ahead of Halifax or any other mutual.

The chairman summed up: the consensus was that conversion was a strong possibility at some stage. Should this remain within Halifax's control or was the 'prize' of *East* sufficiently attractive to bring the decision forward? The 19 October meeting would decide.

At the 19 October board meeting in Halifax the board were joined for part of the meeting by merchant bank and legal advisers. This was the meeting to discuss 'the case for the linked merger and conversion proposal'.

Warburgs saw no need to advise against the linked proposal, but this would need to be discussed with the Building Societies Commission, for whom this would be a difficult issue. The chairman summed up the discussion so far. This was the third formal debate, and there had also been five informal meetings of directors – so there had been ample opportunity to consider all the issues. The Halifax mission implied a significant move away from traditional building society activity towards *bancassurance*. Directors therefore had to consider whether conversion appeared to be a way of fulfilling the mission.

This was the key debate. The advisers withdrew and the chairman asked for the views of the non-executive directors. John Wood, former chairman of the printers McCorquodale, liked conversion more than merger. He was happy about both but if the package was too complex he would support conversion on its own. Professor John Kay, director of London Economics, Britain's leading specialist economic consulting group, had consistently championed the cause of mutuality. He felt that the strengths of mutuality – staff commitment and business focus – might be lost in a plc environment. Nevertheless, on balance, he was in favour of the linked transaction.

Ralph Hodge, recruited to the board following his period in charge of ICI's personnel function during the major rationalisation of its UK workforce, felt that the retention of the *status quo* was not an option and was wholeheartedly in favour of the linked transaction. Nigel Colne, a long-serving Marks and Spencer man, emphasised the difficulty of Halifax remaining number one through organic growth and was strongly in favour of the linked proposal. Colne was to say later that the idea that because Halifax was a mutual it was more in tune with customer service than it would be as a plc was false. Marks and Spencer had been a plc for generations and by comparison, Halifax had a very long way to go in getting close to its customers. It was not plc status that would affect this but attitude and training. Duncan Ferguson, Senior Partner of the actuaries, Bacon & Woodrow, had only just become a Halifax director but he agreed with Colne and said later,

> 'The financial question that applies to insurance companies remaining mutual – passing on benefits to customers in the form of higher bonuses or a discount on premiums – doesn't enter into the equation for a building society. So that argument didn't exist, or at least was easy to consider and then dismiss so far as I was concerned.'

Roy Chapman, former senior partner of Arthur Andersen, was in favour of the merger on opportunistic grounds but felt that there was no need to rush into conversion unless the two could not be separated. Conversion remained a desirable strategic objective at the right time.

On Jon Foulds' 'conversion to conversion', Anthony Coleby, formerly of the Bank of England, said later,

> 'I think his approach was to say, "Well here we have a new situation, we must look at the questions entirely from square one and not allow ourselves to be captives of what was decided in the past in other circumstances".
>
> 'It was clear from a fairly early stage that he actually was quite well disposed to conversion. I have never understood in detail what were the factors, what were the considerations that moved him to that change of view but my private belief is that the prize of the merger with the Leeds was one which he valued quite highly and when he thought about it he decided the prize of remaining mutual was not something he valued as much.'

And was anyone against merger and conversion? Was a vote necessary? Coleby recalled,

> 'We had no one as best as I can recall who was absolutely and totally hostile. We had quite a number who were distinctly reserved about it, including, understandably, some who had been there at the time of the decision in 1988, or whenever it was, to remain mutual.

Whereas I think on the whole those directors who had joined subsequent to that date were on balance more inclined to be favourable to conversion. But I can remember among those expressing doubts, for example John Kay, who perhaps was less committed than some to the objective of size and therefore didn't regard the merger with the Leeds as a prize which should be worth paying anything for, but the way Jon [Foulds] handled it was to say, "Well let's not start talking about conclusions, let us set out the issues as fully, as comprehensively as we can and work our way through them". And that was done with a good deal of input, obviously, from the staff as the exercise unfolded so those who had doubts seemed, I think, to experience a lessening of their doubts and moreover, I think, came to understand that there was a clear body of support among their non-executive colleagues for going ahead with the deal. Those two influences, well managed from the chair, were sufficient in the end to persuade everyone that it should be a unanimous decision.'

Mike Blackburn was later to describe the meeting as 'electric'.

'There was certainly, from my point of view, electricity in the air. Issues were explored, balanced, picked up across the room. Stones were not left unturned. I came out of that meeting feeling I had participated in and witnessed a debate of the highest possible calibre. I felt privileged to have been part of it. If any member of the society had been a fly on the wall he would have flown off saying "Actually, we've elected a bloody good board."'

In keeping with his feelings, Blackburn said to his colleagues, 'The challenge is awe-inspiring but the prize worthy of our efforts, worthy of our predecessors and worthy of our future.' Jon Foulds said that he had been convinced at the beginning of the 1988 discussion that conversion was inevitable but after listening to the arguments, decided he was wrong. Earlier in 1994 he had felt a strong attachment to mutuality but was now convinced more than ever that conversion was inevitable.

The board finally crossed the Rubicon and resolved to continue merger negotiations and, if the merger was implemented, the board would propose conversion to its members.

CHAPTER SEVEN

Unequivocal ... the deal offered excellent value

Negotiations to be continued with the Halifax
The Office of Fair Trading
Stick to its domestic knitting
The rumour is at a level I've only known once before

Negotiations to be continued with the Halifax

B y late October the Halifax board had resolved to accept conversion and that therefore the Leeds requirement of merger with guarantee of conversion (*Option E*) was acceptable. Nevertheless, the Negotiation Agreement put forward by the Halifax, although it 'endeavoured to be accommodating and fulfil all the Leeds' board's requirements', also restricted the Leeds' board's actions during the relevant period of negotiations until 1 July 1995 (or possibly until 30 September 1995 in certain circumstances), although not in a manner that prevented the directors from carrying out their fiduciary, common law or statutory duties.

The advisers' opinion was that signing the Negotiation Agreement meant that the Leeds would have to discontinue any further negotiations, however informal, with third parties. On the other hand the Agreement 'would not preclude the board discussing a clear offer from these bodies, or any others, were any such offers to be received'.

Both of their advisers, Allen & Overy and Hambros Bank, were in favour and Nabarro said that the senior executives at Hambros Bank were 'unequivocal in suggesting that the deal offered excellent value to Leeds members'.

All the directors present expressed in turn their support for the proposal to merge with Halifax. Of those not present, Prue Leith and Chris Chadwick were known to be in favour and although Derek Cook felt that Leeds members should have a payment up-front rather than wait for conversion, he too was in favour.

So, on 1 November 1994, the Leeds board resolved,

'(a) that the Board agree in principle with the proposal to merge with the Halifax Building Society ("the Halifax") by way of a transfer of the engagements of Leeds Permanent Buildings Society to the Halifax under sections 94 to 97 of the Building Societies Act 1986, to be followed in due course by conversion to plc status and flotation of the enlarged Halifax

(b) that negotiations be continued with the Halifax to finalise the terms of the proposed merger with a view to making a public announcement and putting appropriate resolutions to members in due course

(c) the terms of the Letter of Common Intent (11th draft dated 1 November 1994) be accepted and confirmed and that the Chairman be authorised to sign it on behalf of the Society, and

(d) that the Negotiation Agreement (final draft dated 28 October 1994) be accepted and confirmed and that the Chairman be authorised to sign it on behalf of the Society.'

In Nabarro's view the agreement negotiated was acceptable. It prevented Leeds participating in any negotiations or discussions on any major transaction until 1 July 1995 (extended if regulator's action should delay the timetable, to a final longstop date of 30 September 1995). It also included a commitment by Leeds not to allow third-party approaches to delay the timetable to the society's Extraordinary General Meeting on the merger.

In his view, Halifax would not proceed without the agreement. It had decided to float at this stage only if the merger went forward. Once Halifax had announced its flotation plans, even if only to regulators, it would be apprehensive that delays to the merger could leave its flotation process floundering, thus opening the way for third parties to take advantage and make approaches to Leeds.

Nabarro also pointed out that, in spite of many rumours, no other bidder had actually appeared and that the Hambros' desk research,

' ...strongly suggests a bid would not be self-evidently worth more to members than participating in the float of the merged entity.'

There was an exclusion in the agreement which allowed directors, 'to do what they reasonably consider they must to meet their regulatory or legal requirements'. This included communicating a serious definitive offer, if received, to the members in whatever terms the directors considered necessary.

Nabarro concluded,

'On balance, the agreement is beneficial in enabling the *East* board to ignore fishing approaches and – after announcement – the tactical expressions of interest that are likely to follow and may, in reality, only be spoiling actions.'

David Simmonds, *The Economist*
1 April 1995

After all the twists and turns of the previous 24 months, it was a momentous decision and a decisive moment, and Malcolm Barr recognised it as such, graciously acknowledging the hard work of all concerned. He mentioned Roger Boyes and John King especially as those who had negotiated continuously with the Halifax, at times frankly, but at all times in a spirit of courtesy and goodwill.

The Halifax board's resolutions on 19 October 1994 had already cleared the way for agreement to be reached with the Leeds and made the deal a virtual certainty despite the flirtations with other societies and banks in which some of the Leeds directors were indulging. The next priority was timing and organisation but, in the meantime, all concerned needed to be ready in case there were any leaks. A plan was drawn up and circulated to the directors and executive committee of Halifax.

If the conversion issue was raised, the answer was that it was an issue 'regularly examined by the Halifax board' and therefore, by implication, would be examined by any future merged board. There was always the possibility that someone might possess 'hard' documentary evidence of the Halifax board's decision in principle to recommend conversion following the merger. In that case the response would be that this was indeed the view of the current board, that the actual recommendation would have to come from a future merged board, would be some years away and would be subject to a members' vote.

Finally, those concerned were told that liaison was taking place with Leeds to make sure it used the same press statement and questions and answers. It was being emphasised that the Leeds should not say anything more positive about conversion.

The Office of Fair Trading

Both Leeds and Halifax knew there was a possibility that a merger between them would be referred by the Secretary of State for Trade and Industry to the Monopolies and Mergers Commission (MMC). Indeed, as we have already seen, the Office of Fair Trading (OFT) had written to Jon Foulds in July on the basis of a speculative article in *The Observer*.

Subsequently the societies put their case on why the merger should not be referred to the MMC. The document, prepared after close co-operation with the experienced David Hall of Linklaters & Paines, explained that the merger would be governed by the terms of the Building Societies Act 1986 and would result in a transfer by the Leeds of its engagements to the Halifax but would not be an acquisition in the conventional sense. It gave the details – outlined below – of each society.

	Halifax	*Leeds*
Mortgage balances of UK	15.2 per cent	4.5 per cent
Branches	687	453
Estate Agency offices	528	88
Staff — full-time	18,256	4,855
— part-time	6,342	1,462

It highlighted the recent changes in the British financial services sector. Formerly the system had been highly structured with clear demarcation between building societies, banks and other types of financial service provider. Moreover this division had been reinforced by official controls, such as lending constraints, exchange control regulations and a fixed bank rate. The result was extremely restricted competition.

In the 1980s everything had changed and the submitted document quoted from the MMC's own Report into the supply of residential mortgage valuations,

'In summary there have been some major changes in the structure of the industry over the last dozen years. Many smaller societies have left the industry through merger and a number of substantial financial organisations have entered to become significant lenders in their own right. At the same time, those building societies remaining in the market have been able, following the 1986 Act, to expand and diversify the range of financial products they provide. Entry has taken place mainly as a result of the removal of regulatory barriers in 1980, though the boom in demand in the mid to late 1980s was also a major factor in attracting new entrants. There are clearly costs to market entry, particularly the potential sunk costs of establishing the necessary computer systems as well as marketing and advertising costs, but these have not proved to be an effective barrier, at least for the large financial institutions. As regards branch networks, the banks already had such networks in place well before entry into this market, while centralised lenders have demonstrated that a physical presence in the high street is not a necessary condition for successful entry. In part, this reflects the greater importance of intermediaries in this market during the 1980s. These changes have had major effects in the market. The range of mortgage products available has increased. The borrower now has a wide choice between different kinds of endowment and repayment mortgages, available at fixed or variable rates. The recent decline in the housing market, accompanied by continuing availability of funds for lending, has intensified competition between lenders. There has been some switching by borrowers between lenders in search of better terms and a number of lenders have been actively seeking this business.'

The Halifax and Leeds were at pains to point out that, in spite of their significant shares of the mortgage market, they did not consider that the combination of the two societies would have any significant implications for the UK mortgage lending market. Competition from the banks was strong especially when interest rates were low and, in every postal district in Great Britain in which each of the Leeds and the Halifax had at least one branch, other building societies or banks were represented (frequently in considerable numbers). Even in Lancashire and Yorkshire where naturally both societies were strong, the choice for borrowers was still considerable. The societies estimated there were 145 different suppliers in the mortgage market. In their view no single institution dominated the market, nor, given its diversity, was a single institution likely to be able to dominate it in the future.

In looking at retail savings, the two societies pointed out that this too was highly competitive and also fragmented and, at the margin, very price sensitive. In 1993, the Halifax's share of personal sector liquid assets was 12 per cent while that of the Leeds was 4 per cent. Following a merger they expected significant competition to continue for savings from unit trusts, personal equity plans, the stock market, banks, National Savings, other building societies and other institutions.

In the markets of money transmission, credit cards, personal lending and long-term assurance, neither society had a significant share of the market. In the estate agency field the branches of both were spread throughout the country. As there were about 11,000 estate agency outlets in the country, Halifax owned 4.8 per cent and Leeds 0.8 per cent.

Stick to its domestic knitting

Both Halifax and Leeds directors had concentrated hard throughout the negotiating months on ensuring they were going to do the right thing for their members. Neither was yet a public company and although the boards were well aware of the City and the importance of having it 'on-side', Anthony Hotson of S G Warburg wanted to make sure that the case for merger and conversion was well presented from a City perspective.

He assumed that Halifax would call an analysts' meeting. Halifax was quite well known to the market but Leeds barely known at all. He felt that the market might be initially more interested in the impact on quoted companies in the banking sector and cited the fact that the Lloyds/ Cheltenham & Gloucester announcement had more effect on the share price of Abbey National than on that of Lloyds. Halifax and Leeds should be aware that the quoted competition would not sit idly by without comment and that the comment would be designed to undermine the societies' message.

The analysts would home in on three issues. First, they would want to know why Halifax wanted more market share. It would be crucial to show that they were not going for size for size's sake. If size was important they must say why. Second, the market believed, and Jon Foulds had said as recently as last spring, that Halifax favoured mutuality. The market will now want to know why Halifax had changed its mind, especially as conversion seemed to complicate rather than simplify the merger. The City would certainly want to know whether Halifax planned to raise more money on conversion and, if so, how much. Hotson's view of the rationale was that,

'The scale of its profits was becoming inconsistent with mutual status.

Current legislation makes it difficult to remunerate members.

Conversion will enable it to provide economic value to its members.'

He went on to say that the market would be delighted that Halifax did not need to raise more capital. The less capital raised the more its market rating would benefit. In Hotson's view, Halifax should tell the City that it would raise more capital only if forced to by the regulator; it would raise the minimum required; it had no grandiose plans for domestic acquisitions or overseas exploits and that it would 'stick to its domestic knitting'.

The third issue was management and Hotson predicted that at least one of Halifax's quoted competitors would say that the merged societies would not have the stomach or the skills to carry through the necessary rationalisation. Furthermore, apart from the chairman, the management were not well known. Hotson felt that the Halifax should say that,

'The merger is being structured as an acquisition rather than as an amalgamation.'

But Halifax would have to be extremely careful about any comments along these lines. Any mention of the word 'acquisition' would cause uproar in Leeds and could scupper the whole deal. Indeed, Halifax rejected this piece of advice from Hotson, preferring the line that,

'The unique position of *West*'s CEO will prevent the kind of muddled compromises which so frequently hamstring mergers of equals. The rationalisation decisions have been made.'

The rumour is at a level I've only known once before

As we have seen there had been occasional bouts of speculation in the media about a Halifax/Leeds merger and these revived in early November 1994. On Wednesday, 2 November, the 'City Diary' in *The Times* said,

> 'Speculation about a possible merger between the Halifax Building Society and the Leeds Permanent, the United Kingdom's fifth largest society, refuses to die down. The rumour mill went into overdrive yesterday after the Halifax held a national conference for its senior and general managers, the first such event in four years. Mike Blackburn, the Halifax chief executive who occupied the same post at the Leeds until 18 months ago, is reported to have made a mission statement to staff, having toured the society's branches over the past year.
>
> A spokesman denied this included any talk of a merger, but industry observers still believe the two societies are moving closer together.'

Nine days later Pennington said, again in *The Times*,

Hot Leeds
'BUILDING society chiefs are betting on an early marriage between the Halifax and the Leeds. The Halifax, they reason, is desperate to remain the biggest mortgage lender and has just watched the Abbey National gobble up the Household Mortgage Corporation's £1.6 billion mortgage book. Leeds members may be less keen if they see the chance of a bonus from conversion to plc or a take-over slip by.'

Dick Spelman, at that time general manager, Marketing, and on the Halifax executive committee, remembers being summoned by Mike Blackburn in September and having a confidentiality letter thrust into his hands which he was asked to sign so that he could be told something 'confidential'. He had already guessed that something was afoot.

'People were absent in an unplanned way, Gren Folwell particularly, and there were constant *ad hoc* meetings of the board. If you were observant you said to yourself, "Something's afoot!"'

And once he knew, life was not any easier for Spelman. He had to employ all sorts of ruses to obtain information,

'I went to the printer of our passbooks and said, "Look, we think we might have a legal problem in the printing of terms and conditions on our passbooks which might mean we have to re-print them all. If we did, how quickly could you do it?"

Whether he read between the lines he never told me but we got the information, and the books when we needed them. That was the sort of phoney war that was going on.'

By week beginning 21 November the air-waves were vibrating with speculation and on that Monday, Robin Urwin of Leeds sent John Miller a memo, under the heading RUMOURS. He said that the current gossip was that a merger was imminent with both Alliance & Leicester and Halifax, but with Halifax the strong favourite. Leeds colleagues had been at social events where either Halifax employees or their spouses had said the merger was definitely 'on'. Paul Middleton attended a *Top Fifteen* meeting where the Halifax delegate confirmed it. Mike Rowe suggested that 5 December was the date for the announcement. This was based on conversations with a supplier and, again, this was supposedly based on comments from the Halifax. Apparently the rumour was very strong in the field, based on comments made to Leeds staff by Halifax staff. Mike Blackburn and senior Halifax staff had been spotted at an off-site meeting in the Lake District (this last turned out to be false). Urwin concluded,

'The rumour is at a level I've known only once before – just before the announcement last year. Very little of it seems to be internally generated, although people are inevitably putting odd pieces of information together to try and form a picture, e.g. Clive Whitaker being ensconced on the sixth floor, the various pieces of work you have commissioned or brought forward and so on.'

Over in Halifax, Mike Ellis was coming under tremendous pressure from his 'suspicious' Treasury lot.

'Someone said to me a couple of weeks before the announcement, "We know now it is the Leeds". There was nothing I could do at that stage but be very careful and I said, "It's a load of rubbish!"'

On Monday, 14 November, the leading players from both societies, Group 8 (the Chairmen's Committee) – Jon Foulds, John Wood, Mike Blackburn and Gren Folwell from Halifax and Malcolm Barr, John King, Sir Timothy Kitson and Roger Boyes from Leeds – met in secret at Halifax's flat in Jermyn Street. This was the first meeting since the deal was definitely 'on' and there was a certain feeling of euphoria. However, they were all aware that there could still be hitches, and that the announcement would have to be well prepared for and organised. Even the date for the announcement had not been fixed but Monday, 12 December, seemed to be the favourite. Both 15 and 19 December had been considered, but a Monday was deemed to be the best day as it would allow the whole week to field questions, especially from the week-end press. It would allow adequate time for staff communication and was a more respectable distance from the Christmas holiday period than the 15th or 19th.

Roger Boyes was concerned that all the computer systems were in place to cope with the close-off date for membership, thus ring-fencing existing members' entitlements. They should also be ready for 'hot money' flows from speculators.

A programme office had been put in place and Blackburn explained its importance as the 'mechanism of control for pace of work, prioritisation, manpower plans etc.'. The programme would be overseen by the Chairmen's Committee (G8), which would be the governing body determining policy and ensuring that objectives were met. The operational control of the programme would be delegated to the Executive Liaison Group (G6), which would be made up of three executives from each society. The programme office would be manned by further personnel (Blackburn said twelve) and they, in turn, would be supported by six consultants from McKinsey.

The group decided to meet once a week up to the date of the announcement and agreed the dates – 23 November, 29 November and 7 December.

CHAPTER EIGHT

One hurdle after another

Heseltine gives his view
I'm not planning a wager on this one
All we need now is a bloody postal strike!
I need three days to present my case

Heseltine gives his view

The news was out. In chapter one we saw how it happened through a leak to John Willcock of *The Independent*. Halifax and Leeds were going to merge and convert into a public limited company. Fine, but not before a few hurdles had been successfully jumped. The first was to avoid a reference to the Monopolies and Mergers Commission (MMC).

On the announcement of merger and conversion the societies submitted their formal case to the Office of Fair Trading (OFT) why no reference should be made to the MMC. The OFT then had 25 days from 25 November in which to reply. It was thought ill-advised for Jon Foulds to lobby the Department of Trade and Industry (DTI) as the OFT would call on all interested parties such as the DTI, the Department of the Environment, the Building Societies Commission, the Treasury and the Bank of England, and if any of them wanted further information they would ask for it. However, it was thought that an informal meeting between Jon Foulds and the President of the Board of Trade, Michael Heseltine, might be beneficial in order that Foulds could tell the President of the benefits of the flotation, the new company's contribution to the economy and the vast potential for the expansion of share ownership. In the end such a meeting did not take place.

Was there any apprehension in the Halifax camp? Mike Ellis remembered that,

> 'We went through a period just before Christmas when people were getting a bit edgy. This was not helped by *The Independent* saying they thought the merger would be "referred". As they had received the leak some people wondered whether they had received some more information.'

Bleater, *Planned Savings* January 1995

Now the test would come and the indications were that a decision would be made before Christmas.

While they waited, the two societies needed to prepare themselves on how to react when the announcement came. On the same day, Rachel Hirst sent a memo to all the key executives and advisers saying that after discussion, it had been decided that the OFT decision would be immediately communicated to Warburg. In the event of a referral, Warburg would issue the agreed statement to the Stock Exchange Regulatory News Service and no comment should be made to external parties until the announcement appeared on the Regulatory News Service (RNS).

Everyone was fully briefed with answers to every conceivable question should the merger be referred. However, the optimists were proved right. On Wednesday, 21 December, it was announced from Michael Heseltine's office that the merger would not be referred to the Monopolies and Mergers Commission.

I'm not planning a wager on this one

Since autumn 1994 the two societies had been working on the basic terms of the share distribution scheme. Qualifying members, employees and pensioners would be entitled to a fixed number of free shares, referred to as the *basic distribution*, and, in addition, certain investing members would receive extra free shares dependent on the level of their investment. This was to be known as the *variable distribution*. The majority of shares would be in the *basic distribution* category.

The *basic distribution* would go to investing members who held not less than £100 in total in share accounts and/or Permanent Interest Bearing Shares (PIBS) of Halifax and/or Leeds at midnight on 25 November 1994 and remained investing members continuously until conversion, and were eligible to vote on the investing members' conversion resolution. Details of the number of free shares comprising the *basic distribution* would be announced nearer the time of conversion.

On *variable distribution* it was intended that it would be made to qualifying investing members who had a share account with, and/or held, PIBS of Halifax continuously for the period of two years ending on the qualifying day for conversion (a date to be selected by the combined society in due course).

The merger would be conditional on the alteration of Halifax rules to allow members of Leeds, at the time of the merger, to be treated as if they were members of Halifax.

In calculating the *variable distribution*, a member's lowest total balance would fall into a series of narrow bands between a lower limit of £1000 and an upper limit of £50,000. Where a member's balance was over £50,000 the excess would not be taken into account. Extra free shares would be allocated with reference to the band into which a member's lowest total balance fell. Further details of the *variable distribution* would also be announced nearer the time of conversion.

For borrowing members, each would receive a *basic distribution* if he or she was a borrowing member of either society with an outstanding balance of secured indebtedness of not less than £100 in total at midnight, 25 November 1994 and remained a borrowing member through to the conversion date and was eligible to vote on the borrowing members' resolution on conversion.

Employees and pensioners of both Halifax and Leeds on 25 November 1994 would receive the *basic distribution*. Directors would not receive free shares other than as investing or borrowing members. Anyone qualifying in more than one capacity, say as both a qualifying investor and borrower, would benefit in each capacity.

Halifax and Leeds submitted this scheme to the Building Societies Commission before Christmas 1994. The scheme, which had been devised by the two societies and their legal and financial advisers, was believed to comply with the provisions of the Building Societies Act 1986. Because of the known difficulties about the relevant section of the Act, which had come to light in relation to the Abbey National conversion and the Lloyds take-over of Cheltenham & Gloucester, it was thought prudent that the scheme should be reviewed by Counsel. Counsel had initially agreed that the scheme complied with the Act but shortly afterwards had second thoughts. For Graham Johnston this was another low point, perhaps similar to the one he experienced when the merger seemed to be slipping away at the end of the previous August,

'In early December, after a meeting at the Building Societies Commission, a number of us went back to Linklaters' office to do some more work drafting the transfer documents. We received a call from Counsel to say that although they had given advice that the conversion scheme was satisfactory and complied with the requirements of the Act, they were now having second thoughts about whether members of less than two years' standing, and borrowers, could receive free shares. This was a big low point. There were six or eight of us in the room at Linklaters and after this 25-minute conference call John Morris said to Andrew Peck, "Do you think you could tell us in layman's language what Counsel said?" Jon Foulds said, "I'm glad you said that, John, I was just going to ask the same thing."'

They sat and discussed the options. They rang Gren Folwell who was on a train back to Wakefield with Roger Boyes. Johnston remembers they had great trouble getting a decent connection, and Folwell and Boyes had to ring back when they arrived in Wakefield.

'We told them the story and they were gutted, they just did not believe that this could be the case.'

If Counsel's doubts were justified, the scheme would have to be redesigned, which was not only commercially undesirable but was also likely to delay the merger and conversion process. The societies and their respective legal advisers still thought that the proposed scheme fell within the terms of the Building Societies Act but there was now a risk that, without the relevant provision of the Act being considered by the Court, somebody might later claim that the scheme was illegal. The way to establish whether or not the scheme was legal would be to seek a declaration from the Court in a friendly action with the Building Societies Commission.

They went on to Halifax and, with Mike Blackburn, made further calls back to the team in London. As Johnston said,

> 'We wanted the Commission to challenge us in court because if we'd gone out with the transfer document as our conversion scheme and a member had challenged it as not being in conformity with the Act they could have taken us to court and screwed up the whole process. We had to clear all the legal hurdles *before* the issue of the transfer document. You can't sue yourself so we wanted the Commission to do it.'

The Commission was initially reluctant to agree to a friendly action since, paradoxically, it did not appear to harbour doubts about the legality of the proposed distribution scheme. It was not until late January 1995 that it agreed and notified Halifax and Leeds it wanted to seek a High Court ruling.

The problem centred on the section of the Building Societies Act relating to the conferring of rights for members to acquire shares in priority to other subscribers. The Act stated that these rights were restricted to investing members of at least two years' standing on the qualifying date. The question was – who were the 'other subscribers'? Halifax and Leeds said they were only those actually eligible for shares as part of the proposed transfer. Since all of these – investors, borrowers, employees and pensioners – would receive the same fixed allocation of free shares, no one would be receiving rights in priority to anyone else, and the Act would not be breached. The variable element of the share distribution – relating it to balances in accounts – was limited to investors of more than two years' standing and thus did not contravene the Act either. However, the Building Societies Commission argued that the 'other subscribers' could mean the investing public generally. Members of a society, other than two-year-plus investors, should take their chance with the rest of the public and therefore the plans to give them rights to free shares made the scheme unlawful.

The societies pointed out that their proposed conversion scheme was a variation of the scheme used by the Abbey National Building Society at the time of its conversion in 1989. In that scheme equal numbers of free shares were given to qualifying investing and borrowing members, employees and pensioners. The Halifax/Leeds proposals would give extra free shares to certain investing members with two years' continuous membership.

As a result of the court judgement on the Lloyds acquisition of Cheltenham & Gloucester in 1994, however, there was uncertainty about the distribution of free shares to investing members of less than two years' standing or to borrowing members. In the view of the Halifax/Leeds boards, after legal advice, the Cheltenham & Gloucester judgement was not relevant because it related to an acquisition, involved a cash distribution, and was governed by a different part of Section 100 of the Building Societies Act 1986 (described by *Lex* in the *Financial Times* as, 'one of the most ineptly drafted pieces of legislation to have left Parliament in the last decade').

The directors of the societies may have sounded confident about the outcome but they knew it was not a certainty that the Court would give a favourable response. Foulds said,

'I am a betting man but only on certainties. I'm not planning a wager on this one.'

The Commission's new head, Geoffrey Fitchew, who had taken over from Rosalind Gilmore, felt that if a society wanted to change to plc status, the Commission's responsibility and duty was to ensure that the relevant rules and procedures in the 1986 Act were properly observed and if there was any doubt about the meaning of the rules, that Court guidance would be sought. What did Mr Justice Chadwick think? The societies would soon find out although they had to wait from Monday, 20 March, when the Court began its hearing, until Tuesday, 28 March, when the judge announced his ruling.

There was a certain irony that the Lloyds/Cheltenham & Gloucester deal, which was still not finally settled, could be affected by the Court decision on Halifax/Leeds when the Halifax/Leeds talks throughout the second half of 1994 had been seriously affected by the Lloyds/Cheltenham & Gloucester terms. And the judge's decision and rulings would be critical. As Mike Ellis said,

'The court case was interesting because it would determine what we could and couldn't do. We were pretty confident but on the day we were nervous. The court was *packed*. You couldn't get a seat in the place. The press were standing in the aisles and sitting on the carpet. Justice Chadwick said, "To save you a lot of time, trouble and er, some discomfort, I will read the last paragraph of my judgement. This will enable you to do more pressing things." He read the paragraph which effectively gave approval and the place emptied. I stayed on to listen to two hours of the reasons for his judgement but almost everyone else rushed out of the court.'

The judge explained that his decision had been taken in the light of two judgements: the decision in 1989 when Abbey National converted, and the ruling in June 1994 when the High Court restricted the Cheltenham & Gloucester's scheme for distributing the £1.8 billion offered by Lloyds Bank. His view was in line with the Abbey ruling whereas the Cheltenham & Gloucester case raised different issues. Justice Chadwick had been able to take into account Parliament's *intentions*, even though they had not been made clear in the wording of section 100(8) in the 1986 Act. This had been made possible by the Pepper and Hart case, which had established that Courts could take account of relevant documents in matters of statutory interpretation.

The result was that it was all right to give free shares to less than two year investing members but not to give them cash as the Cheltenham & Gloucester had originally requested.

Everyone at Halifax and Leeds was mightily relieved though Jon Foulds said later that he felt no euphoria, in spite of the fact that the outcome had been far from certain. There was too much left to do!

In fact, no sooner had the court risen than the parties left to execute the contract, which provided for transfer of the business of the Leeds to Halifax, and to give formal approval of the documents that Halifax and Leeds would send to their respective members, so that they could be submitted to the Building Societies Commission for the approval needed before these documents were sent to the members of the two societies.

All we need now is a bloody postal strike!

With the Court ruling behind them, Halifax and Leeds could move on to the next major stepping stone, the votes by members of both societies at the two Special General Meetings convened in Halifax and Leeds for Monday, 22 May 1995. Andrew Peck of the legal firm Linklaters & Paines, recalled that it was an extremely tight timetable. As the directors of Halifax wanted the Special General Meeting to be held at the same time as the Annual General Meeting (apart from anything else there would be a saving in mailing costs) there was only just enough time to put together all the documents required by statute for an AGM.

Tension was heightened by a postal strike in the Newcastle area. It made Mike Ellis more careful about what he said in jest,

> 'Once the court case was over and all the documents signed I said jokingly, "All we need now is a bloody postal strike!" and the very next day one was announced in the Newcastle sorting office. We were faced with a real problem. We were required to deliver the merger document to *all* members and all the ones for the Newcastle area were stuck in the sorting office. We were forced to reprint and consider the possibility of delivery through a third-party supplier. The post office management said they could handle the distribution. In the end the strike was resolved and the crisis passed but never again will I say, "All we need now is a postal strike ...", or whatever.'

The members of the two societies would be faced with two resolutions on which to vote, one for investing members and one for borrowing members. For the Leeds members the resolutions were as follows.

1 Special Resolution

To consider and, if thought fit, to pass the following resolution which is intended to be moved as a Special Resolution:

That the engagements of Leeds Permanent Building Society be transferred to Halifax Building Society in accordance with the terms of an Instrument of Transfer of Engagements dated 28 March 1995 a copy of which, signed for the purposes of identification by the Secretary of each society, is laid before the Meeting.

2 Borrowing Members' Resolution

To consider and, if thought fit, to pass the following resolution which is intended to be moved as a Borrowing Members' Resolution:

That the engagements of Leeds Permanent Building Society be transferred to Halifax Building Society in accordance with the terms of an Instrument of Transfer of Engagements dated 28 March 1995 a copy of which, signed for the purposes of identification by the Secretary of each society, is laid before the Meeting.

For the Halifax members the resolutions were similar.

These may have been the formal resolutions but, as we have seen, what the vast majority of members were really interested in was 'when?' and 'how much?', and it is interesting to study the rationale behind the decisions on who should receive what.

Initially, a flat rate distribution was considered because of its simplicity, and the Abbey National precedent. As some 80 per cent of the voters held 20 per cent of the balances and vice versa it would be essential to offer a fairly large flat element to low balance investors. A simple flat structure would also have enabled earlier flotation, which was certainly attractive to the Leeds board, as there would be no worries about two year qualification rules.

On reflection, it was realised that the flat rate structure would not be as equitable as a variable structure. The Abbey system was seen as too crude and it would be unfair to distribute shares, then thought to have a market value of up to £1000 to all investors, borrowers, staff and pensioners irrespective of the size of their balances or the length of their membership. It was therefore agreed that the ideal scheme would be one with a flat rate distribution for all borrowing and investing members and staff and a variable element based on balances of all investing members of more than two years standing.

The People 19 March 1995

In the 42-page document sent to all members of Halifax, Jon Foulds outlined the reasons for the merger – enhanced market position to be the leading provider of personal financial services in the UK – and the reasons for choosing the Leeds – similar culture, strong branding of *Liquid Gold* and *Home Arranger*, and enhancement of West Yorkshire as a financial centre alongside London and Edinburgh.

But what the members really wanted to know was, 'What's in it for us?'.

> 'Members and other customers will have access to the most substantial network of branches offered by any building society today. The combined society will also offer a wide range of products and services, utilising the brands of both societies.
>
> On the Effective Date, members of, and depositors with, the Leeds will become members of, and depositors with, Halifax.
>
> There will be benefits for Leeds investors including improved withdrawal facilities in *Bonus Gold* and *Solid Gold* respectively. For Halifax investors in *Premium Xtra*, the notice period for withdrawals will be reduced on or before the Effective Date. There will be no adverse charges to either the terms and conditions of, or the interest rates payable on, Halifax's investment and deposit accounts as a result of the Merger.
>
> The Investment Schedules ... set out the range of share accounts to be offered by Halifax following its Merger with the Leeds and describe the changes of any significance to their terms and conditions.
>
> There will be no adverse change to interest rates payable by Borrowing Members as a result of the Merger. Mortgage rates, in so far as they are variable, will continue to be variable in accordance with the terms of each mortgage.

This was fine but what they meant was, 'What's in it for us in terms of money?'

For that, they had to read further about 'staff', 'operations', 'directors' and statutory provisions relating to the merger until they reached,

> '**Conversion**
>
> The boards of Halifax and the Leeds have agreed that, following the implementation of the Merger, proposals should be put to members of the combined society, as soon as practicable, for its conversion to a public company which will be authorised under the Banking Act 1987 and whose shares will be listed on the London Stock Exchange. To enhance the value of the shares distributed to members on conversion, neither society will make a bonus payment to members at the time of the Merger. The exact timetable for conversion and flotation will depend on a number of factors, including the satisfaction of certain legal and regulatory processes as well as prevailing market conditions.

It is intended to structure the conversion of the combined society and its flotation on the London Stock Exchange in such a way that the main beneficiaries will be the Investing Members and Borrowing Members who were members of Halifax or the Leeds as at midnight at the end of 25 November 1994 and who remain members continuously until conversion. These benefits will take the form of a distribution of shares to qualifying Investing Members and qualifying Borrowing Members, as well as to qualifying employees and pensioners, of the combined society. It is intended that on conversion, all such persons will receive a basic distribution of free shares and, in addition, that qualifying Investing Members of two years' standing with total share account balances of at least £1000 will receive extra shares based on the size of their balances on certain reference dates. Holders of PIBS of both societies are Investing Members for these purposes.'

Foulds concluded by urging members to vote for the merger proposal. Meanwhile, Leeds members received a similar 46-page document. There was probably more possibility of an adverse Leeds members' vote. The Leeds was losing its name, the head office was moving to Halifax, the chairman and chief executive of the merged society would both be Halifax men. It did, to some, look like a take-over. In his letter to shareholders at the beginning of the document, the Leeds chairman, Malcolm Barr, faced a more tricky problem than his counterpart, Jon Foulds. He explained that Leeds had looked extensively at its strategic options and had concluded that size was becoming increasingly important. Sufficient size would be reached quickly enough by merger and Halifax had been chosen as a partner for its similar culture and Yorkshire base and for the fact that both were recognised as highly efficient operations so that rationalisation (i.e. loss of jobs) would be minimal. Otherwise, his words on merger and conversion were similar to those of Jon Foulds. The Leeds members could see the tangible benefits to themselves and could perhaps live without the intangible benefits of the Leeds name and a head office in the centre of Leeds.

On the day, the Leeds meeting was held at 10.30 a.m. and the Halifax meeting at 2.30 p.m. This enabled those who were members of both societies to attend both meetings. The results of the Leeds vote were therefore known before the Halifax meeting began. Neither society knew how many members would come to the meetings. The usual turnout for an AGM was small, less than 200 in Leeds, perhaps 200–300 in Halifax, but this could be different. Perhaps thousands would come. Arrangements were made for overspill accommodation. They were not necessary. In Leeds, the attendance was about 500 and they all fitted comfortably into the West Yorkshire Playhouse, the total capacity of which, using the Quarry Theatre, the Courtyard Theatre and the restaurant was 1550. In Halifax the normal venue for the AGM was the Victoria Theatre. For this meeting, the theatre, the cinema opposite and the self-service restaurant in Halifax head office were all used. Staff were asked to use the canteen in head office to where the action would be relayed. Plans were laid for a possible attendance of 3000 but only about 700 people came. The AGM followed the SGM.

Although Serge Lourie and Peter Judge were standing for election to the board, due to be voted on at the AGM, most of their questions were dealt with at the SGM.

Judge argued that he had come to do the following.

- Represent the interests of ordinary savers and borrowers.
  (As an alternative to 'privatisation', members should be given every encouragement to participate in the Society's democratic processes.)

- Gain membership rights to all named account holders on joint accounts.

- Enable the Society to distribute part of its surpluses to existing members – for example as extra interest on savings.

'In my view, annual distribution would be better than a one-off sweetener on conversion,' he stated.

'You almost certainly save with, perhaps borrow from, the Society because you got a better deal than from a bank. Why risk change – as the saying goes: "If it ain't broke, don't fix it."'

Lourie wanted,

- a full debate on the proposed merger and conversion to plc, and

- the interests of savers, borrowers and employees to be protected.

'We believe that building societies have not taken enough account of these interests and on issues such as the difference between interest rates paid to savers and borrowers or the right of second named account holders on joint accounts.

We are not convinced that the proposed merger and conversion will improve services. If the merger is to go ahead, stakeholders should receive payment at that point. The delay to conversion is excessive and locks in investors' money.

If conversion to plc is proceeding, we will ensure that existing stakeholders receive the best terms. The board needs independent views.

I agreed fully with Jon Foulds, the chairman, when he said in March 1994 "we remain convinced of the benefits of mutuality".'

At the AGM, they were not elected and indeed both lost their deposits of £200 for failing to collect 5 per cent of the votes cast for all candidates or 20 per cent of the votes cast for the candidate elected with the smallest number of votes.

At the SGM many of the speakers and questioners were critical of the decisions. There was also a tendency to dwell on conversion (the 'when and how much?' theme) even though the meetings were supposed to be about the merger. One member was upset that the cut-off point in the variable element of the share distribution was going to be £50,000. The member said,

'I want to bring to your attention the fact that I have been writing to you and Mr Blackburn and getting answers from the merger unit which have not been terribly satisfactory to me and rather frustrating and exasperating. Now, I would like to say I have been in this society for 40 years … It has been said that we are the owners of the society; well, we are not all the same, we don't have all the same ownerships, some are more equal than others and I would like to point out that for some ludicrous, insane reason a limit of £50,000 has been put upon the *variable distribution.* There is no reason for that. Already people with lower balances are getting a better deal, the higher you get the deal gets less and less attractive and all of a sudden you suddenly arrive at a position where you say £50,000 is to be the limit, nothing after that. But what about a person who has £1 million in the society? It means that 95 per cent of his stake is not being regarded at all. Now, my question is very simple: How can such an unsupportable discrimination be justified? And I will tell you the answer; it can't.'

Jon Foulds' reply to the member was,

'We intend that the majority of free shares will be applied to the *basic distribution*. Now the member who has just spoken finds that, I assume, disadvantageous to him personally. As a board we believed that we had to strike a balance between giving a disproportionally high level of benefits to a very few large investors and next to nothing to the ordinary members who have been the staple of this society for a hundred and forty something years. The average balance, forgive me if the number is not precise, in the Halifax is about £5000, so in taking £50,000 we were taking ten times the average balance. I think that was a pretty fair way of dealing with people who had significant amounts of money with the society.'

While in Halifax, Serge Lourie, Peter Judge and others made their points; earlier in Leeds Leonard Hyde had aired his well-known views,

'I am wearing my Leeds Permanent tie today with very great pride. It may be one of the last occasions on which I can do it. I wonder how much pride there is on the stage today. Because, ladies and gentlemen, I want you to take a long look at the lady [Prue Leith] and the gentlemen sitting there because they are the people who are in the process of destroying the finest financial institution that ever existed in Leeds.'

Hyde went on to say that he felt it unnecessary for the Leeds either to merge or to convert now that,

'The Building Societies Act and the regulations in respect of it have been altered recently allowing building societies a greater range of operations than they had ever had before.'

Malcolm Barr had been expecting a critical question from Hyde and was ready for it. He told the audience of Hyde's 'very, very fine contribution' to the society both as chief general manager and as a director and that he respected Hyde's views. However, the Leeds board had looked at all the strategic options available and merger with Halifax followed by flotation was the best.

Once everyone had said their piece, the votes were counted (most had come in by post). The results on the resolutions regarding the mergers of 1.2 million Halifax savers, 97.7 per cent of those voting, were in favour of the merger and only 30,000 were against. (At Halifax there had been expectations that up to 4 million might vote.) Of Halifax borrowers, 402,000 voted in favour, 97.6 per cent of those voting. A total of 10,000 voted against. At Leeds, 548,000 savers, 95 per cent of those voting, were in favour. Of borrowers, 124,000, 94 per cent of those who voted, also approved the merger.

There were accusations that these numbers were so low as to be meaningless, but this was rejected by Malcolm Barr.

> 'The voting turnout was high; the highest we normally get is 3 per cent for voting for board members.'

For some, even though few doubted that the necessary votes for merger would be received, approval was a great cause for celebration. Mike Ellis said,

> 'I remember the SGM as though it was yesterday. I remember that very well and the feeling of elation after that. I've often said that throughout the merger there was *one* momentous day and that for me it was getting the vote at the SGM. It was just a *key* point. I never doubted, really, that we'd get the vote. It was just a landmark in the process but it was the culmination of something that had been going on for virtually 12 months. It was the culmination of so much effort.'

I need three days to present my case

The Building Societies Act 1986 provides that when the necessary merger resolutions have been passed the societies must obtain confirmation by the Building Societies Commission of the merger.

The role of the confirmation procedures is limited. Section 95 (3) and (4) of the Act provide that the Commission *must* confirm a transfer *unless* it considers that,

(a) some information material to the members' decision was not made available to all the members eligible to vote

(b) the vote on any resolution approving the merger does not represent the views of the members eligible to vote

(c) some relevant requirement of the Act or the rules of any of the societies was not fulfilled.

These are the only grounds on which the Commission may refuse confirmation, or direct the Society to remedy any defects. *It is not the Commission's function to make any judgement about the merits of the proposals which members have approved.* [Author's italics.]

Any interested party had the right to make representations to the Commission, either in writing or in person, and they would be heard by one or more Commissioners assisted by their staff.

There were only 16 representatives and only one that really caused headaches. This complainant told the chairman of the Commission, Mr T F Mathews CBE, that he expected three days to present his case, to which Mathews replied he hoped that would not be necessary.

At the hearing, the complainant claimed *inter alia* that the letter informing him of the SGM had been held up deliberately and that when he received it the words 'HOLD post 22 May JMB'

The Guardian July 1995

were written on it. As we know, and as everyone at the societies and at the Commission knew, JMB were the initials not only of the Leeds chairman but also of the Halifax chief executive. It later transpired they were also the initials of a fairly junior auditor who had visited the security printer of the SGM documents on various occasions. It was a wild suggestion that any of these three should have had any interest in holding up the documents of any member for that matter.

The other representations were of a more straightforward nature, nearly all of which were handled in writing. The Commission produced its report, finding that there were no grounds for refusing confirmation.

'The Commission has considered the applications by Leeds Permanent Building Society and Halifax Building Society for confirmation of the transfer of the engagements of Leeds Permanent

Building Society to Halifax Building Society and, having had regard to the information available to it, including the representations made to it and the societies' responses to those representations and to the Commission's own enquiries, confirmed the transfer of engagements on 11 July 1995.'

CHAPTER NINE

Divide the work into manageable projects

Talk of wholesale closures and job losses is absolute rubbish
Single look at life
Some positive discrimination

Talk of wholesale closures and job losses is absolute rubbish

While the various hurdles were being jumped, the societies had come to the conclusion that work must proceed to bring them together in the hope that there would be no setbacks, and even if there were they would merely be ones of delay. It was a mammoth task.

The management had decided to publish *Converge*, an internal newsletter that was produced jointly and which was published fortnightly. Culling the main news items from it gives us the pace of the merger as it progressed from 25 November 1994 to 1 August 1995, which was to be Day One for the new merged society.

Inevitably, the first issue was rushed out because it had to be brought forward by two weeks. It was dated 8 December 1994 and concentrated on reassuring staff that customers would be given more information: 'Over the next few weeks, a leaflet will be despatched in a mammoth mailing to over 10 million people. It aims to clarify some of the main issues about the deal, although it will *not* include detailed information about eligibility or the benefits that members can expect on conversion to plc, which is not yet available.' As well as a leaflet, *Converge* reminded staff that a telephone helpline had been set up with 230 trained staff and

155

it tried to counter the two or three 'scaremongering' articles that had appeared in the press. There was clearly more nervousness among the Leeds staff and reassuring noises therefore came from Mike Blackburn, now chief executive of Halifax but formerly of Leeds. On the deal being a take-over, he said,

> 'I see this merger as the combination of two very strong societies. Although the Leeds may be smaller than the Halifax, it is an excellent performer as its recently announced results testify.'

And on the fears of job losses he and the Leeds acting chief executive, Roger Boyes, said,

> 'Our absolute commitment is that if jobs need to be *shed* faster than they need to *increase*, the losses will be dealt with through normal turnover and voluntary redundancy. There will be *no* compulsory redundancies as a result of the merger.
>
> Talk of wholesale closures and job losses is absolute rubbish. The organisation we are creating will have so many customers, and so much work to do, that it simply would not make business sense. Highly-trained well-motivated staff are our greatest asset, and we aren't about to let them go.'

The next issue, published on 16 December, explained in broad terms how the merger would be managed. It said that the most senior level of control would be exercised by the Chairmen's Committee (G8) consisting of the two societies' chairmen and vice-chairmen plus executives. This was supported in a more hands-on way by a Programme Steering Group (G6) comprising Mike Blackburn, Gren Folwell and Mike Ellis from Halifax, and Roger Boyes, John Miller and John Morris from Leeds. This group would meet once a week. Planning for all the project work necessary would be handled by one programme office, which would be staffed by senior managers and planners from both sides, all of whom would temporarily give up their usual jobs to concentrate on the merger and conversion plans.

The programme director was the IT specialist and former industrial manager, John Miller, who said,

> 'Almost every single job that has to be done affects others in the chain, so it's essential we organise it carefully. Even so, the approach

is fairly straightforward. First, you design a programme of work, which is watched over by the programme office. Then you divide the work into manageable projects, and allocate small teams to deliver them.'

There were four main programmes. The first was to ensure the members' votes went smoothly including production of the all-important *Schedule 16* document going to members outlining the terms of the merger and details of how to vote. The second, and by far the biggest, programme was concerned with making sure that from Day One of the merger the combined society would offer customers a good service and meet all regulatory requirements. Included in this programme would be other projects such as products, training, computer systems, staff terms and conditions, passbook changes, security, internal post and staff car parking – 170 projects in total.

The third programme would focus on integration of the two businesses after Day One and pilot projects were put in hand in West Kent and London which, among other things, were looking at customer handling and better use of new technology. And these pilots were no small affairs. The West Kent trial under Halifax's Margaret Walkinshaw involved some 400 staff and included the new Service Centre in Chatham, ten current Halifax branches, ten current Leeds branches, nine estate agents and five agents. The experiments were all about eliminating waste, increasing efficiency and achieving more sales.

The fourth programme was about vision and looking to the future as the new society became a leading retail bank.

The third issue of *Converge* noted that the Office of Fair Trading had not referred the merger to the Monopolies and Mergers Commission and explained that staff views on the merger would be researched, sometimes by outside agencies. It emphasised that,

' … employees' individual responses will be confidential, and no names will appear in any of the reports to the management.'

The newsletter found itself still having to counter negative press coverage. This time it was an article in the previous Saturday's *Daily Telegraph*, which had suggested that 'fat' voluntary redundancy pay-offs would be available and that staff were 'queuing up' to take them. The reply from John Lee, Halifax's Personnel director, and David Jarratt, Leeds' head of Human Resources, was,

'The fact is that we have not even started to talk about voluntary redundancy. If we judge that a package needs to be made available, we will make the announcement internally, in the proper way.'

Converge kept the staffs of both societies fully informed of progress through the late winter/early spring of 1995, explaining the intricacies of the Building Societies Commission's friendly court action to test the societies' conversion plans. Once the court had given the go-ahead in late March, *Converge* urged everyone on under the headline **All systems go**. The delay caused by the Court hearing meant there was little time to complete a mammoth task before the Special General Meeting and the Annual General Meeting on Monday, 22 May. By holding both the AGM and the SGM on the same day Halifax would save about £1.75 million. *Converge* stated that,

'The scale of the task is mammoth. About 60 articulated lorries will be required to deliver the paper required to do the printing. The total length of the paper rolls is about 11,000 miles – the distance to San Francisco and back again. Only paper produced from trees grown specifically for paper production will be used.

The documents – each over 40 pages in length – carry information to members about the merger, including how to vote, and the proposed share distribution scheme on conversion. Information packs will have different covering letters, depending on the type of member (e.g. investor or borrower).

Newspaper advertising will start to generate increased awareness of the mailing and urge members to use their vote. The Societies plan different, but complementary campaigns.'

Single look at life

By March 1995 many of the issues concerning which brands in which product areas had been resolved. The March issue of *Converge* was a bumper edition of eight pages as opposed to its normal single sheet, and proclaimed, with a banner headline, **DAY ONE, IT'S TAKING SHAPE**. The first page was all about the management of Halifax and Leeds people. A jobs management unit was to be set up to help ensure management took an,

' … even-handed approach to the placement of staff … and to act as a central resource to match people and job vacancies.'

Every effort was to be made to smooth the path to new jobs, especially if relocation was required. In the past, both societies had offered voluntary severance packages and now a single package was being developed. David Thornborrow of Halifax explained,

'In a change of this scale, voluntary redundancy will probably be needed in some very specific circumstances. However, it is unlikely it will be used widely. There is no question of losing large numbers of people when we have so many business opportunities and so much work to do.'

A new set of terms and conditions was being prepared for the joint society but it was a complex area and would probably take several months to complete. On Day One it was likely that Leeds staff would retain their current terms.

As for the branches, a new area structure was being devised but there would still be eight regions, as under the current Halifax organisation. It was made clear that, although the new head office would be in Halifax, the current Leeds head office would be retained as a major office.

Under the heading, **Single look at life**, it was seen that Halifax Financial Services would combine the existing regulated products businesses of the two societies. The business would use *Halifax Life* and pension products and a joint portfolio of unit trust products.

'However, Leeds *Life*'s innovative approach to product design and customers and its easy-to-read, jargon-free style of literature, should have a strong influence on the company's post-Day One plans.'

The new company would still use General Accident for life administration and S G Warburg for unit trust administration and this should bring few problems as both were already providing the services for each society.

The minimum amount needed in a *Solid Gold* savings account before withdrawals without penalty was to be lowered from £10,000 to £5000 and the period of notice reduced from 90 to 60 days.

Banking services would be very important on Day One and beyond, and *Converge* made it clear that all branches would be offering a range of banking services, including current account facilities and two credit card products: Cardcash and travel money. *Maxim*, Halifax's current account, had been launched in 1989 and had almost a million customers. From Day One, Halifax customers would be able to use former Leeds branches to carry out current account transactions or open a *Maxim* account. Also from Day One customers would be given the choice of two Visa credit cards: a standard card and an affinity card. The affinity card was based on Leeds Visa which, over the previous five years, had raised a staggering £5 million for three charities: Imperial Cancer Research Fund, British Heart Foundation and MENCAP.

Passbooks were going to change. Millions were in the hands of customers and 'the task of moving to one standard format is being tackled right from Day One'. Anyone opening a new account, existing customer or new, would be issued with a Halifax-style passbook. A Leeds passbook used in Halifax branches would be replaced with a Halifax continuation book. Leeds customers using Leeds branches would continue with a Leeds passbook until a new one was needed when they would be issued with a Halifax continuation book.

The two societies would jointly own 1700 Automatic Teller Machines, one of the biggest networks in the country, and these would gradually be altered so that customers of both could use both – but the process would not be completed by Day One.

To allay fears from among staff about their preparedness for Day One, training was being given top priority.

> 'A number of training initiatives are being prepared, including workshops, in-branch training and distance learning, with training specialists being taken from the field and head office. Overseeing the whole programme will be a training steering group, which will look out for any gaps in the training schedules or any possible overloads.'

Halifax's XCEL computer system, supporting mortgage sales and other processes, was going to be installed in Leeds branches, requiring special training for Leeds staff.

Finally, in this March edition *Converge* explained that new corporate clothing was being designed and that the garment manufacturer, Dewhirst, had already started the enormous task of making outfits for around 18,000 or so staff so that they could be delivered shortly before Day One.

Built in the 1970s in the centre of Halifax, the head office
is a fitting landmark to the size and success of the
organisation.

TOP OF PAGE: Board Members of Leeds Permanent Building Society
immediately prior to merger on 1st August 1995.
(Sitting left to right): Sir Timothy Kitson, Malcolm Barr
(Chairman), Roger Boyes and Arnold Ziff. *(Standing left
to right)*: Howard Briggs *(Secretary)*, Geoffrey Armitage,
Prue Leith, Derek Cook, Philip Rogerson, John Miller.

ABOVE: Board Members of the Chairmen's Committee
(or "G8") 1994/5. *(Sitting left to right)*: Mike Blackburn,
Malcolm Barr, Jon Foulds. *(Standing left to right)*:
Howard Briggs *(Secretary to the Committee)*, John Wood, Gren Folwell,
Sir Timothy Kitson, Roger Boyes, John Miller.

TOP OF PAGE: Roger Boyes *(left)*, chief executive of Leeds, with Mike Blackburn, chief executive of Halifax outside The Victoria Theatre *(venue of the Halifax SGM on 22 May 1995)*, the day both the Leeds and the Halifax members voted in favour of the merger.

ABOVE: The sheer size of the operation necessary to cope with deduplication of the societies' registers and mailing documents to them required logistical thinking and planning on the grand scale.

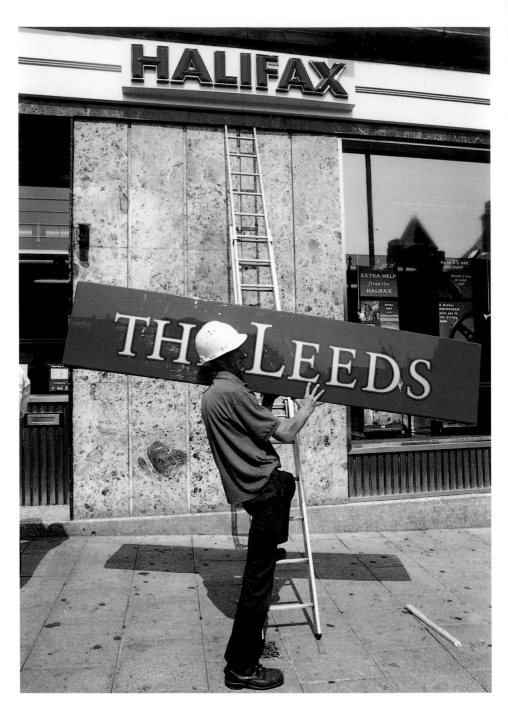

In the 24 hours before the two societies officially merged on
1 August 1995 every Leeds sign had to be replaced with a
Halifax one.

TOP OF PAGE: Chairman Jon Foulds and chief executive
Mike Blackburn sign the document transferring Halifax
Building Society to Halifax plc, 20 December 1996.

ABOVE: In January and February 1997 Halifax ran a heavy
media campaign designed to ensure members voted on the
conversion. The campaign was called "Be part of something big".

The mailing of the Conversion booklet in April 1997
brought yet another heavy response in letters and telephone
calls. A wag posted a booklet on the office notice-board to
keep up morale.

Over the week-end before Vesting Day, 2 June 1997,
every sign in the country had to lose the words
"Building Society".

TOP OF PAGE: *The Sun*, 3 June 1997.

ABOVE: Board Members of Halifax Building Society just after
conversion. Photograph taken on 16 July 1997 outside The Old Cock
Inn, Halifax, where it all started in 1853. *(Front row left to right)*:
Professor John Kay, Jon Foulds, Mike Blackburn, Philip Rogerson,
John Miller, Ralph Hodge. *(Middle row left to right)*: John Lee,
Lord Chadlington, Nigel Colne, Prue Leith, Gren Folwell,
Duncan Ferguson. *(Back row left to right)*: Roy Chapman, John Wood,
Tony Coleby, Roger Boyes, Sir Timothy Kitson, Derek Cook,
Louis Sherwood.

Some positive discrimination

On 10 April *Converge* announced the long-awaited new corporate structure with the names of all the people in key jobs. Under an executive committee the merged society would be set up into four businesses (the building society, Financial Services, Estate Agency, and Treasury and Overseas) and supported by four functions (Finance, Business Strategy and Operations, Personnel and Corporate Affairs, and Secretary and Legal). At the highest level on the executive committee the potential problem of two finance directors was solved by Gren Folwell becoming managing director of the company's biggest business, the building society, while Roger Boyes continued in his role as finance director. John Miller's experience outside the building society movement and his IT skills fitted him perfectly for business strategy and operations. The main marketing role on mortgages and savings was given to another Leeds executive, Judy Atchison, who was appointed to the executive committee. There was certainly no attempt by the Halifax to dominate, with Foulds and Blackburn ensuring that many Leeds executives were placed in key roles. *Converge* also announced the new combined board of directors with Halifax men as chairman and chief executive, one from each society as vice-chairmen, two further Leeds men as executive directors and four as non-executive directors, plus three Halifax executive directors and seven Halifax non-executive directors. This issue was quickly followed by another on 26 April, which gave details of the office locations and the department moves. Halifax's personnel director laid out the ground rules,

"POOR CHAP! HE MUST HAVE THOUGHT IT WAS TO DO WITH THE RUGBY SUPER LEAGUE"

David Banks, *The Independent* 23 May 1995

> 'We will start from the assumption that most people will not want to move. It is also a fact of life that relocating people is very expensive.

Consequently, leaving people where they are and training them to do other jobs is likely to be the better option for both the individual and the society. However, some people may want to move and some specialists will be asked to move. At management level the more senior the position the more likely it is that individuals will need to move with their jobs.'

More people would be moving from Halifax to Leeds than vice versa and, with the growth of new departments such as Halifax Direct, Leeds was likely to experience something of a mini-boom in new jobs with 500 probable in the next 12 months. The society was going to provide generous cash packages for longer travel and disruption.

Ged Nicholls, the general secretary of the Independent Union of Halifax Staff, worked hard on behalf of his members. He had proved himself a shrewd observer of the comings and goings in 1994. During the summer he perceived a discernible change in the corporate response to the intermittent comments in the press linking Halifax to other societies and in August 1994 the union magazine, *Accord*, had printed an article under the title **Laughing all the way to the Leeds?** Nicholls wrote to the staff associations of the other societies, including the Leeds, and suggested they get together to work out a common approach in the event of a merger or wave of mergers. They had agreed and an agenda was formulated. Nicholls then wrote to the board of the Halifax and suggested they get together for discussion. His approach was, 'We will support a merger provided that ... '.

Nicholls noticed that all the key executives had made a point of talking to him at the November conference – before the news became public – including the deputy chairman, John Wood. The general message seemed to be – there are going to be changes in the industry and communication will be more important than ever.

Once the two SGMs were safely out of the way and both Halifax and Leeds membership had voted overwhelmingly in favour of the merger, the *Converge* issue of 25 May gave details of the **Branch Network** and of the programme up to Day One, with workshops and briefings through the remainder of May and the whole of June, and specialised workshops in June and July right up to 1 August, Day One.

In July, in order to prepare customers for the new society, 11 million newsletters were mailed explaining to customers the benefits of belonging to an enlarged society and when the actual merger was taking place. It also gave them guidance on using branches, information on products, told them how existing accounts would be affected and gave them brief details on the next steps towards conversion. And on Sunday, 16 July, a dry run was made with 20 Halifax and Leeds branches and 3 service centres using a 'live' system. This was deemed very successful.

As Day One approached, a new method of staff communication was introduced, *Halifax Television News.* John Lee, interested in finding the simplest and most effective way of communicating with staff in 1100 branches, 700 estate agency offices, 45 business centres and 8 regional offices, saw a television network as the obvious solution. He had been introduced to a business television studio in the summer of 1994 by the Halifax non-executive director, Peter Gummer – now Lord Chadlington.

'I went down there and had my first sight of something I hadn't even realised existed. I was absolutely captivated by what I saw and came back saying, "We've got to do this. If there's an organisation that needs this sort of communications channel it's us. A centre with up to 2000 outlets. This just wires us up."

We formed a project team and gave them three months to tell us how they would do it. By the end of 1994 they'd come back and they'd worked out all the satellite issues and the logistics, all the costs. By the end of January the board had agreed the budget of £4 million and running costs of £250,000 a year, and between February and July we did all the logistics, put up 1500 satellite dishes, created a TV studio in Halifax and hired presenters. Then on 2 August we launched Halifax TV.

And this wasn't Halifax news going to Leeds; this was *New Co.* with its communication channel. And we're on the screen every fortnight – or more often if there's a big issue. Now people don't just get information on paper they *see* the guy saying it and *how* they're saying it. When I go into a branch now people say, "Nice to see you", or "Oh you're bigger than I thought", or, "You're nicer than you look on television". There's a relationship in place, because they are used to you talking to them.

The early programmes will concentrate on news about what's going on in the Society. We're very conscious of the fact that we need to give people hard information that is relevant to them and their jobs. As time goes on we're determined to use its full potential, which will mean developing programmes which are specifically for training purposes or to cover sales and marketing information.'

Paul Martin, in charge of the Leeds branch network, said in spring 1997 that it was,

' … a good facility to have which, to be honest, I think we're still learning to use properly. Overall it was a great communication tool. We could ensure that thousands would hear it at the same time in exactly the same way. You can be sure messages via regional managers cascade down and produce at least four different versions. TV can overcome all that.'

CHAPTER TEN

A feeling of confidence in the new organisation

Will they close your branch?

Why didn't you tell us it was a take-over?

A more 'laid-back' approach

Day One

Will they close your branch?

There is a strong tendency in writing about such enormous events as a merger between the largest and fifth largest building societies to create the country's third largest bank to ignore the views of the 'ordinary people', either staff or customers, who may be profoundly affected.

Fortunately, a young Halifax staff member, Mrs Stephanie Bennett, carried out some research as a dissertation towards her honours degree in financial services and we can reap the benefit of her findings.

Before we look at those findings we should consider the problems that faced the Halifax and Leeds management and see what steps they took to overcome them. The sheer size of the task was daunting – they had eight months to merge 28,000 people with different styles and cultures in 1800 different locations into one unit speaking with one voice. This was only the first step before they had to move on to conversion into a plc and a fully fledged retail bank. Second, the merger and conversion plan was always going to come as something of a surprise to all but a handful of the 28,000. Because of the leak it came not only as a surprise but was revealed in less than ideal circumstances. Inevitably, customers dwelt on the very subjects most worrying to the staff and constantly, mostly out of well-meaning sympathy, asked such questions as,

'Will they close your branch?'

or,

'Will your job be OK?'

The staff and management had to give reassuring answers to everyone while feeling less than 100 per cent secure themselves and also coping with an extra workload. Furthermore, in this particular merger both societies were already extremely efficient and successful, and most staff could not see why they needed to deviate from their chosen path or adapt their culture or successful formula.

These were the challenges. How did management cope? First, there was no 'political' agenda at the top, no hostile intent or predatory undertones. The Halifax chief executive was a former Leeds chief executive. The top team at the Leeds were keen on the merger and the potential for conflict was thereby largely disarmed. Later there were some comments about Halifax being highly procedural with strong control over branches and that the society was status conscious and grade driven with initiative stifled. However, this did not make the key executives of Leeds any less determined to complete the merger.

And it was not only some of the Leeds executives who were concerned about Halifax's management systems. John Lee, recruited from ICI in 1993 to run Halifax's personnel department found the Halifax 'incredibly centrally controlled'. During one of his early branch visits, Lee had the following converstion with one of the branch staff.

Lee:	What do you do?
Staff member:	I'm a grade 9.
Lee:	That's great, but what do you do?
Staff member:	I supervise grade 10s.

That told Lee two things: the emphasis on the structure and the focus on grades.

'The organisation was frozen and locked. It was stuffed full of good people who were having the life-blood squeezed out of them.'

But, of course, it was not all bad. Indeed, Lee was full of admiration for many aspects,

'It was an immensely competent organisation delivering super business results. When I looked into the personnel function, there wasn't much wrong with it. Its policies and procedures, apart from glaring gaps like succession planning and lower management development, were very good and quite far-reaching. However, because of the general climate, they were pretty constrained.'

What did Lee plan to change?

'My agenda has been setting this organisation free so that people can use their own capabilities and Mike's [Blackburn] has been the same. When we compared notes after three months we were aiming at the same thing. We had to help people see their leaders as human beings they could relate to, not Olympian Gods that they were scared of – the difference between First World War generals and the guys who led the troops in the Gulf War.'

The merger helped.

'One of the things the merger has done is help enormously the process of freeing the organisation up. Because the Leeds was a much smaller organisation, everything was much closer, the wiring was simpler, the culture more open and collegiate, more enabling. One of the impacts the Leeds has had has been the encouragement of people who thought like that in the Halifax. We've been able to point out these examples and to use them as part of the process of achieving change.'

And have the two societies come together successfully?

'The overriding success of the merger, despite these different cultures – cultures which made the mistake early on of thinking they were similar – has been the coming together in an almost seamless way and in no time at all, though of course not completely without change and some pain. One of the best things that happened, and I don't know who thought of it, was the use of *Old Co. Halifax* and *Old Co. Leeds,* and *New Co.* People get the sense of *New Co.* as creating something new. *Old Co.* was history.

'The other interesting thing is the new senior team which is full of very different people. I wouldn't want to pretend it hasn't had its rocky patches, because all the bulls have gathered in the field together. But the team has actually come together quickly without any real, fundamental disagreements and people have respected each other's competence quickly.'

A project office was set up in both Halifax and Leeds, and executives swapped so that each office had both Halifax and Leeds management working in them. There were initial problems stemming from Leeds' feeling of insecurity plus a mis-match of experience and levels of management, but fortunately the two project office leaders, David Walkden of Halifax and Clive Whitaker of Leeds, found a common cause and set a blueprint for organisation of the merger programme to move forward.

The management knew that early reactions would be important, and as we have seen, worked hard to try to maintain close contacts with opinion-formers in Parliament, local councils and the media. The internal newspaper, *Converge*, was published fortnightly to keep the staff fully informed about every aspect of the merger. It was felt important to make the 'grapevine' redundant. Surveys among staff were carried out constantly to keep management informed about their concerns. Down the line, managers were made fully aware of their responsibilities to their staff. What are known as 'well-poisoning', 'sabre-rattling' and 'rock-throwing' were all outlawed as was all 'bad behaviour'. A jobs management unit, staffed jointly from the two societies, was set up. Its tasks were to work even-handedly with all staff displaced, whether they were surplus to requirements due to re-organisation or unable to relocate. In fact, nearly all displaced staff moved into alternative roles and fewer than 100 early retirements and voluntary redundancies were necessary out of a joint staff of 28,000. Training was critical, with 5000 needing intensive and over 20,000 substantial training over a six-week period. As we have seen, the need for reassurance was greater among Leeds staff and Roger Boyes, in his capacity as acting chief executive, travelled the country and hosted about twenty-five dinners for local management in the first six months of 1995. Boyes remembered them well,

'There would probably be no more than ten people at the dinners where I and usually one other, either David Jarratt, Ralph Pitman or Paul Martin would have an informal dinner … I found them fascinating and stimulating. I was listening to very articulate, intelligent people, often young men and women only in their twenties and they questioned us very confidently and professionally. I felt very privileged to be there.'

Why didn't you tell us it was a take-over?

In spite of all these efforts, there was inevitably some concern, even discontent. Paul Martin, who looked after the distribution network for the Leeds, said,

'My memory is largely on how branch life coped. One of the main bits of feedback that we got really volubly and fairly regularly from the Leeds side was, "Why didn't you tell us it was a take-over?" "What's this about a merger?" "All our procedures, all our systems, all our products – we're doing things the Halifax way in the branches with their key controls, management structures and so on." They were saying, "Why weren't we up-front?"'

The next problem for Martin concerned the IT.

'There was an awful lot of hype at Leeds management and staff meetings. The phrase was, "With combined technology we're going to have seamless service." Nonsense, for a time Leeds customers went back to hand-written passbooks. So people said, "Why weren't you honest? Why didn't you say we were going to have to take some steps backwards?"

Also the branch system of Halifax which we had to use was behind the Leeds. Not that the Leeds system was necessarily the best, or particularly leading-edge, but at least it was modern. The Halifax system was years old, out of date, old-fashioned, involving a lot of checking which was unnecessary if there was a smarter system.'

Martin did have praise for some of the actions taken.

'We closed branches where there was obvious duplication and people could see the sense of that. What people really wanted to know was that we were being business-like, even if the task was unpalatable. Let's be business-like about it, let's get on with it but don't pretend it's all roses in the garden because it ain't! The feedback was that if we were ever to do something similar, be absolutely straight. Difficult words delivered well will give you a better situation than muddled words delivered in a sloppy fashion.'

Nevertheless, he agreed that a lot of attention *was* given to communications.

Evening Standard 23 May 1995

'The newsletter that was created was good, as were the face-to-face meetings and directors having dinner with a dozen or so branch staff. Quite a lot of that went on and was well-liked as it was a chance to hear things in a less staged way. Communication effort was needed and was delivered quite well.'

What were the results by the time of the actual merger? Business performance was sustained with the two businesses working as one in reasonable harmony and co-operative working relationships. There were no serious industrial relations problems and turnover of key staff was kept to tolerable levels. A new set of terms and conditions including flexible working contracts had been agreed and 100 per cent of staff signed the new contract. In the view of management, the staff had accepted the merger and were looking forward to the future. What did Stephanie Bennett find?

She looked first at the reaction of the Halifax employees to the announcement of the merger which, you will remember, was rushed out on the morning of Friday, 25 November 1994, following John Willcock's article in *The Independent*. Over half the staff learned about the merger by means other than official company channels. They heard through the media or from a third party outside the company. Initially they were a little upset by this but most, on reflection, accepted that, in view of the leak, the announcement was handled well by the society. Subsequent information was also communicated well and allowed them to handle public enquiries with confidence. Regarding the merits of the merger, most felt positive and that everyone in the society would benefit. 90 per cent thought the merger would benefit the society and 75 per cent thought it would benefit the customers. The majority also thought that progress towards the merger in the first few months after the announcement was handled well. The main benefits for staff were perceived as better career opportunities. If there were any concerns, they were in the area of job and career uncertainty as well as the possibility of having to relocate. Integration of staff and systems was also mentioned as a worry.

In Leeds reactions were different. In terms of the announcement, the overall feeling was one of disappointment. News briefs were set up to convey further information but it was felt that these were short on detail. Perhaps the staff at the Leeds felt they needed more information due to their feelings of insecurity from what was initially perceived as a take-over. Nor did the staff feel adequately briefed to cope with public enquiries. When asked whether they thought the merger was a good or bad thing, most staff thought it bad for the customer because many had chosen Leeds as opposed to Halifax because of its smaller size. The staff themselves, viewing the merger as a take-over, suffered greater feelings of insecurity than their Halifax counterparts. Initially, through poor communication, there was a widespread lack of understanding of the reasons behind the merger.

John Morris, one of the Leeds executives on the Group of Six Committee who had worked for the Chairmen's Committee (G8) throughout the summer and autumn of 1994, remembers that there was considerable concern and disappointment among most senior Leeds executives that the name 'Leeds' was going to be dropped. In a weekend at Michael's Nook [sounds an odd venue for a building society managers' conference] in November 1994, where most senior Leeds management were told of the forthcoming merger, Morris noticed that the loss of the name was extensively discussed.

A more 'laid-back' approach

Bennett took the merger period itself as being from 5 June to 1 August 1995. The first official meeting of branch managers was in early June although many managers had taken the initiative to meet their counterparts in the same town. At these meetings in early June, managers were told of the new areas and reporting structures. They were organised by Halifax although several Leeds staff were included in their running. There was general acceptance of the event but 1 August seemed a long way off. (We can be sure that for those in the head offices trying to organise everything for a seamless handover, 1 August was rushing towards them at apparently breakneck speed!)

The managers were issued with an A–Z manual covering the main events leading up to, and beyond, the merger. The managers felt the manual was a great help but that it missed several key issues which engendered doubts about the success of Day One, 1 August. Leeds managers were somewhat taken aback at how prescriptive the manual was and found it difficult to adjust to what they saw as the removal of their freedom to use their own initiative to manage the merger.

A number of staff from the Halifax and service centres were selected to undergo a period of secondment at neighbouring Leeds branches up to and beyond 1 August. This brought home the difference in culture. The Leeds branches were very happy about having the Halifax people but from the Halifax staff perspective it depended greatly on the personality of the person transferred. The main differences they found were in day-to-day procedural duties, for example with regard to security and in the generally more 'laid-back' approach of the administration and managerial control. The secondees faced a choice. They could either drop subtle hints about the way Halifax did things or they could impose Halifax systems immediately. The Leeds people found the latter approach more painful initially but probably in the long run more beneficial. Geoff Jackson, director of distribution in the new Halifax, recalled that many of the Leeds staff found their Halifax counterparts bureaucratic and arrogant and lacking in sensitivity towards customers. They thought the Halifax offices 'over-busy' and while they accepted that many of their offices were in the suburbs rather than city centres (this had been deliberate Leeds policy in their 1970s expansion) and perhaps a little tatty, they were concerned that the improvements instituted by Mike Blackburn would now be submerged. [Slightly illogical thinking as the same Mike Blackburn was now chief executive of Halifax.]

The people transferred felt they had not been given enough time and that their staff were underprepared for Day One. As for the Halifax branches that lost the staff, they felt they had been misinformed about the length of time their staff would be away and were unhappy about losing them during the summer which, with holidays, was a difficult staffing time anyway. Clearly, Bennett had received strong comments on this score, as she wrote,

'This misinformation and the extra workloads caused a great deal of ill-feeling from the older Halifax branches towards the merger and the Leeds branches.'

As for those in the Leeds branches, a major issue that the Leeds staff felt was not addressed was the fact that Leeds staff were more multi-skilled than their colleagues in Halifax branches. For example, cashiers were concerned that they had not been trained in how to open a current account. Some of the Leeds staff became alarmed at the thought of being de-skilled.

All staff went to a one-day workshop within the new business areas. These met with varied reactions. Some thought they were a waste of time that could have been better spent in the branches. However, they did welcome the chance to meet their new colleagues. Staff at clerical level enjoyed the day but the trainers found themselves working hard to counter the widely held belief that it was a take-over, not a merger. On the whole, the feedback from the workshops was positive.

At manager level, weekly project meetings were held to discuss activities within the A–Z manual. This was seen to be a good team-building exercise though there was comment about the time involved. The culture differences showed quite sharply and the Leeds managers expressed concern as most of the change was coming from their side. It was perhaps inevitable but,

'Where a Leeds area manager was appointed, it was felt that a more understanding approach to the changes was taken. For areas where there was a Halifax area manager, Leeds branch managers felt there was not as much understanding given. This appears to be the perspective from the regional level as well.'

The other problem for Leeds administrative staff in the branches was the removal of their head office connection from Leeds to Halifax and the fear that this meant the disappearance of the role. The managers did not seem to be given much guidance on how to counsel these staff.

Budgets were allocated for a social event before Day One so that staff could integrate on an informal level. These worked well and were appreciated, with events ranging from a buffet in the office to a full-blown barbecue and disco at the local golf club. For managers, similar events were organised but with senior regional managers taking question and answer sessions. Many staff felt they were due some official 'thank-you' after the pressure due to staffing levels.

173

A dry run for Day One was organised but was quite heavily criticised for a last-minute change in procedures rendering obsolete the mini-manual that everyone had received. The Leeds staff in particular became nervous about Day One. Several felt that if full computer support had been available for this dry run it would have been more beneficial.

Day One

On Day One, Tuesday, 1 August 1995, the Leeds Permanent Building Society had ceased to exist and it had been decided to close branches on Monday, 31 July in order for last-minute training and the tidying up of records. It was also decided to offer Leeds customers a withdrawal service at Halifax branches despite the merger not having taken place. This attempt to please everyone slightly backfired in that Leeds members wanted to pay money into their accounts and enjoy the full service. This meant that Halifax branches had to deal with many dissatisfied customers who told them in no uncertain terms what they thought of the merger.

On Day One the new Halifax opened its doors hoping to offer a seamless service. Views varied as to whether they did. Old Halifax branches found little difference with just the odd query from former Leeds customers. The main problem was that the computers were not linked up. Indeed they were totally off-line for a period during the morning. This meant that Halifax branches were forced to send former Leeds customers to the nearest Leeds branch. Helplines were not much help often giving formal and standardised answers to personal questions. Leeds branches were extremely busy, partly because they had been closed the day before and partly because the computers were off-line. This caused the former Leeds staff to feel very uncomfortable. They wanted to give perfect service but felt they could not do so.

Bennett carried out further research a month after Day One. She found that in the *Old Co.* Halifax branches there were no issues of significance. 'What merger?' seemed to be the attitude. The only concern seemed to be the continued secondment of staff to Leeds branches.

It was a different story in the Leeds branches where there was a general lack of confidence in the new procedures systems. From managers downwards the staff felt they were starting a new job. Managers felt vulnerable because they did not know all the answers to questions from their staff and the staff felt vulnerable through appearing to be inefficient to the customers.

There were computer glitches. For example, on occasions the system would switch off when a mortgage application was almost complete so that the customer would have to give all the information again. Furthermore, there were some serious gaps in training so that, for example, *Home Arranger* support units had no basic understanding of how the *Home Arranger* service worked, thus putting pressure on the home arrangers in the branches. There was also criticism of the support system for queries with a view that the support was not knowledgeable enough. Additionally, pressure from Halifax branches led to the secondees returning to their old branches three weeks after Day One. This was felt by the Leeds branches to be too soon. The general feeling in former Leeds branches after a month was that they had made a tremendous effort but that they were not giving the service they had hoped to give. They felt they needed further support.

Bennett felt that the managers in the branches were integrating well but that the staff in former Leeds branches felt an 'us and them' situation.

> 'This I find quite alarming, and would suggest that branches do some form of staff swaps.'

From the former Leeds managers' point-of-view the biggest change was loss of contact with the customer. Before the merger they had spent 25 per cent of their time with the customer. Now they spent virtually no time with customers. Looking ahead, many in the Leeds branches felt their branch was under threat and would rather know their fate sooner than wait in uncertainty.

There seemed to be many criticisms in Bennett's survey but, of course, she picked up every single criticism and wrote it down tending to give equal emphasis to one complaint against many expressions of satisfaction. Perhaps realising this, she concluded,

> 'Overall there is a feeling of confidence in the new organisation. Staff are keen to provide service excellence and ensure the future success of the organisation.'

Paul Martin, in charge of the Leeds branch network, broadly agreed with some of Bennett's comments,

> 'Everything *did* work from Day One but not in a systems kind of way. There were a lot of mangled procedures. The resilience of the branch

staff was fantastic. What they can cope with is impressive, whether it's procedures or new products. We still had to compete in the market place and they delivered very, very well.'

In late 1995, Halifax commissioned the London Business School Survey Unit to canvass staff opinion. Questionnaires were distributed to the whole staff (about 33,000 people) and the return rate at 62 per cent was high.

The general response underlined the task that lay ahead for the future combined management. On the merger, a majority (60 per cent) said they had been kept well informed at all stages of the merger and more than half thought it had been well managed prior to Day One, 1 August 1995. About half said they 'often worry about the effect of the merger on my future'.

On customer service a high percentage (73 per cent) thought their particular boss gave high priority to customer service and more than half thought their colleagues tried to meet or exceed customer expectations. They were more critical of the internal support for customer service with only 32 per cent agreeing that 'training on new products and systems is delivered in good time'. Nearly half said that 'procedures take preference over the requirements of customers'.

Most encouraging to the senior management will have been the response to the question about Halifax's vision of its future. In the previous survey in 1992 only 39 per cent thought Halifax had a clear vision of its future. By 1995 this had risen to 73 per cent. On communicating this vision the figures were even better. In 1992 only 24 per cent said they had a clear understanding of the Halifax's objectives and only 19 per cent thought the vision well communicated to staff. By 1995 these figures had changed to 62 per cent and 56 per cent.

This was how the *staff* of the two societies reacted to the merger, to the efficiency of Day One, and to the prospects for the future. But how did the *customers* react?

Market research showed that there was no change in customer perceptions of service; in fact 86 per cent thought it was just the same. For the tiny number who thought the service was either better or worse the two reasons were polite/rude staff and no/long queues. Only 1 per cent of customers using Halifax branches and 2 per cent of customers using ex-Leeds branches experienced problems due to the changes in the way branches dealt with customers since the merger. The vast majority had no worries that the merger might adversely affect service.

The board and management of new Halifax must have been relieved at this positive reaction from the customers. Furthermore, in spite of some criticisms from staff which could be viewed as almost inevitable during a period of uncertainty and insecurity, they could feel satisfaction with the way the merger had been handled.

All the regulatory hurdles had been jumped successfully and the business was moving forward.

In any merger of this kind, jobs and computer systems are the key issues. On both fronts this was a genuine merger, with rapid integration – desirable anyway but necessary in the case of Halifax and Leeds, because of the impending conversion.

The jobs task was achieved without compulsory redundancies. The Jobs Management Unit continued with its essential work through the rest of 1995, placing staff and picking up new job vacancies as new department structures were confirmed. From time to time the whip had to be cracked to stop departmental managers talking to prospective staff directly and bypassing the Jobs Management Unit. But the approach was successful, creating departmental structures with people who integrated rapidly and worked well together, and giving reassurance to those who were temporarily displaced in the process.

The computer systems teams could not have hoped for new and integrated systems on Day One. These would follow up to two years later. But the initial target of a 'seamless service' was achieved. The linkage of the two systems was one of the biggest systems tasks ever undertaken by a UK business, involving over 1000 staff. There were glitches – notably on Day One and later on with passbook processing. But the team 'fixed things as they went' and by October the main systems were reasonably settled.

Interviewed in September, Mike Blackburn said that much remained to be 'bedded down'. He knew that with such changes, and with two former approaches to systems and service, there must be a plethora of bright ideas waiting to be released throughout the new society. So he launched a new and revitalised staff suggestion scheme: 'Why Don't We?'. This turned out to be one of the most successful schemes of its type in any UK company. In the first three weeks there were no fewer than 2500 entries, compared with 3500 a year in the old scheme. Many of these suggestions were implemented, bringing together the best of 'Old Co. Leeds' and 'Old Co. Halifax' practice.

Summing up his reactions after two months, Mike Blackburn was highly optimistic,

'The way the merger has been handled so far gives me terrific confidence that the future will be stronger and more successful than the past.'

However, Halifax could not afford to be complacent for a moment. Leading competitors had mission statements that were similar in terms of market share ambitions, diversification and refocus on the personal sector. And the background was over-capacity, market maturity, less customer loyalty, low entry barriers, high exit barriers and unidentified new competitors.

While they were coping with these challenges, the board of the new Halifax faced a more immediate challenge – conversion to a public limited company.

AUTHOR'S NOTE

Timetable

Many of the significant themes on the journey to transformation from building society to public limited company lasted over a number of months, even years. To make sense of them and how they affected the Halifax's decisions and actions we need to deal with them in a thematic way. To take them chronologically, which would necessitate jumping from one subject to another, would be confusing. Nevertheless, chronology is important and I have listed the key events on the road to conversion, which will provide a reference point for the reader.

Halifax Building Society Merger and Conversion
Key Events and Announcements
November 1994 – July 1997

Date and event	Comments
25 November 1994 Announcement of merger and conversion	Halifax Building Society and Leeds Permanent Building Society announced intention to merge and subsequently convert to a plc. Joint press release issued, outlining merger and conversion proposals, benefits of the larger business, quotes from the two chairmen and background information
25 November 1994 Formal submission of the merger to the Office of Fair Trading	
21 December 1994 Decision by President of Board of Trade not to refer the merger to the MMC	

End January 1995
Building Societies
Commission decides
to seek High Court
ruling on proposed
share distribution
scheme

9 March 1995
Announcement of
the proposed share
distribution scheme
and court action to
clarify aspects of the
scheme

28 March 1995
High Court ruling in
favour of proposed
scheme

End March 1995
Despatch of *Schedule
16* merger
documents to
Halifax and Leeds
members

Covered rationale, structure of merged board,
impact on staff and customers, process, financial
information, investment schedules, and conversion
proposals including an outline of the share
distribution scheme.

22 May 1995
Special General
Meeting of Halifax
and Leeds to
approve merger

Merger and resolutions approved by 97 per cent
majority of Halifax members; 95 per cent Leeds.

11 July 1995
Building Societies
Commission
confirms transfer of
engagements of
Leeds to Halifax

1 August 1995
Halifax and Leeds
merge

6 September 1995
Announcement of reference dates

Halifax told investors that the key dates for identifying balances for the variable distribution would be 25 November 1994 and the date of the SGM. Halifax said the SGM would be unlikely to be before the end of 1996 and that it would give several weeks' notice. This was an important announcement since it allowed savers to withdraw funds provided they re-built them by the SGM date.

3 November 1995
Work starts on the Share Dealing project

The decision had already been taken in principle that Halifax would have to offer its own share-dealing service – nothing already in existence could possibly have coped with initial share sales.

13 December 1995
Announcement of further details of share distribution scheme

This was the important and fairly complex announcement of how Halifax would preserve benefits for successors to deceased accounts. It was this release that first made it clear that successors who were not themselves members would receive only the basic distribution.

25 March 1996
Joint Halifax/ Clerical Medical Insurance Group release announcing proposed acquisition

3 June 1996
Formal announcement of appointment of Royal Bank of Scotland as Registrar

Culmination of decision-making process which looked at a number of contenders, as well as the option of a Halifax 'in-house' operation.

21 June 1996
Clerical Medical approves Halifax acquisition at AGM

23 July 1996
Restructuring

Halifax announced 1000 new jobs; at the same time 1200 jobs to go in Halifax and Leeds.

24 October 1996
Halifax announces further details of conversion plans

This announcement gave forewarning of the planned November/December mailing, to include a booklet, information on share balances and a reminder to keep £100 in the account to retain voting rights. Halifax also announced the January issue of the Transfer Document, February SGM, April/May share allocation, availability of Halifax sharedealing, and probable June float. Additionally, this release announced the switch from the 'specially formed' to 'existing company' route. It reassured members that this would not affect the timetable or the share scheme, but would require a higher voting turnout and would remove the five years' protection.

12 November 1996
Halifax fights announcement on free shares scheme

This was at the peak of the 'shares for the disabled' lobbying and the intention by Douglas French to try to bring in legislation that would affect the Halifax float. The release made it clear that if Halifax had to redesign the scheme it could add at least a year to the flotation date.

30 November 1996
Halifax Conversion – *Next Steps* Booklet published

This repeated information on what would be in the November/December mailing and what members should do to check the information. The reminder to keep a minimum £100 balance was also repeated. This mailing was to 11.2 million customers and ran from 29 November to 6 December. Notification went to 7.9 million qualifying members *and* to 2.9 million members who were ineligible according to Halifax records.

11 December 1996
Halifax prospective executive changes

This put in place the new executive director structure for the plc.

10 January 1997
Announcement –
the final countdown
to conversion

Outlined contents of transfer document/voting
form. Indicated estimated share price at 16
December (390p–450p). Gave table to allow those
with variable distribution to calculate number of
free shares. Gave date of SGM 24 February, last
date for votes 17 February. Gave basic variable
split in terms of total share distribution (65 per
cent to basic 35 per cent to variable). Encouraged
members to vote. Outlined further timetable: 21
March last date for submissions to BSC, 24 April
BSC hearing, late April/May share allocation
forms, June float.

January 1997
TV 'vote' campaign

23 January 1997
Halifax launches
Woodland Initiative

Announced intention to pay for planting 30,000
broadleaf trees in conjunction with Groundwork
and BTCV. Transfer Document back cover
acknowledged environmental impact of heavy use
of paper (actually all from commercial and
renewable sources). Transfer packs used 3400
tonnes of paper.

24 February 1997
Halifax members
voted in favour of
conversion

Results of SGM vote showing 97 per cent in
favour, both borrowers and investors. Investing
members turnout 76 per cent; borrowing members
turnout 66 per cent. Around 6.8 million votes
counted. 1090 members actually attended
the meeting.

21 March 1997
Douglas French's
Building Societies
(Distributions) Bill
and Building
Societies Bill both
receive Royal
Assent

Douglas French and other politicians were keeping
up pressure on Halifax Building Society to change
its scheme because of the 'will of Parliament'.
Halifax continued to resist – decisions had already
been taken.

183

8 April 1997
Further preparation
June conversion

Announced 'share education' campaign –
members to be mailed with share education
booklet. Set out options for share recipients – sell;
keep in Halifax Shareholder Account; put in Single
Company PEP; opt for certificate. Announced
Halifax Sharedealing Service – able to sell free of
charge on listing and for ten days thereafter.

22 April 1997
Halifax set for
2 June conversion

Gave planned flotation date. Contents of mailing:
• booklet
• share allocation statement
• form A to keep
• form B to sell.
(Required to send back form B by 26 May to be
included in initial auction.)
Sharedealing service:
• exclusive to Halifax customers
• telephone service initially for purchases only
• sales by post.
Mailing also gave details of Halifax Single
Company PEP.

24 April 1997
Confirmation
Hearing

28 April 1997
Announcement of
minimum share price

Shares would not be sold if weighted average
auction price was below 415p.

30 April 1997
Halifax announced
further details of
sharedealing process

Detailed special arrangements with Royal Mail to
ensure that sale instructions around vesting day
would be delivered as quickly as possible.

23 May 1997
Building Societies
Commission
confirmation

27/30 May 1997
Halifax confirms members' share instructions

About 569 million shares, 23 per cent of share capital, were sold in initial auction (19 per cent of shareholders decided to sell on vesting day).
Some 69 per cent kept shares; of these, 49 per cent opted for the nominee, 20 per cent for certificates. A total of 8 per cent still unclaimed.
Announced initial auction would close 6 p.m., 30 May for institutions pre-registered with brokers.

2 June 1997
Dealing in Halifax plc shares begins

Weighted average initial auction price, 732.5p (gave value of £1465 for basic distribution; average over £2000). Range of successful bids was 710p to 815p with most weight at the lower end.

6 June 1997
Funds available for withdrawal in branches

23 June 1997
Halifax to enter FTSE 100

3 July 1997
Halifax offers telephone share selling to 3.7 million shareholders

During June a postal service was offered for sellers, with a telephone service for buyers.

CHAPTER ELEVEN

The sheer scale of it all

No fewer than 20 million customers
When and how much?
Everything must change
Eight million shareholders
We learned to cut out adjectives
The spectre in the background
The mailing caused uproar!

No fewer than 20 million customers

The year 1997 marked a period of demutualisation and conversion or, as the *Investors Chronicle* put it in April,

> 'Building society conversions are like buses; you wait years without even a sniff of one, then four come along all at once.'

Four – Alliance & Leicester, Halifax, Woolwich and Northern Rock – were floated on the stock market and one, Bristol & West, was acquired by the publicly quoted Bank of Ireland. In total, the five societies, with 16 million voting members, would represent an expansion of share ownership on a scale similar to that of the privatisation programme of the 1980s and early 1990s, themselves estimated to have created eight million new shareholders. As the Halifax moved towards flotation in June 1997, members and potential investors struggled to cope with the sheer size of the merged organisation. It boasted no fewer than 20 million customers. With a total population of about 58 million in the UK this was a staggering proportion. Assets were £116 billion.

Halifax was the market leader in residential mortgages, its £79.2 billion in mortgage balances with 2.5 million borrowers representing 20 per cent of the market. This compared with Abbey National's 15 per cent, Lloyds TSB's 10 per cent and all the other societies planning to convert with a share of 13 per cent. In the liquid savings market, again Halifax was the market leader with £72 billion in balances in 19 million accounts. This represented almost £1 in every £6 held in UK retail savings accounts.

Roger Boyes was well aware of the size of the task facing the society,

'The conversion process was highly complex. De-mutualising the largest building society in the world, by far, the Halifax together with the Leeds, was a huge constitutional problem. You have two principle regulators to deal with, the Building Societies Commission and of course the Bank of England who will grant the banking licence. So the whole of the regulatory process, not just from a legal and accounting side, but from a logistics side as well, was monumental. So we paused and we said, "How are we actually going to manage all this lot?" We had learned some very, very good techniques from the merger. We were all persuaded that programme management, where you have an over-arching programme that is broken down into logical blocks of work and projects within those logical blocks, charters as we call them, was the way to go forward again. So we planned the approach to conversion along the same lines with an over-arching board committee, the Conversion Committee, meeting monthly. Then we had the programme directors who were Mike Blackburn leading the charge with his three executives, John Miller, Mike Ellis and me who were directly responsible, meeting weekly. We carved up the task into blocks of work, with Mike Blackburn co-ordinating. Then each of us subdivided our blocks into individual projects and each one was written up completely and planned in meticulous detail.'

A committee of programme directors was formed under the chairman-ship of the chief executive, Mike Blackburn, consisting of Roger Boyes, John Miller and Mike Ellis, assisted by David Walkden, Graham Johnston and Ian Stewart. The programme directors met every Monday, almost without fail, from early August 1995 until after conversion vesting day in June 1997. This was the committee controlling the long, complex and highly detailed path to conversion. Within the group, Boyes was responsible for corporate finance and legal and regulatory aspects, Miller for data quality, the members' register, logistics and overall programme management, and Ellis for Treasury, marketing and communication. The conversion programme office managing the whole project was run by the stalwart and dedicated David Walkden who, more than anyone else, kept 'the show on the road'.

The mailing to members schedule was no less daunting. The total between spring 1996 and June 1997 was calculated at 64.6 million separate communications. These included the 1996 AGM notice (7 million), date of birth checks (Leeds 1 million, Halifax 2.1 million), check on accounts (1.5 million), a final data quality check in November 1996 (9 million), the sending of the Transfer Statement and notice of the SGM in January 1997 (9 million), the share allocation mailing in March 1997 (9 million), the 1997 AGM Notice also in March 1997 (7 million), the share allocation and claim document in April 1997 (9 million) and finally a 'Welcome to Halifax plc' in June 1997 (10 million). If the Royal Mail had been a plc, financial analysts would have been telling everyone to buy the shares.

The budgeted costs of the mammoth exercise were not small either. The Logistics box would absorb nearly £70 million and Communications £21 million. The total budget was £150 million or about £20 for every member that would become a Halifax plc shareholder. The eventual cost reached £168 million, mainly caused by a bigger-than-expected load on telephone helplines and correspondence units, and larger commissions and fees generated by the higher-than-expected flotation share price.

Research among members highlighted some of the problems still faced by Halifax if a successful flotation was to be assured. This research showed that as many members did not understand as did understand about conversion. Only one in ten understood completely and two in ten did not understand at all. Nearly 50 per cent said they did not know whether conversion was a good thing. The same number felt the conversion process was taking too long and 40 per cent felt that members were not receiving enough information.

When and how much?

Once people are told they will be given some money they have only two questions, 'When?' and 'How Much?'. In the case of the merger and flotation many members could not believe that it would take from November 1994 until the middle of 1997 for the Halifax and Leeds to be merged, for the combined society to be floated on the stock market, and for them to receive their shares and therefore the possibility of money. Nor could many believe that the societies could not tell them exactly how much they would receive.

Why did the process take two and a half years?

There were four main reasons. The first was the two-stage process, merger and then conversion. The second was the long and highly regulated process dictated by the Act and by the Building Societies Commission, and the time needed for discussions with the Bank of England which would become the converted company's new regulator. Third, a two-year time lapse after 25 November 1994 would mean that every investing member on that date would become a 'two-year member' and would be eligible for the *variable distribution* if their balance was big enough.

However, it was the fourth reason that was the most important. The membership registers of the two societies had to be cleaned up and 'de-duplicated', and this was a truly mammoth task. Both the Halifax and the Leeds held their records by account relationship. Consequently, a single customer with, say, two savings accounts and a mortgage would have three separate records on the computer file. As a result there were no fewer than 32 million individual account relationships with the two societies.

The Building Societies Act required societies to identify members, rather than account holders, for voting purposes. The respective computers were programmed to sort and compare names, addresses and dates of birth, identify duplicates and allocate one vote to one member, however many accounts were held. A simple task we might think, but in practice as many of the addresses had originally been hand-written and many dates of birth were missing, it was not so easy. And the degree of accuracy required for the conversion vote and float was much higher.

It was vitally important that the de-duplication process should be extremely thorough. Votes on both merger and conversion could be challenged if it could be shown that the registers were not accurate, with some members having more than one vote and others none at all. Also the right to vote meant an allocation of shares. It was essential that no eligible member missed out and no one received more than one allocation. Furthermore, once the two individual societies' registers were sorted out, the two needed to be brought together and de-duplicated because, after 1 August 1995, customers who had formerly been members of both societies only had one membership relationship with the Halifax from that date.

The computers rapidly reduced the 32 million customer relationships to 24 million as it eliminated closed accounts and so on, but then the real hard slog began. As far as possible, the computer was used to carry out automatic de-duplication using a clever piece of 'fuzzy logic' programming which picked up near matches of names and addresses. But nearly 3 million records had to be checked manually with reference to branch records in most cases. The staff required gradually built to 350 in head office with another 1000 data quality 'champions' in the branches. The 350-strong central team, made up of head office staff, branch seconds and some temporary staff, made up for the completion of an essentially boring task with a lively social life after hours. No one begrudged them that especially as they finished a month ahead of schedule.

John Miller was able to report the staggering figures to the Conversion Committee in September 1996. Around 32.5 million customer account relationships had been checked. These related to 23.8 million customer records. Of these, 3.5 million were duplicates, 2.5 million were picked up automatically by the computer and 1 million were found by the hard manual slog through 2.8 million doubtful cases.

All this resulted in 20.3 million genuine customers, of whom 14 million were members although not all of them qualifying members. By November 1996, 6.5 million investors and 2.3 million borrowers who qualified had been identified. A number were both and the final count was the 7.6 million people who received shares in June 1997.

After this huge effort the Halifax could at least feel happy that its records were as clean and accurate as anyone could expect and that it had established the highest standards to maintain the accuracy. Furthermore, it now possessed the essentials of a full-scale customer database.

Everything must change

Having made the decision to convert and chosen 2 June 1997 as vesting day, Halifax Building Society had to face the fact that from that date it would be a criminal offence to trade as a building society.

As a result, the words *Building Society* had to be removed from everything – every sign, form, letter-heading, leaflet, business card, computer screen message. (There were, of course, passbooks and plastic cards in the possession of members with Halifax *Building Society* on them but every one issued after vesting day would need the *Building Society* removed.)

Some 2000 Halifax outlets were scrutinised searching out the words, *Building Society*. And they were found not just on normal outside signs but on window notices, letter boxes, business signs, landlords' signs and car park signs. Even signs in office lifts had to be changed. There were over 100 historic plaques and foundation stones to be dealt with though no foundations stones were removed! For some large signs high up on the outside of buildings it was necessary to obtain planning permission to make the change.

Stationery was another mammoth exercise. No fewer than 1,500 forms had to be changed. As with the database, an exercise that had to be performed could be, and was, used as a positive opportunity to make improvements. Research in 1996 had shown that customers felt that the Halifax had far too many products and leaflets and that the language was not as clear or customer-friendly as it could be. Conversion gave the Halifax the opportunity to present fewer but better-designed leaflets and clearer letters.

Implementation and despatch of the changed literature meant that 120,000 parcels, which initially filled a 25,000 square foot warehouse, had to be despatched to the branch network. A round-the-clock despatch operation began two weeks before vesting day with over 1000 tonnes of material, double the normal daily UK parcel traffic, going out in mid-May. The change needed to be made on vesting day itself and it therefore meant, particularly with regard to signage, a massive week-end exercise to be ready on Monday, 2 June.

When it was successfully completed Mike Crowther, creative services manager, said,

> 'It was an enormous task and it took its toll on my hairline, but with the sort of co-operation we have come to expect from Halifax people and suppliers we managed it. We did it all on time and to budget. But please – no more name changes!'

Eight million shareholders

Halifax was breaking new ground in many areas by converting to a public company, but perhaps nowhere more so than in the area of sharedealing. The flotation was due to set up about eight million Halifax shareholders and it was realised that a significant number of those, perhaps more than 2 million, would want to sell their shares at the earliest possible moment. The society decided that it wanted to establish for the longer term its own sharedealing service and by early 1996 it had therefore identified the need for a registrar, a receiving bank to collect and collate members' instructions, a nominee service to solve the unique logistical problems of the Halifax float and anticipate the CREST environment and the sharedealing service.

Selecting a registrar capable of coping with such a huge register of new shareholders was only easy in the sense that the choice was extremely limited. David Walkden, assistant general manager in the Conversion Programme office, recalled that no registrar with its existing structure could have coped. Lloyds Bank registrars were using a system with flat files rather than a database. Barclays wanted to close down its registrar division. Abbey National's system was widely admired but it was felt to be politically difficult for the Halifax to use its main competitor. In the end the Royal Bank of Scotland was selected mainly because Halifax was impressed by its management and by its ability to provide the necessary nominee service electronically.

As with most statistics relevant to the flotation, the numbers involved were staggering. New premises were required to house the extra staff recruited especially for the flotation. The total floorspace used was 74,000 square feet. At the peak the staff employed numbered 1100. Some 300 telephone lines were set up for the Flotation Helpline and another 60 for general use. The maximum number of calls handled in a day was 23,367. The largest number of forms processed in one day was no fewer than 527,313 while the largest number received was 550,000. In total 7 million forms were returned including 1.9 million instructions to sell. This led to payments of £4.5 billion.

The Halifax knew that this creation of about 8 million shareholders, apart from the sheer logistics concerned with registration, was an event that would require very careful planning if the result was not to be complete chaos, with virtually no one able to buy or sell shares because all the existing systems broke down under the strain. Furthermore, such a chaotic situation was likely to lead to volatility in the price of Halifax shares leading possibly to charges of unfairness.

As the scale of the flotation was unprecedented in the UK, David Walkden and Dick Spelman went to the USA to see if an exercise of similar size had taken place there and, if so, how it had been handled. Although they were involved in 40 meetings throughout the country they discovered that the largest had been All America, a mutual assurance company in Worcester, Massachusetts. However, there were only 2 million members when they converted to a public company in 1995.

While they were travelling and discussing the problem of coping with such a large mass of shareholders they came to the conclusion that it would be impossible to cope if every member was given an individual share certificate and the option to sell. Initial estimates had shown that 1 million sales were likely on vesting day with 1.5 million in the first month. (In fact, sales were considerably higher, 1.9 million initial sales and 2.3 million in the first month. This did not include sales by shareholders outside the Halifax shareholder account.) Such a level of activity would make telephone-based selling an impossibility. No provider, not even British Telecom, could have coped. Such a volume would have brought down large sections of its UK network. In the event, on vesting day, it was estimated that 1 per cent of the UK population did telephone and the Halifax telephone system did go down for half an hour at 8.30 a.m.

Walkden and Spelman reviewed Merrill Lynch's experience in handling the pooled nominee system and demutualisation in the USA. They came to the conclusion that Merrill's was not the most suitable institution to handle the nominee system. This system would allow shares to be sold without the physical delivery of a share certificate. It would mean that share sales, including the crediting of members' accounts, could be fully automated with costs reduced to a minimum (in the event Halifax did not charge for sales before vesting day or for 10 days thereafter).

Halifax promoted the nominee by calling the facility the Halifax Shareholder Account, by providing the service free of charge and by guaranteeing that those customers going into the nominee account would be treated in virtually all respects as a conventional shareholder and offering free or competitively priced dealing for nominee sales.

Efficient settlement of the very high volume of early deals was going to depend first, on a high take-up of the nominee option, eliminating the need for certificates, and second, on the Stock Exchange's new 'paperless' settlement system for UK equities, CREST.

Like many new and complex computer systems with little control or discipline over the users, CREST experienced initial problems and there was a great deal of nervousness as to whether it would be able to cope with the settlement of the millions of transactions expected in the Halifax shares.

Given the timing of conversion and the fact that the existing paper-based system, Talisman, was due to be shut down two months ahead of the critical date, there was little that could be done in terms of fall-back or contingency. Discussions were held between Halifax Share Dealing Limited (HSDL), who would be acting for the sellers, and Halifax's brokers, who would be dealing for the institutional purchasers, so that in the event of a CREST failure, some sort of 'off-market' settlement could be effected but this would really have been a 'last resort' measure.

The next concern was the building of demand for the shares to ensure that initial sellers not only received a satisfactory price but also that they all received the same price. In a normal share offer the supply of shares is known and fixed, but in this case the supply, that is sellers, would not be known until just before listing. Demand could exceed supply leading to an illiquid market and extreme price volatility.

The key objective of the offering process was to identify 'natural sellers' in the pre-listing period and direct this supply of shares to institutional investors in a bookbuild offering process. With this process Halifax could hope for a relatively stable market price (so as not to disadvantage members on the basis of the timing of their sale decision), the foundation for a long-term sustainable shareholder base and liquidity. If members felt that strong institutional demand was being brought in the bookbuild and a full and fair price would be struck, they would be more inclined to an initial sale rather than a 'wait and see' approach.

From a range of initial options two methods of facilitating the involvement of institutions in determining a fair price for sellers were eventually short-listed. The first was a bookbuild and the second a real price tender. With a bookbuild the indications of demand would be listed and added up and, using some judgement, a 'strike price' would be determined at a point where all the demand was met and all successful bidders would pay that strike price regardless of the price they had originally bid. Given that the strike price would normally have to be within the range the market expected, the process could lead to inflated, and hence unsatisfied, demand and a subsequent surge in share price. This was something Halifax certainly did not want. Rather, Halifax wanted the best possible price for Day One sellers and to be able to demonstrate that the chosen process had achieved this to the satisfaction of the regulators.

Rather than this traditional method, Halifax opted for a real price tender. This disallowed strike price bids and forced institutions to put a price on their bids. It also encouraged 'stepped' bids. So, for example, an institution wanting a million shares could bid for 100,000 at 760p, 500,000 at 730p, 200,000 at 700p and 200,000 at 680p, knowing they might or might not be successful at each level.

All bids were secret and 'blind' in that bidders had no information on the other bids being made and the whole process was supervised by the regulator, the Securities and Futures Authority. In this way, the brokers could construct a demand schedule and could arrive at the price that was the best possible, based on the weighted average of all the successful bids. Those who bid too low did not get the shares they bid for.

This method did mean that Halifax needed a much more rigorous market education than otherwise, so that institutions had sufficient information to put a price on their demand. Halifax had, in any event, planned an intensive series of roadshows and the extra 'homework' that institutions needed to do led to a higher quality of bids than for a traditional offering as investors formed a clearer view on valuation and did not artificially inflate demand.

We learned to cut out adjectives

Over the last 150 years some bank customers (and even a few building society investors) have lost money through the incompetence or fraudulent behaviour of the supposedly upright citizens handling their money. And every time a scandal occurs the cry goes up, 'Something must be done!'. Furthermore, in 'doing something' existing or new regulatory bodies impose more and more restrictions and conditions to try and make sure that members of the public do not lose their money. As a result, any company trying to float on the Stock Exchange, especially one that was going to be called a bank, would be subject to the closest scrutiny by both the Stock Exchange itself and the Bank of England.

Satisfying both these bodies that the Halifax Building Society, then regulated by the Building Societies Commission, was fit to be Halifax plc to be regulated by the Bank of England, was going to be a long and detailed operation. What the Halifax was seeking was the ability to write in its conversion Transfer Statement,

> 'The Bank of England has indicated that, on the basis of information currently available to it, it would be prepared to authorise Halifax plc under the Banking Act 1987.'

To gain this 'minded to authorise' approval the Halifax had to undertake a daunting number of tasks. The most important was the preparation of a detailed Business Plan in a form acceptable to the Bank. The first draft was produced in late 1995 and was constantly amended before its final submission to the Bank in July 1996.

The Bank required that a *Shadow Section 39* report be prepared on the accounting and internal controls systems of Halifax by KPMG, the auditors of Halifax. This report looked at all aspects of risk within Halifax and identified the areas where shortcomings were evident. Management had to respond to the observations of KPMG, and tripartite meetings were held between the Bank, KPMG and Halifax to agree an action plan to address and resolve the exceptions identified and to monitor progress as conversion proceeded.

Another Bank requirement was the completion of questionnaires on about a hundred senior Halifax managers to check whether the individuals responsible for the day-to-day management were 'fit and proper' persons as required under *Section 9* of the Banking Act 1987.

And while the documentation was being prepared, officers of the Bank made a number of visits to Halifax in order to understand the business in greater depth. The Bank was determined to understand how Halifax controlled its mortgage operations as well as its Treasury operations.

While one team was working on the authorisation process, another was designing a completely new prudential reporting procedure to meet the Bank's requirements. These were significantly different from those traditionally met by Halifax for the Building Societies Commission. This team carried out a huge amount of analysis and implementation work to ensure compliance with the Bank's requirements and, because it needed to demonstrate it could meet these requirements six months before authorisation, reporting began in late 1996.

Yet another team began the preparation of the 166-page Transfer Document, which needed to contain all the information that was material to members in making their decision on how to vote on conversion. The first draft was submitted to the Building Societies Commission in June 1996 and over the following six months went through sixteen further drafts. Every word was checked and adjectives such as 'big', 'small' and 'important' were challenged.

Graham Johnston, controlling the teams working on the regulation requirements, said, 'We learned to cut out adjectives.'

Halifax had hoped originally for BSC approval by 8 January 1997 but wanted, if possible, to have it before Christmas to allow more time for printing and despatch. To its relief, formal approval was given at 3.20 p.m. on 23 December. Christmas, which had been cancelled for the drafting team, was re-instated.

On top of the Transfer Document, it was necessary for the auditors to produce a 'Long Form Report'. This report is intended to be a 'warts and all' description of the organisation and in the case of some companies floating on the Stock Exchange can be highly amusing, noting yachts in the Mediterranean, shooting lodges in Scotland, vineyards in France and flats with highly paid landladies in London. In Halifax's case, of course, no such appendages appeared but it still ran to 900 pages, plus appendices. Just reading it, never mind drafting it, was an enormous load on the relevant project team and key Halifax executives.

Finally there were the Listing Particulars and as Graham Johnston put it, 'If the Transfer Document induced boredom, the Listing Particulars were a cure for insomnia.'

When all was successfully completed on time, Johnston summed it up,

> 'We in the team were very conscious that we were central to the whole conversion process. If we had not succeeded in delivering on time any of the documents required by the various regulatory bodies, the whole conversion process could have been put back by weeks or even months. Draft, draft, draft, check, check, check – boring and tedious it may have been but the fear of failure concentrated our minds.'

The spectre in the background

As we have seen, Halifax was not the first building society to demutualise and float on the stock market. In 1989, the Abbey National had gone through the process and established a number of precedents. The one that the Abbey National directors would like to forget, and which would serve as a constant reminder and warning to Halifax, was the loss of a substantial number of share certificates. Furthermore, Halifax's number of qualifying members, at around 8 million, was almost twice that of Abbey National's 4.3 million, bringing even greater pressure on the mailing houses involved.

Nevertheless, sorting out and posting 4.3 million share certificates was a mammoth exercise and, as everyone now knows, it went horribly wrong. John Fry, the Abbey National director masterminding the flotation, recalled with horror the growing realisation that what had seemed a small glitch probably caused by the usual postal delays was in fact a full-scale disaster.

Things became so desperate Fry sent for Lloyds and the Post Office and said to them,

> 'Something is terribly wrong. Lloyds is telling me it's delivered all the certificates to the Post Office, every single one of them. And you, the Post Office, are saying you've delivered them all. This cannot be, because we are still inundated, we're getting branches under siege, telephone switchboards under siege.'

And it was not getting any better as the days went by. Fry said later,

> 'We had branch staff being spat at, some actually physically assaulted. Telephonists had to be sent home in tears and I had several people on the phone who were incredibly rude.'

As Abbey and Lloyds investigated, the ghastly truth emerged. Huge numbers of certificates had been burned and it was eventually calculated that 530,000 of the original 4.3 million certificates had gone missing.

As almost all the affected members/shareholders were customers as well, the potential for damage was severe and if, on any occasion, those involved in the Halifax conversion were tempted towards complacency, a mention of what had happened at Abbey National would surely have them checking and re-checking their systems and procedures, and reinforcing the already strong arguments in favour of the nominee route.

The mailing caused uproar!

From the announcement in November 1994 of the plan to merge and convert until vesting day in June 1997, a period of over two and a half years, it was essential that the societies kept their members informed and they were fully aware of this need for constant communication. As we have seen, in that two and a half year period over 75 million merger- and conversion-related packages were despatched. For the conversion exercise alone there were over 65 million – collecting date of birth and other information during 1996, checking the accuracy of addresses and account balances in November and December 1996, the Transfer Statement mailing in January 1997, the share education mailing, the share allocations and claims mailing and finally the welcome pack. On top of these were the normal statutory mailings such as notices of Annual General Meetings, accounts statements and tax statements. There was a constant stream of communication with members. And yet some still complained that they were being kept in the dark.

Some mailings brought more reaction than others. One was the mailing in November 1996 which included a booklet, *Next steps to conversion – How it affects you*. With such headings as, *Are you a member of the Halifax? Will you be a qualifying investing member? Will you be entitled to the variable distribution?*, it was bound to bring a big response both in telephone calls and correspondence.

The Halifax had anticipated a large response and had planned for it. The helpline system was set up so that the majority of calls would come into an automated unit. This was called an Interactive Voice Response Unit (IVR). It would operate 24 hours a day supplying answers to the most popular general queries. Backing up the IVR would be 250 operators handling relatively simple queries and behind them would be 140 core staff handling more complex and account-specific queries either over the telephone or in response to written enquiries. At peak periods, help would be given by 50 operators from Halifax Direct. But, whereas the large numbers anticipated and planned for at the Special General Meetings had not materialised, in this case the numbers expected proved to be an under-estimate. In the words of Valery Duggleby, programme support manager, 'The mailing caused uproar!'

Although experience gained in the merger process had warned the Halifax that mailings would bring an upsurge in enquiries both at branches and head office, this was one area where the society underestimated the impact.

In the November 1996 mailing, it was not the qualifying members who caused the problem – only 150,000 out of 11.2 million members required corrections to their records – but the 2.9 million members who would not qualify for shares. In the first week of December, the telephone helplines received over 300,000 calls with 96,000 on one day, 5 December. A vicious circle built up. As queues built, callers rang and re-dialled, building even longer queues and creating an 'abandon rate', which at times reached 20 per cent. To add to everyone's frustration, the helpline operators were heavily constrained in their replies, having to stick to legally approved 'scripted' responses. Some of the callers were so abusive they reduced many of the operators to tears. Many of the temporarily hired operators worked for a day or two and decided not to return. During the month of December a total of 728,119 telephone calls had been received.

That champion of the people, *The Sun*, was soon in on the act. Under the headline,

THE HELL-IFAX
400,000 furious callers jam Halifax phones over bonus

The Sun, claiming this was an 'Exclusive by Isabelle Murray, City editor', noted that there were some mistakes discovered in the 13 million letters sent out. Inevitably such publicity exacerbated the situation increasing the number of telephone enquiries.

Ged Melling, *The Times* 9 August 1997

A great deal was learned from the November mailing and resources were put in place to minimise queuing on the helplines. The Transfer Document mailing in early January caused another upsurge with calls running at 30,000 a day by the end of January. At the same time letters arrived by the sackload and the Halifax aim of replying within a few days became impossible to achieve. Many letters were long with complex histories of account relationships necessitating detailed checking, both centrally and at branch level. Despite replying to 1500 letters a day, the backlog grew to over 20,000 by the end of December. Letter-handling staff were increased from 50 to 75 and the response rate grew to 15,000 a week. Nevertheless, the backlog built to 50,000 by the end of January with the surge in letters following the Transfer Statement mailing. Gary Marsh told the programme directors' meeting on 27 January 1997 that an increasing number of members were contacting the press when they did not receive an immediate reply to their correspondence.

By 10 February the backlog reached 60,000 letters, but that was the peak. By separating out the complex deceased estate cases and putting in extra resources to handle them, a steady inroad was made into this backlog.

By the middle of March it was fewer than 20,000 and the Conversion Information Office expected to clear it completely by early April. However, another problem was highlighted by David Walkden when he told the programme directors' meeting of 24 March about the increasing number of County Court summonses being issued against the Halifax by disgruntled members and borrowers. Everyone agreed that these must be robustly defended by properly briefed local solicitors. No one had any doubts about the public relations damage if a case was lost.

The early April clearance target was not achieved and Walkden reported on 1 April that 9749 letters were still outstanding. Furthermore, concern was now being expressed at the likely influx of telephone calls and correspondence when the April mailing went out and the 309,000 members, who had disenfranchised themselves, realised they had done so.

The response to this mailing almost overwhelmed the conversion office and some wag posted an amended cover of the booklet sent to members on the office notice-board [see photo section].

Amid all the anguished letters and telephone calls received by the Halifax there were occasional letters which brought a smile to the lips of the harrassed staff. One such letter came from the Reverend Rosie Bates (see next page).

The Parishes of North Hinksey, Botley and Wytham.

The Rev'd Rosie Bates
Priest-in-Charge
The Vicarage
81 West Way
Botley
Oxford OX2 9JY
Tel (01865) 242345.

19 April 1997

H Jon Foulds
Chairman
Halifax Building Society
Trinity Road
Halifax
West Yorkshire
HX1 2RG

Dear Mr Foulds

Thank you for your letter and enclosures recently received. As an impoverished vicar of Botley, I am more than delighted to have a bit more money in my account. I have been endlessly pissed about by Barclays for the last five years and will be especially delighted to transfer my account to Halifax as soon as appropriate.

I wish you all the very best at what must be a pretty exhausting time for you.

Yours sincerely

Rosie Bates

Rev'd Mrs Rosie Bates

Of the phone calls, one was from a woman who was separated from her husband. While she was still making the monthly mortgage repayment she noted that he, as the first name on the account, would receive free shares. Outraged, she told the Halifax that if they did not make her the recipient, she would put his budgerigars in the gas oven and present the carcasses to him in the certificate envelope.

Valery Duggleby could not deal with every telephone call herself or even one in a hundred, but if a caller was particularly persistent or seemed to have a particularly complex and intractable problem, he or she would eventually be passed from BT operator to BT supervisor to

Halifax operator to Halifax supervisor to her. She remembered one caller who said,

> 'I have said repeatedly that I want to speak to a manager.'
> 'I am a manager, Sir,' replied Duggleby.
> 'But you can't be, you're a woman!'

Many telephone calls were from women incensed that they were not going to receive shares because their husbands were the first-named on the account. However, one was from an anguished man who did not want any more correspondence from the Halifax because his investment provided him with 'pin-money' and was a secret from his wife.

The main problem for both telephone callers and correspondents was that they could not grasp the *fundamental* difference between the share allocation rules and those governing their accounts. With an ordinary account the Halifax could, and sometimes did, bend its own rules and customers did sometimes achieve concessions by persistence or appeal to a higher authority. With the share distribution, the details had to be set out in the Transfer Document and could not be varied, otherwise the whole conversion process could have been challenged. There could be no *ex-gratia* payments, no special treatment, no compassionate payments and no taking account of long-established relationships going back for generations.

However, some members just would not take no for an answer and many of the telephone calls and much of the correspondence reflected this.

When it came to posting the Transfer Document in January 1997, the statistics boggled the mind. Each transfer document weighed 400 grammes and postmen were limited by health and safety regulations to delivering a maximum of 25 a time. Someone calculated that if they were all piled on top of one another they would make a tower 56 miles tall and if all the pages were laid side by side, they would cover 160,000 miles or 5 times the circumference of the Earth.

Christian Slater, *Evening Standard*
7 January 1997

The mailing used 5000 tonnes of paper with 30 million items being sorted into almost 8 million envelopes. Some 150 lorries were used to transport the paper from the mill to the printers and 13 printing sites across the country were used tying up 60 per cent of the UK's printing capacity. Some 18 mailing houses were used (and, mindful of the Abbey National experience, were carefully vetted). Around 12,000 Royal Mail cages were needed and as they only owned 5000, the Royal Mail needed to buy another 7000. The Royal Mail also increased its trunking vehicle requirements by 30 per cent. Perhaps most daunting of all for the Royal Mail, and by implication for the Halifax, only 10 per cent of letterboxes in the UK were large enough to accommodate an unfolded A4 document.

In such a mammoth exercise did anything go wrong?

CHAPTER TWELVE

Something ought to be done!

A capital problem

Human error

A hell of a job to establish the equity

Frivolous and vexatious

It's a very confusing form

A capital problem

B efore we see what went wrong or what boulders there were on the highway, there was a major technical issue that the Halifax directors needed to face. This technical problem could have been of great consequence for the further development of the business of the society once it had become a public company.

We have already seen that the 1986 Building Societies Act had brought almost as many new problems as solutions to the needs and desires of the building societies and in 1994 it was realised that one of its sections would need to be addressed. This was the section on the Priority Liquidation Distribution Reserve (or for those who prefer a really user-friendly acronym, PLDR), an idea imported from the USA, following their experience of 'thrift' society conversions in the 1970s and early 1980s. The reserves of mutual societies were there for the protection of the members. Some US conversions took place without any distribution of reserves or benefits to members and the new management then moved into more risky ventures. Some converted 'thrifts' went into liquidation and the reserves, which would have been there to help bail out members, were no longer available as the capital belonged to the new shareholders. As a result the idea was conceived of 'ring fencing' the transferred reserves for the benefit of the former members. When the idea was imported into the UK and inserted into the 1986 Act, those drafting the Act did not think there would be 'windfalls' for members and wanted this ring fencing to protect the members.

The PLDR in the 1986 Act gave former investing members a claim on the reserves of the former building society, to be triggered in the event of the liquidation of the successor company. The claim on reserves was proportional to size of balance at the time of conversion, and was reduced by any withdrawals and not increased on any receipts – hence the concept of a steady run-off of the PLDR.

The essential problem for the Halifax was that the Bank of England would need to set a capital ratio for Halifax plc, but the capital that could be counted towards this ratio would be reduced by part of the amount of the PLDR. At best, this would mean that Halifax plc would be very tightly constrained in terms of possible acquisitions in the early years. At worst, it could have required Halifax to raise additional capital at the time of conversion. This would have been ludicrous, because counting in the PLDR the converted society was over-capitalised already, and it was readily predictable that the PLDR would largely run off in three to five years.

The PLDR was identified as a real problem early in 1995 and, although everyone including the Bank of England agreed that it was a legal frustration, for the moment the requirement stood and it could not be ignored.

In August 1996 a paper, *Existing Company Route versus Specially Formed Company*, argued that it would be legally possible to avoid PLDR by arranging to be taken over by an existing company and, furthermore, that there was no legal reason why the existing company should not be a subsidiary of Halifax Building Society.

The Conversion Committee had to decide whether all the problems associated with this late switch in the route to conversion, which would include the necessity of a much higher voting turnout – more than 50 per cent as opposed to 20 per cent – and the loss of Section 101 BSA protection against take-over within five years, were worth the avoidance of the extra capital problem. It decided that they were and indeed media and institutional reaction was favourable.

Human error

In spite of all the checks put in place, inevitably mistakes were made. One of them occurred with the mailing of the share allocation forms in April 1997. The error came to light when calls were received on the Conversion Helplines and when the affected members contacted their branches in Basildon. In this case all the members had received the share allocation form which contained their own personalised letter, their own personalised 'keep' form but a neighbour's personalised Share Allocation Statement and personalised 'sell' form.

The complexity of the mailing, with four personalised items in one pack, never tried before, had caused concern at the planning stage and as a result the control procedures had been thoroughly tested and signed off by KPMG. In addition to manual checks by the Halifax's internal auditors and the main contracted mailing house, Chorleys, an Optical Character Reading camera system had been bought for £50,000. This camera could read marks on all four personalised items and reject any packs where the four items did not match.

It transpired that during a half hour one evening an operator had not carried out some sample checks and allowed the defective packs through. The camera, although switched on, did not pick up the error because it occurred between the camera and the collating area. Once the Halifax identified the source of the problem everyone relaxed but those in charge of the operation had been apprehensive for a time. Basildon was, after all, in Essex where people knew their rights and were likely to demand compensation. However, worse was to come. David Walkden remembers receiving a telephone call at home on a Saturday morning a few days after the discovery of the Basildon problem to say that the helplines were 'going ballistic' and nearly all the calls were from the Guildford area. The information was somewhat sketchy but it seemed that the same problem that had hit Basildon had now hit Guildford. As Walkden put it,

> 'This was really scary. Guildford was 300,000 forms further on than Basildon. Were 300,000 mailings wrong?'

Fortunately it transpired, after thorough checking, that the problem was limited to only 354 members in the SS14 postal area of Basildon and 649 in the GU1 area of Guildford. Action was promptly taken and no further erroneous mailings came to light.

A hell of a job to establish the equity

In such a large pay-out of shares, easily transferable into money, it was inevitable there would be disgruntled people who felt they had been unjustly excluded. Indeed the bigger the pay-out, and consequently the greater the publicity, the more aggrieved some of the excluded would feel.

It seemed reasonable when merger and conversion were announced that the Halifax and Leeds should say,

> 'The main beneficiaries will be the investing and borrowing members of Halifax and Leeds who are currently members of either society and remain members continuously until conversion.'

This made clear that non-members, though they might be customers with deposit money-transmission accounts, would not benefit from any share allocation. Successors to deceased estates was a more complex issue and it was not until December 1995 that the Halifax was able to finalise its proposals.

Essentially, the second-named would receive the share entitlement of the first-named if the first-named died, and the personal representative of a sole share account holder would receive all or part of that sole member's share entitlement, including the variable distribution if the successor was a two-year member, but just the basic distribution if the successor was not a two-year member.

Another pressure group built up behind the claims on behalf of children (under 18s). Children fell into two categories – those whose parents held accounts 'in respect of' their children, and accounts held in the child's own name. In the first case, the parent was in effect a trustee and would get free shares, but, of course, only one distribution. The account balance would be aggregated with any other account the parent held. Children with their own accounts were minors and therefore non-voting members.

There were two main reasons why the second group should not receive shares. First it would have broken with the guiding principle, the link between the right to vote and entitlement to free shares. Second, the Building Societies Act said they must receive the statutory cash distribution, which, in the case of the Halifax, was 9.4 per cent of the account balance. It would have been unreasonable and unfair to give them both benefits.

The Halifax was only too well aware that this was a tricky area. Children were, after all, its savers and borrowers of tomorrow. And pressure from some parts of the media was unrelenting. *The Mail on Sunday* ran a campaign throughout the summer and into the autumn of 1997 under such headlines as **Touchy Halifax still won't pay under-18s**. However, the Halifax remained steadfast. A share distribution to minors would have been unprecedented and was never a possibility.

In the summer of 1996, the media woke up to the fact that the building societies faced a tricky problem in handling share allocations in the case of the disabled. And, of course, it was a good news story – hard-nosed and large financial institution depriving the weakest members of society.

The Building Societies Act (by common consent not a very well drafted act) stated that only the first named on an account, whether family member, trustee or carer, was the member. As *The Times* pointed out in August 1996,

'The shares or cash to be handed out by the society will go to the named individual rather than directly to the disabled person. This discriminatory system not only deprives handicapped people of their rights. It may also oblige them to tackle the trustee or other person responsible for their money to ensure the building society payout is handed over.'

Ray Ward, a public relations executive with a mentally handicapped son, wrote to Peter Lilley, the Secretary of State for Social Security, and also Angela Knight, Economic Secretary to the Treasury, the minister responsible for building societies. Knight herself wrote to Lilley saying that the Building Societies Act 1986,

' … does not prevent societies from giving more than one allocation of shares to each member in particular societies.'

The Royal National Institute for the Blind also protested,

'The provisions of the Act [Disability Discrimination Act due to come into force in December 1996] make it clear that disabled people should not be refused a service unreasonably or treated on different terms. There is a real possibility that the current rules for building society conversions could run contrary to the spirit, if not the letter, of the Act.'

The Bishop of Beverley, John Gaisford, whose son was disabled, added his voice to the protest and his letter to *The Times* was published on Saturday 29 March 1997, under a photograph of the Bishop and a headline, **Halifax board has moral duty to disabled**.

The letter concluded,

> 'Acknowledging that the Halifax is "awash with money", there is a moral responsibility on the board to make the necessary allocation to those who are at present barred from receiving the basic distribution.'

The real problem arose in the case of severely disabled people living in residential homes where one member of staff ran the accounts of all the residents. The disabled lobby found it difficult to understand why each disabled person should not receive an individual allocation. However, as the group solicitor, Chris Jowett, pointed out,

> 'We would have to look behind every account to see if there was a deserving beneficiary who would be eligible by whatever criteria we had adopted. If someone happened to be the principal of a residential care home it's easy to establish that but if someone came along and said "I've got five accounts and they are for five relatives who are all incapable of looking after their own affairs and I'd like you to treat them separately" it would be a hell of a job to establish the equity of that. As a solicitor I am conscious that there are many firms of solicitors, and also accountants, who have held accounts for clients and they're only getting one whack of shares for all those clients. They've known that since the Abbey days and they ought to have said to themselves, "I ought to rearrange the accounts which I am holding for clients to maximise the potential share benefits." For whatever reason a lot of them never did that; in fact very few of them did.'

Others in the legal profession might not agree. They did not feel that there was any duty of care, following the Abbey National Flotation, to hold building society accounts on a basis that would maximise distributions in the hope that there might be a distribution on conversion. Indeed, because many individual entitlements to monies held in professionals' building society accounts would be quite small, professional advisers might run the risk of liability for not pooling the funds and maximising the interest return.

By November 1996 pressure was building up and the Shadow Cabinet Minister for Disabled People, Tom Clarke, demanded a full-scale enquiry. To counter growing protest the Halifax issued a press release under the heading, **Halifax fights threats to free shares scheme**,

'The question of the position of the disabled in relation to building society conversions and the issue of free shares has been the subject of recent media and political comment. Halifax wishes to make it clear that its proposed share distribution does not discriminate against people with a disability.

On conversion, the Halifax scheme will principally give shares to qualifying investing and borrowing members. Each member has one vote. This principle is carried across into our share distribution scheme and one member receives one set of benefits only. This reflects the basic principles of mutuality. The Halifax does not discriminate against any group in society, and certainly not the disabled.

Many disabled people are members of the Halifax and will receive free shares. Those disabled who are beneficiaries of trustee accounts are in no different position from beneficiaries of other trustee accounts – for example, solicitors' or accountants' client accounts, parents' accounts for children, local organisations such as scout troops and so on.

Our lawyers have considered the Disability Discrimination Act. We have a very firm legal opinion that our scheme does not contravene this Act.

Under the present scheme, separate treatment of disabled savers, on a case by case basis, is not possible. Any such individual decision could give rise to a legal challenge to the entire conversion process.

More than a third of the adult UK population now have expectations of significant "windfalls" in 1997. We sincerely hope that these plans will not be disrupted.'

On 26 November the National Disability Council issued a press release of its own claiming,

'Notwithstanding the technical legal arguments, the Council considers the present arrangements to be discriminatory and totally unacceptable. It is of the view that the current flotation proposals would leave many disabled people, who are not the first-named on their accounts, at a considerable disadvantage over their first-named counterparts.'

On 4 December a debate took place in the House of Lords in which Lord Ewing of Kirkford, the former Labour Member of Parliament for Falkirk East, pressed Lord MacKay of Ardbrecknish, the Minister of State, Department of Social Security on whether the government had any plans to make representations to the building societies on behalf of the disabled,

> 'There are cases where one charge nurse is the first-named on upwards of 30 accounts. The building societies are saying that they can have only one allocation of shares. Does the Minister accept that this is neither a political nor a financial matter, but a moral matter? It is wholly wrong of the Alliance & Leicester and the Halifax building societies to treat these unfortunate people in this immoral way ... '

Lord MacKay replied,

> 'The issue is a bit more complex than at first appears ... It is for the building societies themselves to decide which scheme they feel is most appropriate, and, of course, for the building society members to decide.'

By the middle of December 1996 it was becoming clear that Douglas French, Conservative Member of Parliament for Gloucester, was planning to propose a Bill under the ten-minute rule, which would force the building societies to give bonus payments to disabled savers. It was extremely unusual for a Bill introduced in this way to become law – only five had succeeded in twenty-five years – but one of those five had been a Bill introduced by Douglas French in 1995 whereby second-named account holders of building society accounts could inherit the membership rights of the first-named member on the death of the first-named account holder.

And on Tuesday, 11 February 1997, it was announced that French had won Government backing for his Bill. It was due to return to the Commons later in the week, and with support guaranteed from the Treasury Ministers and the Labour leadership it stood an excellent chance of passing through all the necessary House of Commons stages in one go. If it did so, the Bill would go to the House of Lords on 28 February and would stand a good chance of becoming law by the end of the Parliamentary Session – that is, by Easter.

The Halifax response to this situation and the receipt of a letter from French to chief executive Mike Blackburn, claiming that the Halifax's refusal to think about payments to second-named disabled savers was 'untenable' and 'a betrayal of the ethos of mutuality', was to warn that the whole conversion process could be delayed by a year.

Blackburn said that if French's Bill became law and was retrospective, the conversion would be 'delayed by at least a year and at great expense if we have to re-do documents. That will mean 8.5 million people, many of whom are disabled, will have to wait for bonuses they are expecting.'

French's Bill became law and received Royal Assent in March. However, it did not apply to those societies already on the path to conversion. That seemed to solve the problem but the issue was still alive in the autumn of 1997, months after the flotation. MENCAP was still demanding special arrangements for those it maintained had lost out. However, Halifax had steadfastly refused to make exceptions which might have opened the floodgates to demands from every group of 'special' cases and, at the cost of more hostile publicity, continued to refuse to concede to any particular group. The society knew that as a company it would only run the risk of claims from many others, prolonging the debate over free shares for many years to come.

Another group that brought some anxiety to Halifax were those members living overseas, although the society had anticipated some difficulties. Halifax members lived in almost every country in the world. Each country had its own local laws and its own regulations concerning the issue of shares. To avoid an impossible burden of work, which could have threatened the conversion timetable, the board decided at an early stage to identify those countries where Halifax had a material number of customers and where the distribution of free shares 'would not result in a breach of local laws or require compliance with regulatory require-ments which Halifax considered onerous'. This resulted in a list of 26 countries, including 13 of the 15 European Union countries, but excluding the USA because of the complex securities regulations in that country.

The Transfer Document, sent out in January 1997, made it clear that a registered UK (or permitted territory) address at midnight before Vesting Date in June 1997 *would* entitle the member to shares (if otherwise qualified). So for those who could properly do so, there was ample time to establish a different address. Yet there were complaints from many members in other countries that this information had not reached them at all, or had reached them late. They argued that Halifax should not have used normal State postal services (especially US Mail) and should have made the 'warning' much more prominent.

Others argued that they did have a right to the shares and that Halifax should have battled its way through local regulations – at whatever cost and whatever the implications for the timetable – in order to meet their needs. Once again, this became a media issue, complaints were vociferous and litigation was threatened. But unlike some of the other groups, there was little evidence of widespread sympathy for the excluded 'overseas' members.

Frivolous and vexatious

In early March, David Gilchrist received a telephone call from a Michael Hardern. Hardern was already well known throughout the building society world as 'the champion of the carpet-baggers'. A butler by profession, he had recently dedicated himself to winning the best possible deal for members of those societies that planned to convert and to trying to force those that wanted to stay as a mutual into converting. He now told Gilchrist that there was the possibility of a group of members attempting to requisition a Special General Meeting to try to persuade the Halifax to amend the share distribution scheme to take account of French's Building Societies (Distributions) Bill. This threat had to be taken seriously and Gilchrist consulted the society's solicitors.

On 17 March the Halifax solicitor, David Gordon, set out the conditions necessary for members calling a Special General Meeting. To begin with, it was too late for members to propose new resolutions for the Society's AGM due on Monday, 21 April. Under the Society's rules, the members could require the Society to call an SGM at the written request of at least 200 qualifying members who would each need to deposit £50. If the Society received a valid requisition it would be bound to put the resolutions to the members within 56 days and must give 21 days' notice of calling the SGM. The Society need not call an SGM if the members' right to requisition is being abused for 'frivolous or vexatious' purposes.

Gordon made it clear that if a valid requisition was received before vesting day, the planned conversion timetable would be threatened. Malcolm Waters, Counsel, was asked his opinion and his advice was

214

that 'the Society would have a strong legal argument for refusing to call the meeting and rejecting the resolution'.

As well as significant problems that needed to be tackled with efficiency and careful attention to detail, it was inevitable in such a huge exercise that there would be errors in misallocation of shares, wrong addresses, mixed up account numbers and so on. We have already seen the potential for disaster if a mailing house failed to carry out the checks that had been put in place. As chief executive Mike Blackburn pointed out, make a mistake that affects only 1 per cent of the members and you would upset 80,000 people, enough to fill Wembley Stadium; make a mistake that affects 10 per cent and you are talking about filling a town the size of Manchester.

Perhaps frustrated that all seemed to be progressing smoothly towards a highly successful flotation, the press grabbed at any crumbs they could find. Under the headline, **Halifax facing its share of problems,** *The Daily Telegraph* highlighted the woes of some disgruntled members,

'Yesterday saw a fresh batch of complaints about administrative bungling – not all of them concerning delays or disputes about under-allocation. At least one error was in favour of the account holder.

Robyn Anderson, 14, from Holme-on-Spalding Moor, York, was surprised to receive an allocation of 208 Halifax shares – despite the Building Societies Act prohibition on stock being issued to minors. Her mother, Helen, had set up an account for Robyn on an "in re" basis; so the passbook is marked "Mrs Helen Anderson in re Robyn Anderson".

Mrs Anderson, a lunch-time school supervisor, noted the warning in the Halifax literature that criminal proceedings could follow false claims for stock and said "Someone at the Halifax has clearly made a mistake and I imagine we could have claimed Robyn's shares and acted innocent in the unlikely event of the error being detected.

"But that is no excuse and, although Robyn is morally just as entitled to her shares as anyone else, I do not believe that right justifies dishonesty on my part."

Robyn's father, Steve, called on Halifax directors to "remedy an obvious injustice and give all non-qualifying customers a cash bonus equal to that of their non-existent shares.

"If such a step means reduced dividends for all shareholders, then that would seem to be a small price to pay for righting such an unfortunate wrong."'

It was very irritating for those concerned but it hardly merited such a misleading headline. Gary Marsh said,

> 'We knew we were going to get some flak dealing with millions of people who were going to get shares and a smaller number, but still many thousands, who were not eligible but thought they ought to be and thought that something ought to be done about it!'

As well as the tricky situations that arose with deceased members, there were plenty arising from those who had already divorced or were in the throes of a divorce. We have already seen how one woman threatened to put her husband's budgerigar in the gas oven. *The Times* discovered another unhappy divorcee,

> 'A new disenfranchised group has emerged: divorced borrowers who have paid their mortgages faithfully but will not benefit because their former spouses remain the first name on the loan. Under the rules of all conversions, only the first-named account holder is entitled to a payout. Among those affected by this ruling is Frances Russell, a *Times* reader from Ealing, West London, who has now remarried after divorce from her first husband.
>
> Although Mrs Russell has been solely responsible for the payments on her Halifax loan, taken out four years ago, she will not receive the basic distribution of shares because her former spouse was the first-named account holder. The entitlement to a payout has now been entirely lost because he has now taken out a new loan with another lender. However, Mrs Russell does not gain the right to a payout because she was not the first-named holder on the all-important qualifying date of November 25 1994.
>
> Mrs Russell said: "In June 1993 I took out a Halifax mortgage with my first husband. But, as we parted before we could begin living in the house, I moved in alone with my son, Franklin, who is now ten, and paid the mortgage myself from the beginning. Even though I was managing very well by myself the Halifax would not allow me to transfer the property into my sole name as they considered that I did not earn enough."
>
> She was surprised to discover that, had her first husband taken out a mortgage with the Halifax immediately after having his name removed from the joint mortgage, he would have been entitled to free shares.

When Mrs Russell wrote to challenge the decision, the Halifax replied that although the ruling did "produce winners and losers, there was no practicable alternative". However, Mrs Russell feels that this does not answer her question nor address her specific case. "I find it difficult to believe that the building society can just elect to treat borrowing members in an unequal way," she said. "This has made me feel very much like a second-class citizen."'

It's a very confusing form

The Halifax was caught between a rock and a hard place when it came to the design of the share allocation forms for its flotation. On the one hand the form needed to conform to certain regulations, while on the other it needed to be simple enough to be easily understood by investors, many of whom had never owned a share in their lives. Inevitably some complained. On 21 May 1997, the *Daily Express* under the headline, **Halifax forms spark fresh storm**, complained about the misleading nature of the share allocation forms,

'Investors are complaining that the document misled them into putting their shares into the Halifax's own accounts rather than opting for share certificates. To make matters worse, they have been told by the Society that it is now too late to get the errors corrected in time for the June 2 flotation.

Because they do not have a certificate, they will not be able to take advantage of the expected price surge by selling on the first day.

The problem came to light after an article in *The Sunday Express's* "Money" explaining how to fill in the Halifax share allocation forms, which have to be returned by May 26.

Following the article, *Express* "Money" was inundated by calls from readers complaining the complex forms had bamboozled them into making the wrong choice, causing them to miss the deadline.

Josephine Pollen, of Broadstairs in Kent, intended to request a certificate for her 200 shares, but inadvertently asked for them to be placed in the Halifax shareholder account. Shares in the account can only be sold by post, taking several days.

Pollen discovered her error on April 29 and asked the Halifax for a new form. However, it took three weeks to arrive, and with it was a printed form headed "Important Notice". This said "Unfortunately you will be unable to respond within the time scale set out in the accompanying letter". In other words, her form will not be processed by the May 26 deadline, so she will not be able to sell her shares on the first day of trading.

"I'm disappointed," Pollen says. "If the Halifax price goes up sharply in the first couple of days I may well want to sell. But I won't be able to if I haven't got the certificate.

"It is a very confusing form, particularly for novice investors. I'm annoyed it took so long for the Halifax to get me a replacement."

Financial experts accuse the Halifax of deliberately making the forms confusing to lock investors into its own single-company PEP or its shareholder account, a deposit account for shares.

Other PEP-providers, desperate to sell their products to the millions of new shareholders describe the Halifax forms as "nothing less than disgraceful". They believe many investors will not realise the error and will end up in the Halifax PEP by default.

The Halifax denies attempting to deceive investors, saying the forms are very straightforward and reassures investors who miss the deadline that they will get their share certificates once their applications have been processed.

A spokesman says: "There is no question of investors' wishes not being respected. People have three years to claim their shares, and even if they miss the deadline, certificates will be sent out within a few days."'

CHAPTER THIRTEEN

The advisers

Propitious advice
Our relationship was not deal-driven
Pulling clients by the nose
Some blue blood on the side

Propitious advice

In a flotation where almost every family in the land is affected, the necessity for the very best advice was easily understood. Furthermore, those chosen would be delighted at the honour. There would be many hours of work involved and the fees would also bring a warm glow to accompany the honour.

One of the problems all companies and institutions based outside London face in using London-based organisations is, for want of a better term, what we can call the capital complex. Because many, perhaps most, of the country's largest companies as well as Central Government and the head offices of all the charitable, cultural and advisory institutions are based in London, an attitude has unfortunately developed over the years among many Londoners that they are automatically superior to those who have the perceived misfortune to live and work elsewhere. It can take some a long time to realise that this superiority complex is misplaced. As we shall see, it was the cause of some friction in the march towards conversion.

In spite of its position as the incumbent company, Shandwick was still asked to make a presentation on how it would handle the run-up to conversion in early 1997 and, on 16 October 1995, the Shandwick team that would work on the Halifax account presented its case to the senior executives of the Halifax. As background, Shandwick pointed out that its clients included 50 of the largest companies in the country representing 10 per cent of total stock market capitalisation. It was involved in a flotation approximately once a quarter, including the recent flotation of Northern Ireland Electricity, which it felt to be of particular relevance as there had been a low understanding of privatisation in Northern Ireland with an unsophisticated investor base.

Shandwick saw the main challenge as delivering City and media endorsement with the main goal of achievement of a positive and convincing vote from the members in favour of conversion. Regarding the City and media, it advised that there was a small number of opinion-formers and it was essential to win them over. Halifax senior management would need to meet City editors as soon as possible. Regarding members, Shandwick advised against 'wall-to-wall' advertising or the members would charge them with wasting 'their money'. Most unsophisticated investors thought that companies controlled their own share price and some stock market education would be necessary. Early appointment of an Investment Relations Manager was advised and the thorny issue of directors' remuneration was raised with a view to having a clear explanation of the Society's policy.

And how did Shandwick find Halifax as a client in this mammoth task of conversion? Rachel Hirst, the Shandwick director responsible for the account, found those involved extremely responsive and decisive,

> 'The response was incredibly good. There was a mechanism whereby we had these twice weekly conference calls. There were very clear responsibilities ... They were a dream client from that point of view. They were incredibly decisive and there were very short lines of communication.'

And how did Halifax find Shandwick as an adviser in this critical period? The conclusion to the Communications – Media/Political section in the *Post Implementation Review* reflected the Halifax's satisfaction both with its internal team responsible and its external advisers.

> 'The Media/Political project broadly achieved its objectives. No catastrophes hit us and we did not have the degree of media criticism which was made of both the Abbey and the Cheltenham &

Gloucester at the time of their conversions. We have managed to maintain our reputation with the media.'

Corporate Affairs director, David Gilchrist, said,

'They were very good, both in the area of strategic advice and in the hard slog of agreeing press releases and question-and-answer briefings. They shared our view of problems, opportunities and solutions. We worked well together.'

The Halifax's legal adviser, Linklaters & Paines, had also given excellent service during the merger and was retained for the conversion. The firm is one of the largest law firms in the UK with a significant corporate practice and had been chosen to advise the society when it looked at the conversion option in 1988. A senior partner, Len Berkowitz, had led the Linklaters team at that time and, although there had only been a relatively low level of continuing relationship in the ensuing years, he had been the obvious choice for Mike Blackburn to telephone in May 1994 as talks with the Leeds got under way. Berkowitz had been assisted in 1988 by Andrew Peck, who subsequently advised the society on the establishment of *Halifax Life*, so Berkowitz brought him on to the team for the new project and he took over the major advisory role when Berkowitz retired from the firm and moved to the Bank of England as adviser to the Govrnor and head of the legal unit.

As we have seen, the various hurdles to be tackled during the merger – dealing with the Office of Fair Trading, the *Schedule 16* court case and the Building Societies Commission Confirmation hearings – had also been safely negotiated.

However, it is not only private individuals who become frustrated with lawyers, whom they tend to see as overpaid and unnecessarily adversarial. Business organisations also become impatient of their ways but perhaps for different reasons. The very act of starting a business is a positive one based on the participant's optimistic view of what he or she is going to achieve. Executives usually assume things will go well considering only the upside and ignoring the downside. Lawyers, on the other hand, have to deal with the downside. Very few of their clients ring them and congratulate them when a deal or a contract goes well. Almost all ring them for help when things go wrong. Furthermore, lawyers know who could receive the blame when matters do not turn out quite as well as hoped.

These different approaches can lead to friction as the lawyers insist on checking and re-checking, and taking the time to consider all the possibilities of any action. The *Post Implementation Review* reflected this dilemma perfectly.

Halifax said of Linklaters & Paines,

> 'Linklaters & Paines generally produced timely advice, although their definition of meeting a deadline of 5th June is 11 p.m. on 5th June! They were not ambiguous, they seldom changed their view and we have great confidence in their advice.'

However, some at Halifax felt that Linklaters put some of its own staff under too much pressure.

Advisers at Linklaters & Paines, in contrast with some of the other advisers, produced a comprehensive report when asked to contribute to the *Review*. Needless to say, their perspective of the conversion programme was different.

They also complained that they were asked to advise on topics where they had not been fully involved when they could have been.

However, in spite of these criticisms of some of each other's methods, Halifax was certainly happy with Linklaters & Paines – 'great confidence in their advice' – and the legal firm was fulsome in praise of their client,

> 'The Conversion Process was a project on a grand scale … The fact that conversion was delivered on time and with relatively low levels of complaint or errors testifies to the robustness of the project planning and the professional manner in which those plans were implemented both by project directors and those working for them.'

The auditor, KPMG, was, of course, closely involved in all the major aspects of the conversion process. As it happens, it had been auditors to both societies before the merger. Its role, as with all auditors, was slightly tricky in that, on the one hand the auditor is in place to advise its client and is appointed and paid by the client while on the other, it has a statutory duty to make sure the client handles financial matters in the correct way. Long gone are the days when the company chairman could do and say as he liked in this area and when his auditor stood up to protest at the AGM was told,

> 'Nay lad, sit down, tha's just the scorer.'

KPMG was the natural choice for skilled accounting support for the conversion. KPMG was the end-product of a merger during the 1980s of Peat Marwick International and the European firm, Klynveld Main Goerdeler. As auditors of several of the top banks, it had an extremely strong position in the sector.

Support for the conversion process ranged from high-level regulatory and technical advice to vote scrutineering, and KPMG had a major role in validating the 'de-duplication' of members' records and establishing the complex voting procedures needed for conversion. Through its work in reporting on Halifax systems of control, KPMG was also extensively involved in the key task of obtaining the banking license from the Bank of England.

As with Linklaters & Paines we would have to say that as everything passed through on time and with very few errors or complaints the accountants performed their task to everyone's satisfaction.

Would that life had been so simple when it came to choosing banking and broking advisers and working satisfactorily with them!

Our relationship was not deal-driven

The rise of S G Warburg was one of the great success stories of the City after 1945. Founded in 1946 by Siegmund Warburg, a refugee from Nazi Germany, by the early 1990s it was viewed by many as Britain's leading merchant bank. But Warburg had not found it easy. The City 'Establishment' of the 1940s and 1950s had despised him. In 1980, in a rare interview, he said,

> '"Do you know this fellow Siegmund Warburg? He starts in the office at eight in the morning." That was considered contemptible. Most of them came to the office at ten in the morning. I was awful. They looked down on me with the most awful snobbism.'

The turning point came in 1959 when Warburg advised Tube Investments (now TI) in its successful take-over of British Aluminium. In doing so Warburg defeated Hambros, Lazards and Morgan Grenfell, announced its presence and marked the 'beginning of the end of the old City ways' according to Lord Cairns, Warburg's deputy chairman in the early 1990s. After mergers with the jobbers Ackroyd and Smithers, brokers Rowe and Pitman and the Government broker, Mullens, at the time of Big

Bang in 1986, Warburg entered the 1990s as perhaps the most-respected merchant bank in the City.

The bank had advised Halifax during the merger negotiations with the Leeds, and all at Halifax agreed that the Warburg team led by Anthony Hotson had carried through an excellent job. Hotson's experience as private secretary to the Deputy Governor of the Bank of England and his secondment as Assistant Commissioner to the Building Societies Commission had proved especially relevant. Nevertheless, flotation was a different process from merger and Warburg was asked to make a presentation in a 'beauty parade' alongside Schroders and Deutsche Morgan Grenfell in the summer of 1995.

To general astonishment it was announced on 8 March 1996 that Halifax would not, after all, be using Warburg as its adviser during the flotation period nor indeed would it be employing Warburg's stockbroking division as its lead broker alongside Merrill Lynch. What had gone wrong?

In the merchant banking world, the early 1990s brought the same challenges and pressures that were affecting many other businesses. Globalisation was becoming increasingly prevalent and to compete, size was becoming more important. British merchant banks were too small and undercapitalised. This was starkly emphasised in March 1995 when Barings was swept away overnight by the activities of one rogue trader.

In their book, *All that Glitters – The Fall of Barings*, John Gapper and Nicholas Denton wrote that the then chairman of Schroders, George von Mallinckrodt, and his chief executive, Win Bischoff, speculated that the emergency call from the Bank of England (to discuss Barings' problems) might be because a large bank was in trouble and that they thought it might be Warburg. Warburg was not in trouble but it *had* just reported lower profits due to 'rough' financial markets and it had begun discussions with a number of other investment banks. In December 1994 it had announced a merger with the US investment bank Morgan Stanley. Unfortunately, before the marriage was consummated, the deal was called off with a Morgan Stanley director, Steve Waters, declaring, 'We only wanted Warburg for MAM.' [Mercury Asset Management.]

This was extremely harmful to Warburg. As Rachel Hirst said later, 'They were sort of left standing.'

In combination with the Barings collapse, this period of uncertainty led to a split between Mercury Asset Management and Warburg prior to Warburg accepting a take-over offer from Swiss Bank Corporation.

Clearly the old Warburg that its clients had known was now a different animal, and many clients watched with some trepidation to see what sort of animal it would be. *The Independent* said on 9 March 1996 under the headline, **Halifax sacks SBC Warburg as float adviser**,

> 'There have been expressions of concern elsewhere about the bank's approach to client relations, which are now much more product-driven, adopting SBC's American investment banking culture, rather than the relationship-style that made Warburg the envy of the City in its heyday. Halifax's decision follows the desertion of the bank by a long list of other clients, including Wessex Water which dropped Warburg as its financial adviser ahead of its bid for South West Water this week. In addition, Boots and P&O have recently replaced Warburg as their stockbroker.'

The real problem from Halifax's point of view seems to have been a loss of the close relationship at the top. No one was disputing the fact that the bank was doing an excellent job on a day-to-day basis. Mike Ellis, who was working closely with the Warburg team, said later, 'The team at Warburg were very good. There was no concern over them.'

However, chairman Jon Foulds had become increasingly worried by the changes at the top of Warburg, where a number of key contacts had left the bank or were removed from close contact with the Halifax. Of those involved in the 'beauty parade' of mid-1995, Nick Verey had been diagnosed as having leukaemia (sadly he has subsequently died), Anthony Brooke left Warburg to join BZW and, perhaps of most significance, Derek Higgs left Warburg to join the Prudential. As *The Daily Telegraph* put it rather succinctly,

> 'After 15 months of dealing with Higgs & Co., the Halifax has apparently decided that if it has to start explaining the process all over again, it may as well explain it to a new bank.'

The final straw as far as Foulds was concerned was Warburg's acting in a transaction involving another building society and, furthermore, not telling him for several weeks.

Although Foulds was reluctant to take the steps that would lead to the replacement of Warburgs, he knew that if he was going to make a change, it would have to be made without delay in order to give the new team at least a year in the saddle before flotation. He called a board meeting, put the facts before the directors and the result was a unanimous decision to make a change and Deutsche Morgan Grenfell was the choice.

Morgan Grenfell did not have long to celebrate its appointment before it needed to get to grips with the massive task in front of it. The bank had grown very rapidly in the 1980s and was acquired by the German bank, Deutsche Bank, as the globalisation in banking gathered pace. It had performed strongly again in the 1990s. By 1996 it employed 9000 people in 45 countries, spanning every aspect of investment banking. It took some time for the bank to realise that conversion was being handled from Halifax rather than its office but, in view of the limited time available to get to grips with such a massive flotation, Halifax accepted that it performed its role satisfactorily.

Pulling clients by the nose

On 18 October 1995, Jon Foulds had written to Merrill Lynch enquiring whether it would be interested in becoming joint broker to the Halifax in the forthcoming flotation planned for the early summer of 1997. Needless to say, the chairman, Christopher Reeves, replied that indeed Merrill Lynch would be interested and would present its 'credentials' on 15 November.

Reeves became chairman in 1993 and used his undoubted talents to help make Merrill Lynch the best choice to act as joint broker for the Halifax flotation and lead broker from March 1996.

The flotation was going to be unique, not only because of its size but also because initially virtually every shareholder would be a private individual, a voting member of the building society. Whoever was appointed broker would have the difficult task of satisfying individual shareholders who wanted to sell some or all of their shares, individual shareholders who wanted to retain their shares and, on the other hand, UK and international institutions who wanted to buy shares.

There were very few stockbrokers with the international strength to be able to satisfy these criteria. Merrill Lynch was one of them. Initially an exclusively US broking operation, Merrill Lynch expanded throughout the world in the 1980s and, in the 1990s, placed even more emphasis on its global spread. In its presentation to the Halifax in November 1995, it laid out its relevant experience and qualification for the task of handling the flotation.

It showed it had built up substantial experience in handling UK offerings with a major retail component. It had also gained considerable demutualisation experience through having acted as adviser to, and lead manager of, more demutualisations of financial institutions than any other organisation. It had handled 49 demutualisations since 1985 and had acted as lead manager of more than 25 per cent of all the conversions in the US. This experience in the US, which was substantially similar to the conversion process in the UK, made the bank feel it was qualified to help Halifax manage its conversion process in the most effective manner.

Philip Southwell, one of Merrill Lynch's corporate brokers, believed the firm was chosen as joint broker because of its position as the largest market maker in the UK with a market share in excess of 25 per cent, its strong US axis and, most importantly, its emphasis on retail business. He also felt that the broker's cause was helped by having Richard Coleman (who just happened to be a Yorkshireman!) as its banking analyst. Coleman was probably the most highly rated banking analyst in the City.

In spite of all its qualifications to handle the flotation, perhaps because of them, tensions arose between Merrill Lynch and the relevant team at Halifax. As we have seen, Halifax planned the merger and flotation meticulously with every angle and scenario considered. Merrill Lynch's approach was different. As one of the other advisers said,

> 'They would rather say to a client, "Just leave it to us", whereas the Halifax wants to plan everything. When it decided on the real price tender for the allocation of shares to institutions, Halifax wanted to talk it through but Merrill Lynch said, "Leave it to us, it's our job."'

We have already seen countless examples of Halifax's meticulous analysis of every problem and structured approach to finding the best solution and, above all, of its determination to be closely involved in every major decision. Roger Boyes was to say later,

> 'This meticulous approach caught the advisers by surprise, particularly the merchant banks, because merchant banks traditionally pull their clients by the nose. They drag you through the complex world of flotation. What the Halifax said was, "We don't need you to drag us by the nose. We are perfectly capable of organising

ourselves. What we want you to do, merchant bank, is to feed us with the technical stuff that we have to build in as well."'

At times, the Halifax became frustrated at the broker's approach. It wanted to be assured that members who sold through the proposed auction system would get the best price. In fact, after the Alliance & Leicester flotation where members could have received a much better price if they had sold in the market on the first day, it became a serious issue. The truth was, no one could guarantee what would happen to the price when the shares were traded on an open market, but it was felt to be essential that members received a fair price and that it should be carefully and logically explained to them. The *Post Implementation Review* highlighted again the Halifax's problem with some of its London-based advisers,

> 'Philosophically, it has always been the desire of Corporate Finance to manage our advisers rather than letting our advisers manage us. Advisers have an extremely important role to play in Corporate Finance activities, but they are merely advisers.'

Some blue blood on the side

When Halifax dispensed with SBC Warburg as its merchant banking adviser in March 1996, it also relieved the company of the post of lead broker to the flotation, and throughout the summer and autumn of 1996 made no move to ask anyone else to become joint broker with Merrill Lynch, now the lead broker. Nevertheless, it was always seen as a necessary step and in early November, Roger Boyes and Mike Ellis met Christopher Knight of Deutsche Morgan Grenfell and discussed the possibilities over dinner. Knight pointed out that while it was 'not essential for you to appoint a second broker, it would be desirable to do so'.

There were several reasons. It would provide improved service through competition, and increased depth and breadth of expertise, avoid the possibility of conflict of interest if only one broker was retained, especially if the client was acquisitive, and provide a wider range of institutional contacts and a different perspective on the market – particularly helpful in the context of fund raising or an acquisition. Boyes said,

'You've got to look at the size of the Halifax. We were attempting to get as big a spread as possible, as much influence in the market as we could. At the same time, you've got to listen to different points of view. Merrill Lynch could have a point of view and we wanted to be able to compare and contrast that point of view with somebody else.'

So much for the theory. The tricky task was to decide the firm. One possibility was to appoint several firms not formally as joint brokers, but as members of a small syndicate, along the lines of arrangements that were put in place for international equity offerings. This would broaden Halifax's approach to the market and allow it access to several firms before selecting one to act as joint broker.

In the end Cazenove *was* selected as joint broker. It had presented to Halifax at the same time as Merrill Lynch in autumn 1995 when the society was holding a 'beauty parade' to select its lead corporate broker. Halifax had not been particularly impressed by Cazenove's presentation and, at the time, Merrill Lynch and Warburg had been the preferred candidates. Perhaps Cazenove's heart was not in it. David Mayhew, a partner with Cazenove, said later,

'I was luke-warm about getting involved. I thought Halifax was a dull business.'

Compared with some of Mayhew's former clients, Halifax was perhaps a little dull. Certainly it had avoided the fast and apparently glamorous dealings that had characterised parts of the City in the 1980s.

Cazenove itself is a long-established stockbroker situated in Tokenhouse Yard, just behind the Bank of England, and had long been considered the most distinguished stockbroker in the City. In its original presentation to the Halifax it described itself as 'London's leading corporate stockbroker'.

Amid all the City mergers, alliances and acquisitions that took place at the time of the Big Bang in the autumn of 1986, Cazenove remained aloof and 'independent in the form of a partnership'. There were 65 partners and 850 staff based in 11 offices around the world as well as in Tokenhouse Yard. It already acted as broker to 51 of the FT-SE 100 companies. Cazenove prided itself in being different from the new integrated investment houses,

'We have not built our business around the marketing of proprietary or investment banking proposals to our clients. As a consequence of our extensive deal flow and daily experience of dealing with Stock Exchange matters, we are well placed to provide you with this information.'

Its experience in handling large privatisations and initial public offerings in the previous 15 years was second to none. It had acted as joint broker in the privatisation of British Aerospace, lead broker and distributor in the privatisation of BAA, British Airways, British Gas, Jaguar and Enterprise Oil, and joint broker in the privatisation of BT, Britoil, Cable and Wireless, National Power and Powergen and the UK Electricity Generators and Regional Electricity companies.

On 23 January 1997, Halifax confirmed Cazenove's appointment as joint broker. Rob Thomas, the building societies analyst at UBS, commented,

'Halifax already has the big international broker in Merrill Lynch. Perhaps it has chosen Cazenove to get a bit of blue blood on its side and escape its northern image.'

By early 1997, all the advisers were in place, and the scene was set for the biggest flotation the world had ever seen. Would anything go wrong?

CHAPTER FOURTEEN

At the front

Problems with the helplines
Shall I keep them or sell them?

Problems with the helplines

We have seen how the helpline system put in place by the Halifax was almost overwhelmed by the number of calls in December 1996, following the mailing designed to establish all the members' correct account details. In the branches the staff were also made aware of many members' frustration. Claire Wilson, a manager at Halifax's branch in the Strand in central London, said,

> 'The helplines weren't a help! A customer would come in and say, "We have been holding on for 30 minutes only to be told to go to our own branch." So they would be annoyed even as they came into the branch.
>
> I'm not sure, but I don't think the people on the helplines were Halifax staff. Someone 'phones up, they wait for 30 minutes and then they get a scripted answer. When they ask what that really means, they get the scripted answer again!
>
> And the staff helpline wasn't much better. If we had a customer we couldn't help, we'd ring our staff helpline and you'd be there with the 'phone, doing your work while it was singing whatever it was singing. That was frustrating for us so it must have been awful

for customers who, of course, thought they were paying for the call even though it was free.'

'Nightmare' was Kevin Wilson's word for the immediate aftermath to the mailing,

'"Nightmare" would be the word for that! I think you've probably got two things to say about it. The first thing is that right from Day One we never ever said that shares were going to be paid on merger, but everybody expected they were going to get shares straightaway. We kept getting remarks like, "When am I going to get my shares?"; "You're holding me to ransom and I can't take my money out"; and "You're going to have to lower interest rates". [Presumably this complaint came from savers rather than borrowers.]

However hard you tried to defend the position, and the competition took full advantage with advertisements saying, "The Halifax is keeping its interest rates lower because it's got you tied in", the criticism kept coming. Blatant lies were being put around here in Huddersfield.'

Shall I keep them or sell them?

The November/December 1996 mailing was designed to pick up queries, mistakes and problems and, in the final analysis, the percentage of accounts that needed correction was very small. The mailing was designed to clear up the mistakes and there were still six months to go before vesting day.

The mailing in April 1997 telling members how many shares they would receive and what to do if they wanted to sell or retain them was different. By this time members expected that their queries would have been sorted out and, *if they had raised them* after the November/December mailing, they should have been. As we have seen there were still a few, a very few, that had not been, but of course a whole new lot of queries arose from members who seemed not to have read any of the earlier mailings and who now, with money in the offing, at last started to take a detailed interest in their accounts.

As vesting day approached, the queries in the branches came not only from members who felt there was a mistake on their account or who felt disgruntled because in some way they had disqualified themselves, but also from people who wanted advice. The staff were told that they should not give financial advice but it could be difficult. As Claire Wilson in the Strand branch said,

> '"You can't say this, you can't say that" but what do you do when an 86 year old comes in and says, "Shall I keep them or sell them?"; you have to say, "Would you like money or shares?" and then he says, "What would you do, my dear?" It's very difficult.'

And of course, members wanted to know how much their shares would be worth and some were not happy with the answer, 'I'm afraid we can't tell you that. It depends on the state of the market at the time.'

One cause of many complaints was the failure of many members to realise that to qualify for shares, they needed to have at least £100 in their account on 24 November 1994 as well as on the date of the SGM, 24 February 1997 and on 31 December 1996. Although all the members were told of this condition some did not read the correspondence and failed to comply.

Of course, there were the funnies because many of the members, perhaps the majority, had never owned a share in their life. (Apparently a number of early BT shareholders thought that their first dividend cheque was their telephone bill and sent a cheque for the amount to BT.) One Halifax member in Walsall, when he was told he would be receiving shares worth around £3000 asked, 'When do you take the money from my account?'

Another said, 'I've sold my shares, but I've changed my mind. Can I have them back?'

The fact that those under 18 could not receive an allocation of shares caused widespread complaint in spite of the fact that they received a cash bonus. Even this problematic area had its funny moments. One cashier told a customer, 'Accounts in the name of a minor will receive a cash bonus', and was startled by the reply, 'But that's discrimination, I'm a welder!'.

Clearly some were enjoying the whole exercise. One woman took the proceeds of her sale in cash and then paid the money straight back in to her account. 'I just wanted to see it!'

In spite of all the publicity and letters to members, one told a cashier when asked to make her cheques payable to Halifax plc in future, 'Well, you haven't written to me telling me you're changing so how should I know?'

In spite of the extra work in the branches was there any real unhappiness? In Kevin Wilson's opinion there was not. When asked if he thought the bottle of champagne and £40 to spend on a night out which were given to all staff was adequate compensation, he said,

> 'Generally speaking, yes. It's a nice gesture added to the 200 free shares, the opportunity to join the Shareholder schemes and other staff benefits as a result of the conversion. And the Halifax staff mortgage scheme is better than the old Leeds scheme. I don't think staff have got anything to complain about over the last couple of years. The working week has been reduced from 37.5 to 35 hours. It has been exceedingly hard work but good things have come out of it. There was a nice bonus paid to everyone in March. From a staff point of view there haven't been too many problems. People have maintained a positive approach all the way through.'

As D-Day approached, Halifax took the precaution of monitoring carefully the Alliance & Leicester flotation, which took place on 21 April. Halifax staff in the branches were put on alert to observe activity in Alliance & Leicester branches in the days following its flotation and any contacts with Alliance & Leicester were used to pursue enquiries.

Paul Crump, manager in Temple Row, in Birmingham, studying his local Alliance & Leicester branch said,

> 'I noticed they had huge queues once the sale proceeds were in the accounts. They were queuing on the pavement past our branch. On 6 June, if the same percentage as at the Alliance & Leicester are sellers (27 per cent), that will mean over 2 million people nationwide. Friday 6 June is fixed in my mind because I know we're going to be in a similar position. People will be queuing to draw their money out, close their account or have their passbook made up to date and, if it's anything like next door, a lot of people will close their accounts. They will have their shares, thank you very much, and they'll be off!'

As a result of these observations, instructions were given to Halifax branches that all counters should be fully manned where necessary.

'There will inevitably be queues within our branches, but the customers will generally accept this if they can see that every effort is being made to deal with the queue.'

Halifax also advised customers in its mailings of the anticipated increased traffic and told them about extended opening hours.

Clearly, there would be a need for extra cash in the branches, which caused the Halifax to plan daily cash deliveries, if necessary, to every outlet. The £600 limit that each customer could withdraw per day was to be retained, although managers were given authority to be flexible. The objective was to avoid customer irritation, anecdotal evidence of which had been reported from the Alliance & Leicester flotation.

There would be security implications of extra cash in the branches, and with all the attendant publicity, those with criminal intentions would be well aware of the possibilities. Branch premises were already protected by security equipment and staff were fully trained in procedures to be followed in the event of a raid. The use of extra security guards was considered but rejected on the grounds that it would not only highlight the presence of extra cash but also possibly confuse existing staff as to whether they should follow established procedures.

In spite of the increased workload, staff at the branches were coping admirably. John Lee, ultimately responsible for their welfare, said later,

'It's been massive, but people have delivered, without any angst. If there's any concern around it's driven by "Is the organisation helping us to do this, can we deliver this properly?" and not "Bloody hell, what are they doing this for, why are they breaking our backs?". They are saying, "We're Halifax and we want to do it properly" and they have.'

CHAPTER FIFTEEN

The great day is coming

Consumerism is back

In desperate straits

Going public the right way

Be part of something big

The nap for 1997

An orderly market

A market crash?

Joy for millions

1.9 million sellers on Day One

Consumerism is back

The major economies of the world rarely operate in synchronisation. As the business cycle waxes and wanes, the USA, Japan, Europe and the UK are usually slightly out of step with each other. However, in early 1997, virtually the whole world was enjoying economic growth. In January, the Organisation for Economic Co-operation and Development (OECD) predicted that, for the first time since 1985, all its 29 member countries would enjoy GDP growth in 1997. Furthermore, it predicted that the economies of developing countries and Russia and Eastern Europe would also grow as well.

And if the whole world was growing, Britain itself was beginning to grow at a pace many economists believed was unsustainable. All the signs of a gathering consumer boom were in place by the end of 1996. Retail sales grew at 3.9 per cent in the year, unemployment fell to under 2 million for the first time since 1991, and house prices rose by an average 7 per cent between the fourth quarter of 1995 and 1996. Most were predicting even faster rises for 1997. Certainly the talk of late 1995 that inflation was dead and house prices would never rise sharply again seemed a distant memory.

But was another housing boom getting under way? Had the British learned the lesson of the 1980s boom and the early 1990s bust? The bust had certainly been nasty enough. Nominal house prices fell in 1990 for the first time in twenty years and fell again in each of the following three years. In real terms they fell every year from 1990 until 1995. The fall in nominal terms pushed many people into negative equity, in 1993 no fewer than 1.7 million households. Between 1990 and 1996 almost 400,000 houses were repossessed. However, many 'experts' believed that the lessons would not be learned. When prices are rising it is difficult as an individual to take the stand – 'I'm learning the lesson of history and not buying'.

Sam Smith, *Daily Express* 5 March 1997

By early 1997 there was no doubt about the improved financial position of most of the country's population, especially those who had borrowed most in the 1980s and had therefore suffered most in the early 1990s. By the time of the General Election on 1 May, it was clear that the 'feel-good' factor, which the Conservative Government had worked so hard to engender, had returned. It did not help the Conservatives on Election Day but it was certainly fuelling consumer spending, and the windfalls enjoyed by members of the Alliance & Leicester, which floated on the stock market in April, Norwich Union and Woolwich, due to float with the Halifax itself in June, would fuel it further. As *The Economist* put it,

'Suddenly, consumerism is back in fashion. Forget all that guff about the nervous, financially prudent 1990s. The British are feeling flush

HERE are ten ways to spend £1,500:

① Trendy Tamagotchi cyberpet toys cost £14 so you could get 107.

② Pay off 3¼ months of an average £60,000 home loan.

③ A family of four can have a holiday in Los Naranjos, Menorca.

④ Put enough money aside to cover the gas bill — for five years.

⑤ Try an à la carte meal for 24 at London's Savoy — or 815 Big Macs.

⑥ Buy four season tickets at Southampton FC costing £360 each.

⑦ Have a night out for 12 at the Royal Opera House in posh box seats.

⑧ New motor? How about a 1992 J-Reg Seat Marbella 900.

⑨ Sweet tooth? Buy 605lb of Pick 'n Mix from Woolies at £2.48 a pound.

⑩ Open another building society account — you might land another windfall.

The Sun prior to flotation

with cash again, and ready to use it. This week's flotation of the Halifax … provided ample evidence of the new up-beat mood.

Over a quarter of the 7.6 million Halifax savers and borrowers who received shares worth on average £2200, traded them for cash at the first opportunity. *The Sun* newspaper helpfully listed ten ways to "spend the dosh".

In May the consumer confidence index jumped by seven percentage points to its highest level since 1988 – the last time consumers went on a spending spree.'

The recipients of the windfalls could leave the economists to worry about the adverse effects. They had only to decide how to spend their money or indeed whether to spend it all rather than save it instead.

According to a report from the Henley Centre after the Alliance & Leicester flotation, 50 per cent of the recipients saved the money, but of those anticipating windfalls, only 42 per cent expected to save them. Maeve Geraghty, an associate director of the financial services practice at the Henley Centre said,

> 'What is interesting is that of those who had received their windfalls, a lot had saved them, but of those who anticipated getting them, the percentage of

Financial Times prior to flotation

those intending to save has dropped. Holidays and home improvements have particularly done well ... the majority were anticipating treating themselves.'

In desperate straits

When, in late November 1994, the Halifax and Leeds committed themselves to merger and subsequent conversion, it was always likely that the next General Election would have to be considered as a factor in the actual timing of flotation. At the time, the Labour Party was enjoying a 20 per cent lead in the polls and most people felt certain that it would win the next Election.

A Labour Government, traditionally the friend of the workers and enemy of business, was considered to be harmful to the stock market. At the very least, it was expected that an Election would produce a period of caution and possibly a sharp decline in prices. For example, in 1992, fear of a hung Parliament, or worse in the eyes of the market, a Labour victory, knocked 6 per cent off share prices in the month before polling day. It was impossible to predict the timing of the Election.

Roger Beale, *Financial Times*
26 February 1997

In theory the final date when one had to be held was June 1997, but only governments in desperate straits hold on until the last minute and in practice the likely date was the autumn of 1996. The task of preparation for the flotation was so enormous that Halifax decided second-guessing the Government was a waste of time and that it had better get on with flotation and let the politicians worry about the timing of the Election. It became clear that the summer of 1997 was the earliest that the society could be ready for flotation. It also became clear to the Conservative Party that it was in desperate straits – Labour's lead in the polls remained stubbornly around 20 per cent – and that it would cling to power until the last minute, which was also the summer of 1997.

However, the importance of this political influence on the timing of the flotation diminished as New Labour went out of its way to reassure

239

the City, big business and the middle classes that New Labour was their friend. Enterprise and wealth creation would be encouraged, taxes would not be raised and the unions would be kept in check. The stock market, by now convinced along with everyone else that Labour would win the Election, did not take fright. Halifax could plan vesting day according to its own timetable and not worry about the Election. A Gallup poll of City fund managers, published on 14 April 1997, showed that 60 per cent thought shares would be unaffected by the Election result.

Going public the right way

Everyone was moving steadily towards 'conversion' but someone needed to decide on a specific scheme. What would be the actual method used whereby members would receive shares and the society would become a public limited company with its shares traded on the London Stock Exchange?

Once it had been decided to adopt a share allocation scheme with both a *basic* and a *variable distribution* and one in which the majority of the free shares would be applied towards the *basic distribution*, Halifax needed to decide the nominal price of the shares, the number for *basic distribution* and the scale for the *variable distribution*. It was essentially a mathematical calculation.

Assuming that Halifax would have net assets of approximately £7.25 billion on vesting day and that the number of members receiving shares was 8.26 million with 200 shares going to members as the *basic distribution*, the distribution would be worth about £860 if the shares traded at £4.30, which was 1.5 times net assets.

The recommendation put to the board was that the *basic distribution* comprise 200 shares and that the *variable distribution* comprise two shares per £100 balance with the previously agreed cut-off point at £50,000.

Be part of something big

Just as Special General Meetings had been called in 1995 to approve the merger of the Halifax and Leeds, an SGM was also called in February 1997 to approve the Halifax's conversion to a public limited company (plc). Whereas the previous SGMs had been held locally, in Halifax and Leeds, this one was held in the much grander setting of the Sheffield

Arena, scene of the Labour Party rally a week before the 1992 General Election, which was seen by some in retrospect as triumphalist and thereby a factor in Labour's failing to win in that Election. By this time, few doubted that the members would agree to conversion but you will remember Halifax had increased the number needed to vote in favour by changing its method of converting.

Even before the Halifax had made the decision to use the 'existing company route', thereby introducing the need for 50 per cent of the investing members to vote in favour, Mike Blackburn had set an 'emotional' target of achieving such a vote.

In round numbers the Halifax would need 3.35 million votes in favour but given the possible votes against and adding a comfort margin the society set itself a target of 5 million. Such a voting response was unprecedented in building society history, and, although Halifax was somewhat reassured by turnouts of 70 per cent and more in other conversion and acquisition votes, it felt that a major press, television and campaign was necessary.

From Christmas 1996 into early 1997 it ran the heaviest promotional campaign the society had ever undertaken. To contrast with the verbose and ponderous Transfer Document, the campaign, *Be part of something big*, was light-hearted and humorous and appeared to be well received. And, more importantly, it worked. By the end of January, 5.7 million voting forms were received and by the final deadline in mid-February, 6.7 million, 78 per cent of those eligible. This meant a massive vote-counting operation. The votes went initially to two mail-handling companies before being transferred to the Normanton Data Centre where staff from KPMG used computerised

The Guardian January 1997

scanning equipment to read each form. Teams worked up to 18 hours a day, 7 days a week, during the 30-day proxy voting period, processing up to 400,000 forms a day. All were counted in plenty of time for the SGM.

Of the 8 million members about 1100 came to the meeting. The vast majority sent their votes by post. The votes of those present would not be taken until the end of the meeting when the results of the postal vote would also be announced. In the meantime, those present could ask questions or, as our old friend, Serge Lourie, established with Jon Foulds who was chairman of the meeting, make a speech.

> **Lourie:** Would you please rule whether it is permissible for people to make speeches on this issue?

> **Foulds:** Yes it is admissible; I find the word speech slightly formidable and I can imagine us all being here until midnight if everyone makes a speech. Please keep it short.

Lourie himself was the first to make a speech and repeated his arguments in favour of mutuality and reminded everyone that Jon Foulds himself had said in the Halifax Annual Report in 1994,

> 'Our ability to maintain healthy reserves is helped by the fact that building societies unlike public companies do not have shareholders to whom they pay dividends.'

Foulds did not answer Lourie's points because, he said,

> 'I could detect that what you said had echoes of interest round the room [there had been constant applause and some cheering for Lourie's points] and I have no doubt that we are going to come back to some of the points.'

And indeed the point about the benefits of mutuality was raised again, by a Marilyn Johnstone,

> 'I have yet to be convinced that your move is actually going to generate the long-term improved rates compared with other building societies who intend to stay mutual.'

Foulds replied,

> 'I think the kernel of my answer is really competition. Some of our fiercest competitors, and this is a fiercely competitive marketplace, are already plcs and they do have the obligation to pay dividends.

242

So the fact that the organisation will assume the responsibility of paying dividends does not mean that it will be less competitive either in terms of the rates which it offers to savers or which it charges to borrowers ... The key to our future success is our ability to meet our customers' future expectations and I suggest to you that it's right that profits should be shared and not just accumulated.'

Foulds also pointed out that members with shares would receive an additional source of income through dividends and Mike Blackburn, answering another question, argued that as the Halifax expanded into more risky areas capital provided by equity shareholders was more appropriate than reserves effectively owned by members of a mutual society.

Graham Allen, *Daily Express* 4 June 1997

One of the most erudite speakers was a Jacob Ziegel who had flown all the way from Toronto in Canada to complain about his exclusion from the share distribution because he lived in Canada. Blackburn explained that it had proved extremely difficult to obtain a speedy reply from financial regulators in a number of countries and that residents in those countries had therefore been excluded. He pointed out that it was possible for such people to register an address in the UK.

The questions and speeches continued, some to the point, some not, some amusing, some not, until Peter Judge, Lourie's old sparring partner, came to the podium and adopted his usual aggressive tone using pejorative words and phrases such as, 'engineering a cheap sell-off of our asset'; 'haven't ruled out nice fat bonuses, fairy-tale salaries'; and 'I think that is despicable'.

After a long ramble about the iniquities of privatisation in general and this Halifax 'privatisation' in particular, Foulds felt obliged to ask if he was going to put a question. The two bandied back and forth until Judge gambled by asking the audience to applaud if they wished to hear him further.

There was some applause, but Foulds effectively called his bluff by asking the audience to clap if they wished Foulds to cut Judge off if he went on too long. This brought a much louder applause.

After more questions and speeches, many of them critical of the idea of conversion, the former chief executive, John Spalding, came to the podium and in a quiet, thoughtful but authoritative manner, supported the resolution to convert,

> 'One reason today why I am incredibly glad to have retired, is that I did not have to get involved in a distribution of shares scheme. It is not a thing which I think can satisfy all the members ... if you satisfy one group you will dissatisfy another, and I honestly think that the scheme you have produced ... is one which is fair and as reasonable as you could have achieved.'

He reminded his audience that the committee on which he was chairman, the Spalding Committee, had made recommendations that the powers of the building societies should be increased to enable them to compete with the banks. Those recommendations had been enshrined in the 1986 Building Societies Act, which itself had opened the way for conversion. He concluded to considerable applause,

> 'I say it with the greatest regret and I have the greatest sympathy with those speeches that have been made in favour of retaining mutuality, but I am quite clear in my mind the day of the great mutual national building society is over. Its days are not just numbered, they are over and there is no alternative that I can see to conversion. I, therefore, support the motion.'

After a few more questions and answers Foulds called a halt, with some protest from those who had not put their questions, and a vote was taken. For the record the results were as follows.

- Around 6.82 million voted by proxy and approximately 1100 attended the meeting.

- Of the 6,960,000 eligible investing members, 5,150,000 voted in favour of the resolution to convert while 110,000 voted against. Of those who voted, 97 per cent were in favour and those in favour represented 73 per cent of those eligible to vote.

- Of the 2,290,000 eligible borrowing members, 1,520,000 voted in favour and 40,000 against. Again, of those who voted, 97 per cent were in favour and those in favour represented 66 per cent of those eligible to vote.

As a result, the votes received substantially exceeded the 50 per cent of all investing members necessary for the resolution to convert to be approved and it also passed the 75 per cent of all investing members who voted. For borrowing members a simple majority was required.

The nap for 1997

As the two and a half years between the announcement of conversion in November 1994 and actual flotation in June 1997 progressed, the two questions that members asked Halifax more than any other were 'When?' and 'How much?'.

By January 1997 they knew the answer to 'When?' but they still did not know exactly 'How much?'. By then, of course, the personal finance sections of the press were beginning to make predictions, and members also knew how many shares they were going to receive. The likely price of each share when they were floated on the stock market in June became clear in January 1997. Halifax's financial advisers thought the price would be between 390p and 450p. This meant that the minimum allocation of 200 shares would be worth £780 to £900.

The average allocation would probably bring a benefit of around £1300, a somewhat higher figure than the one that the press had been bandying around for the previous two years. At this price most financial commentators thought the shares would be a bargain and encouraged members to retain their shares rather than sell them. For example, Melvyn Marckus in *The Sunday Express* described the Halifax as 'the nap for 1997'. He, like every other financial commentator, knew that the Halifax was so big it would be in the top quartile of the FT-SE 100 index and that every fund manager would have to buy some. He rather rashly gave the Halifax *at its closing quote on the first day's trading* as his nap of the year.

During the spring of 1997 a virtuous circle, at least as far as Halifax members were concerned, began to form. The British economy continued to grow steadily without any apparent signs of rising inflation. The US economy was certainly performing well and prices on Wall Street continued to surge ahead. This encouraged the London stock market in spite of the uncertainties of the forthcoming General Election and the increasing number of profit warnings being issued by companies affected by the growing appreciation of the pound. It appreciated by nearly 40 per cent against the Deutschmark between the summer of 1996 and the late spring of 1997, imposing a severe profit squeeze on British exporters as well as on companies with large overseas interests. At the same time, bank shares, unaffected by worries about the pound, began to outperform the rest of the market and within the banking sector the only converted building society, the Abbey National, performed exceptionally well. This led to increased expectations for the opening price of Alliance & Leicester, due to float in late April, and for the Halifax. This led to further purchases of banking and Abbey National shares by institutions concerned about their weighting in banking shares, which led to increased expectations for Alliance & Leicester and Halifax and so on, and so on. By May 1997, even before the Halifax boosted the sector further, the market capitalisation of the banking sector overtook that of the whole of what are termed 'general industrials', effectively the whole manufacturing economy. Three years earlier it had been valued at only half of the producing sector.

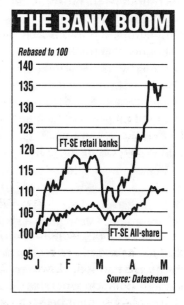

THE BANK BOOM

Rebased to 100

FT-SE retail banks

FT-SE All-share

J F M A M

Source: Datastream

While this background activity was taking place, Halifax pressed on preparing both itself and its members for life as a public company. In the middle of April 1997, it sent every member eligible to receive free shares a booklet called *What shares are about*, which gave basic information about the London Stock Exchange and how shares could be bought and sold. The booklet had been prepared in conjunction with the Stock Exchange and Proshare, the organisation set up to encourage the individual ownership of shares.

At the same time, Halifax announced the launch of the Halifax Shareholder Account. This was designed as a 'convenient and secure way for members to hold their Halifax shares after conversion'. The Halifax Share Account would 'make the holding of shares as easy to manage as having a savings account'. It would also be free of charge for at least three years. Significantly, it would enable customers to buy, sell and hold shares without having to keep a share certificate thereby reducing costs and eliminating all the inconvenience when a certificate was lost. However, customers would be sent regular statements to enable them to check their holdings, purchases and sales. Customers would also have access, initially exclusively, to the Halifax Share Dealing Service, which would provide a quick and low-cost method of buying and selling Halifax shares. Although the service would only deal in Halifax shares initially, it was planned to extend the service to other shares.

For ten days after vesting day, members would be able to sell their shares free through the Halifax Share Dealing Service. Thereafter, costs would be highly competitive at 0.5 per cent (most stock brokers charge 1.95 per cent to private clients) and a minimum charge of £7.50.

Halifax wanted as many members as possible to opt for the Shareholder Account in order to reduce the administration in dealing with certificates and it gave those who chose such a route virtually all the rights of certificated members including the right to an annual report and to vote at the annual general meeting.

And, of course, Halifax set up a Halifax Share PEP in the form of a single company PEP investing solely in Halifax plc ordinary shares. Although it provided a tax-free environment for the holding of Halifax shares, the society made it clear it was really only of interest to higher rate taxpayers or those likely to have to pay capital gains tax.

An orderly market

Most of Halifax's work on the conversion process was aimed at ensuring that all its members received the correct number of shares to which they were entitled. However, the society needed to work also towards a smooth flotation whereby the financial institutions could purchase the shares of those members who wished to sell their shares. The institutions would not receive any of the free allocation and, as all shares initially would be allocated to members, nor could they apply for any. If they wanted shares they would have to buy them in the market. The potential for volatility, not to say chaos, as well as considerable cost, was obvious and a method was devised to ensure a more 'orderly' market.

In June 1996 Merrill Lynch, the lead broker, presented a document called *The Offering Process*. The document outlined the four main objectives which were: to maximise the value for selling members, offer a fair and workable choice for members with a simple and easily understood mechanism, initiate the building of a long-term institutional shareholder base, and minimise the risk of a price spike and volatility.

As Merrill Lynch pointed out, the four objectives were self-reinforcing. If members thought they were receiving a fair price they would be more likely to sell ensuring that demand would not completely outstrip supply. It was clearly vital to create institutional demand in order to accommodate members wishing to sell.

There were three main types of financial institution – the tracker or passive funds, the active funds and the overseas investors. There would also be some demand from individual investors.

The normal approach to measuring and satisfying demand for a large new issue had been what was called 'the bookbuild'. It had been used in all UK privatisations over the previous four years, in nearly every international IPO, and was becoming increasingly popular in every UK new issue with appeal for overseas investors such as BSkyB and Orange.

As part of the bookbuild process, the four key board members, Jon Foulds, Mike Blackburn, Gren Folwell and Roger Boyes, undertook a roadshow accompanied by investor relations manager, Charles Wycks. For five solid weeks, from Monday 28 April until Friday 30 May, they presented the merits of Halifax past, present and future, to institution after institution, mostly to those based in London but also to others in Edinburgh, Glasgow, Paris, Frankfurt, Geneva, Zurich, Eindhoven, Rotterdam, The Hague, Madrid and Dublin.

The roadshow team emphasised the Halifax's capital strength and the fact that it enjoyed the strongest credit rating of any UK financial services institution and was now of a size to remain a winning player within a consolidating financial services industry. Within that industry its customer franchise was second to none, and in mortgages and savings it was a focused market leader. They showed the institutions that the Halifax had moved decisively into the growth field of retail banking and consumer credit as well as personal lines insurance and long-term savings. It was a low-cost producer and distributor with a high quality earnings stream. Its management had a first-class record of delivering a consistent stream of growing earnings and was now widely experienced both within and outside the industry. The smooth integration of the Leeds had demonstrated its acquisition skills.

The method chosen for allocation to institutions was a competitive real-price auction. This meant that shares would be sold to the institutions that offered to pay the highest prices and that they would pay the price at which they bid and the proceeds would be passed on to the members in full. Members would receive the weighted average of the price bid by institutions. The initial auction would close on the Friday night before conversion for the shares of the members who decided to sell immediately and whose sale forms were received by the Halifax the previous Monday, 26 May. For those whose sales forms were received after that date up to and including conversion day, their shares would be sold on the first day of dealings and again would be sold to the institutions offering the highest prices.

A market crash?

It seemed extremely unlikely in view of the strength of the stock market generally and of the banking sector in particular, but it was possible, that some serious event would occur and that the conversion process would be placed in jeopardy. There was, after all, an unhappy precedent that had occurred less than ten years earlier when the stock market crash of October 1987 had thrown the selling of a Government holding in BP into chaos and the Government had been forced to guarantee a minimum price to share applicants.

In the booklet *Your Share Allocation Guide*, members were told that instructions to sell would not be activated if the price fell below the 415p level published in the press on 28 April.

As it happened, later in 1997 there were some wild gyrations on the stock market as the financial problems in the Far East began to have an impact on markets in the USA and Europe. On Tuesday, 28 October, the *Financial Times* 100 Share Index fell by over 450 points in the morning before recovering in the afternoon. Such conditions would have provided a very difficult environment for the Halifax flotation and the mind boggles as to what would have happened if the Halifax price on vesting day had been 416p, just above the no-sell level, only to move up sharply in the following few days.

Joy for millions

In the event, 23 per cent of members' shares were offered for sale in the post by Monday 26 May, a total of 568,641,878 shares. (This was not as high as the 27 per cent of Alliance & Leicester shares but was still higher than many estimates. Indeed, Merrill Lynch had predicted in 1996 that only 10 per cent of members would sell on vesting day.)

This huge block of shares satisfied all the institutional bids down to a price of 711p, itself a price way above estimates of only a few weeks earlier. The weighted average was 732.5p. Some institutions had bid as high as 815p. Melvyn Marckus, who, you will remember, had given the opening price as his nap of the year back in January now referred to it as a tongue-in-cheek exercise. His view now was,

> 'Those who wish to purchase stock at upwards of 700p should only do so with long-term investment in mind.'

The Daily Telegraph, constantly a critic of the Halifax demutualisation, had still been carping in October 1996. When it was announced that Halifax would forego protection from take-over *The Telegraph* wrote,

> 'Yet, while the Halifax may be the big cheese of the building societies, by the standards of banks today it is small beer. Just as significantly, it is looking distinctly peaky as its merger-and-float programme grinds on. Abbey National, which is about the same size, is valued by the market at £8 billion. That may add up to nearly £1000 per head for the Halifax's current owners, but Lloyds Bank is now valued at £20 billion. It could have the Halifax for lunch.'

When Halifax floated, far from looking 'distinctly peaky' at a capitalisation of £8 billion, it was capitalised at the opening price of 774.5p at about £19 billion. No one, and certainly not another British bank, was having that for lunch.

Its sister paper, the *Sunday Telegraph*, seemed to have a better grasp of where Halifax would be positioned.

> 'The company sees itself as a retailer of financial products but shows a clean pair of heels to the big retailers such as Sainsbury's (capitalisation £6.5 billion), Tesco (£8.2 billion) and even Marks

and Spencer (£14.5 billion). Among banks, it is neck and neck with Barclays and only HSBC and Lloyds TSB are more highly valued.'

Finally, after two and a half years of grind and slog and meetings and long evenings and ruined week-ends, the great day arrived,

Monday, 2 June 1997 – Vesting Day
Halifax Building Society is dead
Long live Halifax plc

And there were no last-minute hitches. The market did not collapse – though the Footsie did fall sharply on the previous Friday, especially the banking sector. And the shares opened at 774.5p, a priced undreamt of only a few weeks earlier. The media were full of praise. The *Financial Times* said,

'Halifax is a fine institution with handsome prospects.'

The Guardian liked its management,

'The Halifax is notably more impressively managed than some of the clearers.'

The *Daily Express* noted the huge extension to private share ownership,

'More members became private sharholders at 8.30 a.m. yesterday than the Tories managed to create in more than a decade of government privatisations.'

The Independent was full of praise for the method of coming to the market,

'That pays tribute to a process that achieved much better value for Halifax members than the Alliance & Leicester early sellers achieved.'

This was all a bit tame for *The Sun* which shouted,

HALI-FATCATS
Joy for millions as bank shares payout soars past £2500.

The headline of its sister paper, *The Times*, seemed designed to give the opposite impression,

'Debut drop for Halifax as members take windfall.'

The Times was technically right in that the shares opened at 774.5p and closed at 734p, remarkably close to the 732.5p that the 23 per cent of original sellers would receive from the previous Friday's auction.

'Now – I suppose you're going to do something really sensible with the Halifax money.'
Daily Star 3 June 1997

Some thought the price far too high. David Pontney, banking analyst at stockbroker, Panmure Gordon, said,

'This is midsummer madness. Though I would advise paying up to 700 pence a share, there are a lot of large sheep in the market willing to pay over the top. This is a guaranteed way of losing money in the medium term.'

Richard Coleman, Merrill Lynch's highly rated banking analyst, was more circumspect,

'The sector has taken a good beating in the past week or so, but my view at the moment is with interim results coming up soon, we're going to see some upgrades, and the sector is still well under-pinned.'

1.9 million sellers on Day One

As we have seen, Halifax had decided that it must have its own share-dealing service and had invested a great deal of money and effort into making sure Halifax Share Dealing Limited (HSDL) was up to the standard of the rest of the organisation.

Everything about the Halifax conversion was big. As the chairman put it,

'All the numbers are *Guinness Book of Records* stuff!'

And the Halifax Share Dealing operation was not likely to be any different. When it was planned, Halifax had no idea what the volume of share transactions would be or how many members/shareholders would want to buy and sell Halifax shares in the first days of trading. But they did know that there would be around eight million shareholders.

The aims of the service Halifax would give were set out as:

- simple to use
- inexpensive
- easy to understand
- branded Halifax
- capable of further development
- configured to meet regulatory and agreed internal standards
- communicated to all target audiences and efficient in retaining customers and facilitating the return of share sale proceeds to the Group

One of the key tasks was to recruit a manager with experience of share dealing and the person chosen was Sue Concannon, who had been the business development director of the successful Sharelink, the first telephone-based, execution only, share-dealing service and the company that set the pace for every other similar operation.

When she arrived in Leeds (Halifax Share Dealing Limited is based in a former Vickers tank factory in the centre of Leeds) on 20 January 1997, Concannon found that,

'A lot of the planning work had already been done, some of the office established and some of the management team recruited. The

253

budget had been ready for a year and most of the software delivered so we were just into testing it and making sure everything worked.'

But, of course, not just anyone can start up a share-dealing service.

'To conduct share dealings, the company had to be regulated according to the Financial Services Act. We needed to be regulated by the Securities and Futures Authority and there were various stages of membership we needed to go through. The Securities and Futures Authority, KPMG and our auditors were looking over our shoulders for months and, after many stages, we reached our regulatory sign-off only two weeks before Vesting Day. It was a little bit tighter than we would have liked but the wheels take some time to go round.'

The time in the months leading up to Vesting Day was spent working with the registrars selected by Halifax, Royal Bank of Scotland, and the brokers, Merrill Lynch and Cazenove. Concannon remembered it was,

'Testing, testing all the systems to make sure they worked, end-to-end testing of everything from cutting the database for those members who were eligible, sending that off to Royal Bank of Scotland and producing the allocation warning, or the dummy allocation warning, and pretending to send that out and filling in forms, sending them back to RBS so that they could practise all these things and we could practise our bit, and Merrill Lynch and Cazenove could practise their bit.'

HSDL was sharing a building with Halifax Direct and it used the sophisticated telecommunications structure that had been installed for that part of the organisation. As HSDL needed to record every telephone call, Halifax Direct helped it to set up the system.

Recording every telephone call was not a Stock Exchange or SFA requirement but virtually every share-dealing operation used such a system. Sue Concannon explained the reason,

'You can monitor what's been said to clients and if there's a dispute about a deal, where maybe a customer said, "I told you to buy a 100 and you bought a 1000" and the price has gone west since, we can actually listen to the recording and say, "No, you did say 1000 and we can read it back to you or we can send you a recording if you like." It means we can settle any disputes like that very quickly.'

How did it all go on Vesting Day and in the first 10 days?

As with all numbers to do with the Halifax flotation they tested the capacity to think of them in real terms.

There were 1,910,165 sellers on Vesting Day involving 568,641,878 shares at an average price of £7.32521349. The share price was stable with the closing price around £7.35. More than 20 per cent of shareholders – that is more than 1.5 million members – requested share certificates and these were despatched, as well as opening nominee statements, within 10 days.

Some £3.52 billion was credited to 1,497,656 customer accounts and £646 million of cheques were issued.

And it was not just the members who might have found all these numbers difficult to cope with. Bank note suppliers struggled to provide the £1 billion in CASH that Halifax required for its branches on the Friday after Vesting Day. It wanted all the money to be in £50 notes until it was pointed out that many Halifax members were not used to buying papers and milk with £50 notes!

CHAPTER SIXTEEN

A tidal wave of change

Well recognised for good standards
Further consolidation
Banking is no passing fad
Rifle instead of shotgun

Well recognised for good standards

O n top of all the activity and workload involved in consolidating the Leeds merger and preparing for conversion, Halifax acquired Clerical Medical or, to give it its full title, Clerical, Medical and General Life Assurance Society.

Founded in 1824, Clerical Medical had prospered steadily and by the early 1990s employed 2500 staff with assets under management of £15 billion. In early 1995 the decision was taken to demutualise. As Robert Walther, the chief executive, put it,

> 'The reason for our decision to demutualise was the need for capital. We felt our investment policy was becoming steadily more constrained by this lack of capital and we were having to invest more in fixed interest and less in equities which would eventually be to the disadvantage of our policy holders.'

Clerical Medical chose the route of selling itself to another financial institution and after drawing up a very long list of possibilities narrowed it down to about 15 by the summer of 1995. Halifax was one of the 15 and Walther met Mike Blackburn and James Crosby at the end of August.

During the autumn the Clerical Medical board decided that a full tender process would be the best way forward and six institutions known to be interested were asked to bid.

A number of stakeholder interests had to be considered. Walther summed it up,

> 'The board took the view, very strongly, that they had to look after the interests of the policy holders and therefore they must accept the most generous financial terms for the policy holders. On the other hand, from a management point of view, I was very concerned that all stakeholders should benefit from the transaction.'

The management favoured the Halifax because they could see that *Halifax Life* outsourced the vast majority of its operations and that the level of integration and redundancies would be lower than would be the case with most of the other bidders. Fortunately, Halifax also offered the best financial terms.

Terms were agreed in January 1996, and due diligence reviews and further negotiations took place through February and into March until the announcement was made on 25 March. Walther recalled that everyone was taken by surprise,

> 'People were not surprised that Clerical Medical was being taken over, but no one had put our name alongside that of the Halifax so I think confidentiality was very well maintained throughout the exercise.'

Most had assumed that NatWest would be the winner. Indeed, on 26 February, *The Daily Telegraph* had written, **NatWest favourite for Clerical Med**.

On the announcement, some commentators, Alex Brummer in *The Guardian* and *Lex* in the *Financial Times*, wondered if Halifax had paid too much – the price was £800 million. In the light of developments over the following 12 months the truth was that Halifax probably secured itself a bargain. And indeed *Lex* conceded as much,

> ' ... the price tag of £800 million does not look excessive. It represents a premium of £140 million above the value of the funds. But there will be some cost savings. *Halifax Life* farms out its administration; bringing that in-house is expected to save an estimated £10 million or more a year. The internal review under

way at the Clerical should yield further savings. The question is whether Halifax should have waited for a larger prey. But prices are likely to go up, as competition for the few reasonably large mutuals on the block intensifies. And the deal is strategically sound. At flotation, Halifax will be a broad personal financial services company, well-placed to adapt to a rapidly shifting personal savings market.'

Halifax and Clerical Medical had different motives in discussing the price. Clerical Medical wanted to say it had negotiated a very good price for its policy holders. Halifax wanted to say it had secured a bargain although it also wanted to deter other bidders and was therefore reasonably content if the media said it had paid a very full price.

Why did Clerical Medical put itself up for sale rather than opt for a public flotation, a route taken so successfully by the mutual building societies and Norwich Union? Walther's answer in 1997 was,

'In 1995 conditions within the life assurance industry were difficult. We were not writing new business on a profitable basis. We felt we would get more money for the with-profit policy holders if we found a single buyer and if we found the right buyer we would have more control over our own destiny. If we had floated, by now we would have been taken over but we would not have been in control of our own destiny.'

And what was Halifax's thinking?

As part of the merger with Leeds, *Leeds Life* and *Leeds Unit Trust* businesses had been merged with *Halifax Life* and its fund management and unit trust business. Once that was done, as James Crosby put it, 'We were immediately faced with having to get on and develop this business.' Long-term savings and protection were seen as strategically attractive in terms of growth. Furthermore, Halifax felt it lagged its competitors in its diversification into these areas. The possibility of building up distribution of *Halifax Life* and unit trust products through independent financial advisers (IFAs) was seen as too slow and there was also the feeling that they would not be enthusiastic about selling Halifax branded products.

As the Halifax moved in its thinking towards growth in this area by acquisition rather than organically, one or two potential candidates sprang to mind. As we have seen, discussions with Clerical Medical began in August 1995, and through the autumn the benefits became apparent. Crosby remembers that the love affair took time to develop,

> 'It was surprising because it took quite a few meetings, maybe two a month for two or three months, before we fully understood the quality of the fit that we could achieve here and started to really believe that we should go for it in the sense of actually making it happen. I suppose that was October 1995.'

And what was so attractive about Clerical Medical?

> 'It had a very established franchise in the IFA sector. It had a brand that was well-recognised for good standards of dealing with people and high business values. It also had a complementary focus in that we aren't specifically an upmarket brand in the IFA sector. It also has a very important off-shore business and that's an essential part of being a leading IFA office in the UK today, so that was an important factor as well.'

Was it a problem fitting the acquisition in to the conversion timetable?

There was a small window of opportunity in the spring of 1996 and Halifax had to convince Clerical Medical that this had to be seized, because although Halifax became progressively more enthusiastic about the acquisition it was not prepared to jeopardise the conversion in any way. As Crosby said,

> 'The one thing that would never move was the timetable and we would walk away the moment it looked threatened. I guess we would have done because we had the benefit of knowing that the conversion project was much, much bigger and much, much more important in that context.'

Further consolidation

The whole exercise of merger and conversion was designed to position the Halifax for a profitable future. On 3 June 1997, the future was here. What was the Halifax going to do with it?

There were plenty of people willing to offer their advice. Most, especially in view of its strong cash position, were expecting acquisitions.

Back in January 1997, the *Financial Times* was anticipating where it might strike,

> 'In theory, the Halifax should be able to find a good home for that money. With a 20 per cent share of the mortgage market, it could snap up a further 5 per cent – in effect any one of its old peer group apart from Nationwide – before hitting monopoly constraints. The scope for cost savings makes this an attractive option, but willing victims at the right price will be hard to find. It might also make sense to buy a life assurer, given Halifax's goal of becoming the UK leader in personal financial services.'

The *FT* went on to suggest that Legal and General would fit nicely with Clerical Medical or the more bold step of a merger with Prudential to create a rival for Lloyds TSB. However, it cautioned against such a risky venture reminding Halifax of the disastrous TSB acquisition of Hill Samuel. It concluded,

> 'Halifax will have to come up with a watertight business case if it wants to justify an acquisition rather than handing spare cash back to investors.'

There was no doubt that the City expected further consolidation in the banking sector. Jon Leonard, banking analyst at Salomon Brothers, spoke for many when he said,

> 'Everybody is talking to everybody else and everyone is doing numbers on everybody else and everybody is watching everybody else. The scene of UK banking could change quite quickly.'

With or without acquisitions or merger, the Halifax was in a very strong position to grow organically. It could move forward on several fronts. In the mortgage area, it was immensely strong with no less than £79 billion loaned to 2.5 million people. In the liquid savings market, its share was 16 per cent. In retail banking, it had only been allowed to participate since 1986 but nevertheless already enjoyed a share of 4 per cent of current accounts, 4 per cent of unsecured loans and 3 per cent of the credit card market. In personal life assurance, it was already the largest arranger of building and contents policies and the necessary analysis of all its members and customers during conversion would enable it to sell in future to those 20 million customers rather than just its mortgage holders. In long-term savings, Halifax held a 3 per cent share but, through Clerical Medical and *Halifax Life*, expected to double it to 6 per cent within five years.

And Blackburn firmly denied that satisfying shareholders would mean a bad deal for former members or customers or that plc's were the only organisations capable of necessary tough decisions,

> 'Both *Old Co. Halifax* and *Old Co. Leeds* prided themselves on being commercial and the evidence for that was in the cost-income ratios of the two organisations. When I was at the Leeds, we closed about sixty branches which was very counter-culture to building societies at the time. It was quite a statement. The Halifax had also taken a number of steps to reduce its cost-income ratio.
>
> As a plc there will be an even sharper focus and a continual quest for cheaper and more cost-effective ways of delivering service to customers. But I would like to think that our focus on the customer will not be blunted by the requirement to satisfy shareholders because I really do think that unless you've got the customer propositions clear and you've got the staff correctly recruited, trained, motivated and rewarded, then you don't stand a cat in hell's chance of satisfying shareholders. However, the one big difference will be the constant foot on the accelerator which plc will demand.'

Banking is no passing fad

Halifax had always emphasised how competitive were the marketplaces in which it operated. It was now a bank and competing with the leading clearing banks, Lloyds TSB *et al.* But it will also be competing with supermarkets. As *The Economist* said in January 1997,

> 'Bread, milk, mortgage? ... by the middle of this year, shoppers at all Britain's main supermarket chains will find the combination on offer ... Supermarket bosses insist that banking is no passing fad.'

Marks and Spencer has already established a substantial business covering charge cards, consumer loans and investment products, and in 1996 Tesco extended its customer loyalty card scheme to include debit and savings facilities. Its ClubCard Plus account pays a highly competitive interest rate of 6 per cent on cash balances. Following Tesco, Sainsbury launched Sainsbury's Bank in October 1996 and Safeway launched a debit card that its customers could use in several retailers.

And by the autumn of 1997 Tesco and Sainsbury were beginning to make an impact. Under the headline, **Tesco serves up a tasty 6.5 per cent**, it was commented,

> 'The extremely attractive rates offered by Tesco's new savings account, launched this week, and Sainsbury's existing account are putting the building societies and banks to shame.'

Banks began to react in different ways. NatWest struck a deal with Tesco to administer its accounts (albeit not for long) and Bank of Scotland negotiated a stake in Sainsbury's Bank. On the other hand, Sir Richard Greenbury, chairman of Marks and Spencer, and John Gildersleeve, a Tesco director, both left the board of Lloyds TSB, because of conflict of interest.

Halifax, along with the other banks, will have to counter this competition and the supermarkets themselves will undoubtedly make some serious mistakes in learning their new trade. They will remember that the long-established American retailer and mail-order company, Sears, nearly bankrupted itself when it diversified into financial services in the 1980s.

At least the banks and the newly converted building societies will start from a very profitable position. In 1996 the five leading clearing banks – Abbey National, Barclays, Lloyds TSB, Midland and NatWest – produced a combined pre-tax profit total of £8.4 billion or £180 for every British adult. Their average return on equity was over 22 per cent compared with 15 per cent for the USA, 10 per cent for Germany, 6 per cent in France and a negative return in that country of banking success, Switzerland.

Will the good times last? As Alliance & Leicester, Halifax and Woolwich all converted from mutual building societies to shareholder-owned banks, the High Street is looking seriously overbanked. All have branches nationwide and all have put forward plans to expand aggressively into pensions, insurance and consumer lending. Competition on interest rates has been muted in the last 12 months because the societies effectively locked in their savers and borrowers waiting for their windfall. That period has now ended and competition on this front is likely to intensify.

Apart from supermarkets, the main competitors to the banks, new and old, will, of course, be those building societies that have remained mutual. They have learned to state their case strongly and the main plank of that case is that as they do not have to pay dividends to shareholders they will be able to offer their borrowers lower rates and their savers higher rates. They have received some support in their contention, the first of which came from the Building Societies Ombudsman Council, which said in June 1996 that there was considerable evidence to suggest that,

> 'Over the longer term, a mutual building society which is run solely for the benefit of its members is likely to provide house buyers and savers with a better deal than a publicly quoted company.'

The Council was supported by the March 1997 edition of *What Mortgage?* which had found that out of 72 lenders, the top 25 offering the best value to customers were all mutual building societies.

One of the results will surely be greater consolidation with the remaining large mutuals acquiring their smaller rivals and banks trying to acquire building societies to build market share without sacrificing margins. Roger Boyes was not alone in predicting the end of the mutual building society industry when he said,

The Guardian 12 January 1996

> 'They are a dying breed. There will be one or two small ones which I am sure will survive with a local franchise. If the middle ground is there in 20 years I will be astonished. You'll get all the "We'll fight them on the beaches" stuff from the Nationwide and others but at the end of the day economic forces will overwhelm them.'

263

In what sort of shape did the Halifax emerge to take on and beat all the competition?

Rifle instead of shotgun

From April 1994 until June 1997 some people at the top of the Halifax had been almost totally absorbed in the merger and conversion process and almost *everyone* in the organisation had been involved from 25 November 1994 until June 1997. As we have seen, this had meant increased work for everyone, and for some a seven-day-week regime for months on end. When it was all over, Boyes said,

> 'The merger and flotation have been all-consuming even though we have tried not to make it so. There hasn't been a day nor a week-end these last two years when I haven't had to do something on flotation. In the last three months I don't think any of us has had a week-end off at all. We were working seven days a week on documentation and everything that went with it. It was quite stressful. I think everyone was getting a bit jaded towards the end.'

Mike Ellis said,

> 'An enormous debt of gratitude is owed to the front line staff who have coped so magnificently throughout the merger and conversion process and to customers, the majority of whom have shown considerable patience and understanding. David Walkden and his team at Head Office worked miracles and the impact on all our personal lives, and that of our families, over such a long period would hopefully not be repeated. However – never say never again.'

But Boyes, Ellis and everyone else were well aware that the existing business had to be run in the knowledge that competitors would quickly take advantage of any lapse. Did anything beneficial emerge from all the extra work apart from the general positioning of the society for the future which was the motivation for the whole exercise?

John Miller was convinced that it did,

> 'Conversion forced the society to reorganise its data around individual customers rather than products. Halifax now has the ability

to see at a glance the customer's full "relationship" including a credit history.'

Jon Foulds agreed,

'De-duplication of the Leeds and Halifax registers occupied 1500 people for most of a year. That gives you some feeling for the sheer scale of the operation. But the benefit that comes out is that we are probably the only financial organisation that knows exactly how many customers it has got. It is an auditable number. We know how old they are and we know what their transaction history is. In other words we have a database of unequalled quality and part of our challenge now is to use that database to mount a series of rifle shots to offer products to people at a time in their lives when they are most likely to want it instead of using a shotgun approach offering 16 different products to anybody and everybody.'

Some, notably Prue Leith, were concerned that the pressure of competition and the need to provide ever-growing profits to satisfy financial institutions – a situation not helped by the high and therefore demanding share price on flotation – could lead the Halifax to make decisions that would boost short-term profits but which would not necessarily be beneficial to the company in the longer term.

Roger Boyes refuted the argument about short-termism,

'Prue has a point. There is the temptation to go for short-term profits but if you are delivering outstanding customer service, if you've got your business advantage, if you are the employer of choice, if you do have an outstanding working relationship or form of partnership with your suppliers, what you've actually got there are the ingredients of an outstanding business. If you've got all that in place, really got it, not just talking about it, then you will have the wherewithal to satisfy shareholders. You may have a mismatch in terms of timing but I think that is manageable. Providing you keep telling the market what you are doing and why you are doing it I think the market is not quite as short-term as a lot of people believe it is.'

And did the windfalls given away by the building societies and Norwich Union create a consumer boom so feared by many economists and analysts? The Bank of England commissioned the polling organisation,

MORI, to conduct a survey among recipients of windfalls. Its conclusions, published in early September 1997, suggested that of the estimated £35.9 billion effectively given away, only £5.9 billion was spent immediately on consumer items. A further £5.9 billion went into various forms of savings, £700 million went on debt repayment and the vast majority, £23.4 billion, was left in the shares of the demutualising society or insurance company.

In October 1997, it is impossible to say how much difference to the British economy the demutualisation programme would have. In theory, no one was any richer. If members' holdings were worth £30 billion now, they were worth £30 billion, or close to it, last year.

The Guardian 8 January 1997

In practice the difference was liquidity. In 1996 members could say 'I've got a holding in the Halifax worth £2500'. In 1997 they could say 'I've got £2500 in cash'.

The British economy is in better shape than it has been for a generation and scarcely needs a boost. However, if the survey above is correct, and most beneficiaries of demutualisations continue to treat their holdings as long-term savings, the overall effect will be negligible. Furthermore, the possible harmful, inflationary boost in spending has been so well flagged that a newly independent Bank of England will surely act through interest rate rises to slow the economy down if it feels the necessity.

In the autumn of 1997, Jon Foulds as chairman and Mike Blackburn as chief executive could look back on three and a half years of monumental effort with enormous satisfaction. In truth, the whole process of merger and conversion had begun many years before that. If we accept that in the world of commerce only the efficient, and those who adapt to changing circumstances, survive, it was inevitable that the Leeds Permanent Building Society was not going to survive as a separate entity. Blackburn, Boyes and Miller understood that. Once Blackburn had gone to Halifax, Boyes and Miller made the strategically sound decision to seek a merger and worked hard and skilfully to ensure that it was with a compatible partner.

Foulds understood it too and put together a board at the Halifax where every member possessed experience and expertise pertinent to the Halifax's future aim of being the country's biggest and best personal financial services provider.

The overwhelming reason that the merger and conversion went through so smoothly was that a small group of people understood the need for an absolutely professional organisation and were able to convince everyone around them. It did not make for a comfortable life. Fortunately they had the strength to change.

APPENDIX

House prices, average earnings and retail prices, 1956–97

Period	Av. price new houses		Av. price all houses		Earnings ratio
	£	Increase %	£	Increase %	
1956	2,280		2,133		3.08
1957	2,330	2.2	2,181	2.2	3.00
1958	2,390	2.6	2,258	3.5	3.00
1959	2,410	0.8	2,258	0.0	2.86
1960	2,530	5.0	2,373	5.1	2.81
1961	2,770	9.5	2,593	9.3	2.91
1962	2,950	6.5	2,765	6.6	3.02
1963	3,160	7.1	2,966	7.3	3.09
1964	3,460	9.5	3,243	9.4	3.14
1965	3,820	10.4	3,578	10.3	3.23
1966	4,100	7.3	3,865	8.0	3.27
1967	4,340	5.9	4,085	5.7	3.34
1968	4,640	6.9	4,449	8.9	3.37
1969	4,880	5.2	4,640	4.3	3.26
1970	5,180	6.1	4,975	7.2	3.14
1971	5,970	15.3	5,632	13.2	3.23
1972	7,850	31.5	7,374	30.9	3.78
1973	10,690	36.2	9,942	34.8	4.45
1974	11,340	6.1	10,990	10.5	4.16
1975	12,406	9.4	11,787	7.3	3.57
1976	13,442	8.4	12,704	7.8	3.34
1977	14,768	9.9	13,650	7.4	3.29
1978	17,685	19.8	15,594	14.2	3.30
1979	22,728	28.5	19,925	27.8	3.64
1980	27,244	19.9	23,596	18.4	3.56
1981	28,028	2.4	24,188	2.5	3.23
1982	28,508	1.7	23,644	−2.2	2.89
1983	31,678	11.1	26,471	12.0	2.98
1984	34,160	7.8	29,106	10.0	3.09
1985	37,308	9.2	31,103	6.9	3.05
1986	43,646	17.0	36,276	16.6	3.29

APPENDIX

Period	Av. price new houses		Av. price all houses		Earnings ratio
	£	Increase %	£	Increase %	
1987	51,290	17.5	40,391	11.3	3.40
1988	64,615	26.0	49,355	22.2	3.82
1989	73,820	14.2	54,846	11.1	3.89
1990	77,556	5.1	59,785	9.0	3.87
1991	75,989	−2.0	62,455	4.5	3.74
1992	73,441	−3.4	60,821	−2.6	3.43
1993	76,143	3.7	61,223	0.7	3.34
1994	77,074	1.2	64,762	3.9	3.40
1995	78,983	2.5	65,649	1.4	3.33
1996	81,716	3.5	70,537	7.4	3.45
1997 (est)	89,888	10.0	75,958	7.7	3.55

INDEX

Abbey National 116
    compared with Halifax 250
    conversion scheme 143
    ends cartel 44
    flotation 197
    increased share purchases 246
Accord, union magazine 162
ADL 84–8
    suggest Leeds merge 86–7
advertising, banks 46
advisers *see* ADL; Cazenove & Co;
    Merrill Lynch; Warburg
AGM 150, 158
Allen & Overy 128
Alliance & Leicester 87, 95, 228
    flotation monitored 234
    Halifax compared with 251
    share price 246
announcement of merger
    accounts, new 21, 23–4, 25–6
    computer system, modifying 23–4
    control room 24
    forced 18ff
    and government 32, 33
    helpline 22, 25
    planned 107–8
    press 21, 22, 23, 25
    speculators, stopping 22
    staff, concern for 23
    story, *The Independent* 18–20
    television 26
Archer, Ronnie 66
Arthur D Little *see* ADL
assets
    Halifax BS 48, 49, 74, 100
    Leeds 52, 100
Atchison, Judy
    against merger with N & P 82
    appointed to Leeds 77
    helpline script 25
    marketing role 161
ATM machines 160
auditors *see* KPMG

bad debt problem, Halifax 69, 70
bancassurance 98, 125
Bank of England 45, 101
    capital ratio 206
    Halifax flotation 195–6
    MORI poll 265–6
bank status, Halifax 118
Banking Insurance and Finance
    Union *see* BIFU
banking services, new Halifax 159–60
banks
    advertising 46
    give mortgages 44–6
    restricted 43
    supermarkets acting as 261–2
Barings Bank 224
Barr, Malcolm
    against early merger 88
    board appointments 80
    merger talks 104
    at SGM 151
basic distribution, shares 140, 240
Bennett, Stephanie, research 165, 170
Bentley affair 50–1
Berkowitz, Len 221
best practice
    Halifax 76
    Leeds 78
BIFU 34
bird codenames *see* Project Aviary
Birmingham Midshires BS 115
Birrell, Jim
    background 69–70
    conference summary 64
    pro-merger 73
Blackburn, Mike 19, 22–3, 75, 127
    appointed to Leeds 55
    background 70–1
    on banks 43–4
    comment after merger 177–8
    on conversion, SGM 243
    on diversification 76
    Halifax 72, 81

270

Leeds 55, 77–9
    joint letter to MPs 33
    meeting on merger 100
    on merger 91
    on plc 261
    report on 94–5
    staff reassurance 156
    talks to Miller 97–8
Blue Book, The 8–9
board of directors, new 161
Boleat, Mark, book 40–1
bookbuild 248
boom *see* building boom; consumer
    boom
borrowers
    drop in numbers 49
    Leeds/Halifax 100
Boston Consulting Group 80
Boyes, Roger 20, 21–2
    on advisers 227, 228–9
    on conversion 187
    joins Leeds 77
    joint letter to MPs 33
    management dinners 168–9
    meeting on merger 100, 105, 107
    with advisers 109
    merger dossier 101
    mutuality, end of 263–4
    National Provincial merger 82–3
    retains post 161
    short termism 265
    spokesperson 31
    staff reassurance 156
    work load 264
Bradford & Bingley 95
branch overlap after merger 104, 124
Briggs, Howard 53
Britannia BS 54
brokers *see* Cazenove & Co; Merrill
    Lynch; Warburg
building boom 49
building societies
    assets
        in 1939 38
        in 1994 42

banks, competition from 44–6
    borrowers, number of 42
    desire for home ownership 37
    history 37–45
    legislation 38
    lending, growth in 45
    mergers commonplace 84–5
    monopoly on finance 42
    mutual 263
    period of growth 38
    reduction in number 39
    restrictions, lifting of 62, 116
Building Societies Act 38
    became law 61
    free shares 141–4
    merger rules 152–3
    restrictions lifted 61–2
Building Societies Association 50, 115
Building Societies Commission 152–4
    Transfer Document 196–7
Building Society History, The 40
Building Society History in Transition,
    The 44

capital
    and conversion 117
    need for 65–6
carpet-baggers 25–6
cartel 42, 44
Cazenove & Co 64, 229–30
Chadwick, Chris
    appointed to Halifax 77
    subterfuge 106
Chapman, Roy 126
cheque book operation, Leeds 102
Cheltenham & Gloucester 95–6, 114–16
children's share allocation 208–9
Clerical Medical 256
    Financial Times on 257–8
clothing *see* uniforms
Cobden, William 37
Colby, Andrew 126–7
Coleman, Richard 227
Coles, Adrian, BSA 115–16
    on Blackburn 71–2

Colne, Nigel 125–6
competition 44–6
computer systems
   integration after merger 177
   modifying 23–4
   problems after merger 174, 175
Concannon, Sue 253–5
consumer boom 236–8
Converge 155, 157–8, 168
conversion
   accepted 128
   committee formed 187
   costs 188
   discussions 59–67, 111, 117–27
   documents 196–7
   initial reactions 26–30
   key issues 117–18
   mailing to members 188
   meetings with advisers 109–10, 112
   package deal 122
   possibility agreed 125
   put off 67, 72
   rumours 17–18
   scheme 140–4
   timetable 179–85
Conversion to plc 124–5
conversions, other 116
Cook, Derek 80
Cornwall-Jones, Mark
   dinner host 18
   pro-conversion 66
corporate structure 161
council houses sold 42
Coventry BS 115
credit cards 160
CREST 193–4
Crowther, Mike 191
Crump, Paul 234
customer base 265
customers
   benefits 162–3
      see also share allocation
   letters from 199–203
   questions 165–6

Daily Express 217–8, 251
Daily Telegraph, The
   complaints 215
   on flotation 250
   Halifax redundancies 157
   on merger 28
   and Warburg 225
database clean up 189–90
Day One of merger 174–8
deceased estates' share allocation 208
Denham, Algernon 50–1
Dept of Trade & Industry *see* DTI
Deutsche Morgan Grenfell 226
Dewe Rogerson 64
directors, after merger 161
disabled, share allocation 209–13
dissertation *see* Bennett, Stephanie
divorcees share allocation 216–7
Dodson, Eric 66
Drake, Leigh, book 44–5
DTI 138
Duggleby, Valery 199, 202

earnings, average 268–9
economic growth worldwide 236
Economist, The 237–8
   supermarket banking 261
Ellis, Mike 20, 23–4, 106
   asked to provide 'brief' 103
   legality, conversion scheme 143–4
   meetings on merger 100, 105–6
      with advisers 109
   memo to Blackburn/Folwell 108–9
   on postal strike 145
   praises staff 264
   pre-merger nerves 139
   pressure from Treasury 136–7
   on SGM 152
employees *see* staff
enquiries from customers 165–6, 171
ERM 68
estate agency, Halifax 73, 74
Evening Standard 26–7

Ferguson, Duncan 126
Fford, John 66
Financial Services Staff Federation 34
Financial Times 27, 30, 31, 251
  Clerical Medical 257–8
  Halifax plc future 260
Fitchew, Geoffrey 143
flotation 191ff
  The Daily Telegraph on 250
  helplines 199
  letters from members 200–1
  mailing 198–203
  others 186
  USA study 192
  see also conversion
Folwell, Gren 20, 21
  for conversion 65
  meetings on merger 100
    with advisers 109
Foulds, John 19, 20, 21, 138
  advocates wider powers 89–90
  on conversion 66, 77, 111–12
  on customer base 265
  new Halifax chairman 69
  on merger 90, 104
  on mutuality 105
  at SGM 242–3
  on variable distribution 150–1
  on Warburg 225–6
friendly societies 38
future of new Halifax 176

G8
  control of merger 156
  meeting 32, 137
General Accident 159
general election 239–40
Geraghty, Maeve 238–9
Gibbs, Sir Roger 18
Gilchrist, David 20
  concern for staff 23
  for conversion 64–5
  on merger 90, 122
  and Michael Hardern 214
  on mutuality 123

  on Shandwick 221
  told of merger idea 100–1
Glendale Federal 58
government
  bill, disabled savers' shares 212–13
  housing policy, 1940s 49
  and merger announcement 32, 33
Group of Eight *see* G8
Guardian, The
  Clerical Medical 257
  on flotation 29
  quote Blackburn 91
  Vesting Day comment 251
Gummer, Peter 163

Halifax (before merger)
  assets
    in late 1880s 47
    in 1903/39 48
    in 1940s 49
    at initial merger talks 100
  background 46–52
  bank status 118
  best practice 76
  budgets, lack of 59
  conversion agreed 128
  estate agency 73, 74
  Foulds appointed 69
  Halifax Equitable, merger with 48
  meeting with Leeds 31, 32
  merger with Leeds
    agreed 128–9
    considered 56–7, 91–6
    feasibility of 79, 86–8
  Mission Statement 72
  objectives 89
  rigid structure 101, 166–7
  services offered 72–3
  staff reaction to merger 171
  valued on stock market 65
  see also under conversion
Halifax Action Group 35
Halifax Financial Services 159
Halifax Life 118, 258

Halifax plc
  Abbey National, compared 250
  Alliance & Leicester, compared 251
  banking services 118, 159–60
  Clerical Medical acquisition 256–9
  computer
  integration 169, 177
  problems 174, 175
  customer
  contact down 175
  reactions 176–7
  Day One 174–8
  executives 107
  future, views on 176, 259–60
  key positions 124
  managers' meetings 171–2
  manual 172
  strategy 107
  summonses 201
Halifax share dealing service
  see HSDL
Halifax Television News 163
Hambros Bank 79, 128
Hardern, Michael 214
Harrington, Tom 54
helplines 231–2
  Day One of merger 174
  flotation 199
  merger announcement 22, 25
Hemingway, Peter
  legislation 71
  replaces Walker 54
Hepburn, Robin 20
Heseltine, Michael 138
Hill, Enoch 48
Hirst, Rachel 18, 20, 220
Hobson, Oscar, book 38–9, 47, 49
Hodge, Ralph 125
Home Arranger service, Leeds 79
Hornby, Dick 57–8, 67
Hotson, Anthony 133, 224
house
  ownership, growth 37, 41–2
  prices 68, 75, 268–9
housing market, boost 42

HSDL 194, 247, 253, 254
Hundred Years of the Halifax, A 38
Hyde, Leonard
  critical of merger 36
  on destruction of Leeds Permanent
    general manager, Leeds 53, 151

Independent, The
  on flotation 251
  news of conversion 17–18
  reaction 28–9
  on Warburg 225
Independent Union of Halifax Staff 34
  see also Nicholls, Ged
inflation 40
insurance 73
interest rates 39, 67–8
Interest Rates Undertaking 44
investors advised 114–15
IT after merger 169
IVR 199

Jarratt, David 157–8
Johnston, Graham 106, 121–2
  conversion
    documents 196–7
    scheme 141, 142
Jowett, Chris 210
Judge, Peter
  against conversion 243–4
  critical of merger 35–6
  at SGM 149

Kay, Prof. John 125
King, John 80, 121, 122
Kirkbright, John, Project Aviary 92
Kitson, Sir Timothy 32, 81
KMPG 222–3
Knight, Christopher 228
Knight, Michael 70

Labour government, election 239–40
leak to media 17–18, 20
  see also under announcement of
    merger

Lee
  David 66
  John 101, 157–8, 163, 166–8, 235
Leeds
  assets
    1920s/30s 52
    at initial merger talks 100
  background 52–5
  best practice 78
  Blackburn appointed 55
  cheque book operation 102
  conversion, study on 79
  direction, lack of 85–6
  expansion 43
  Halifax, merger suggested 88
  loss of name, reaction to 171
  meeting with Halifax 31, 32
  merger with Halifax
    agreed 128–9
    considered 56–7, 91–6
    feasibility of 79, 86–8
  and National & Provincial 81–2
  new savings accounts 80
  Southdown, merged with 80
  staff
    lack of confidence 174
    reaction to merger 171
    reassurance 22, 31
  strategic plan 77–80
  and Woolwich 52–3, 54, 95
Leeds and Holbeck 54
legal issues
  conversion scheme 142
  merger 108–9
legislation 38, 40
  disabled savers and shares 212–3
  see also Building Societies Act
Leith, Prue 80, 265
lending
  free market 58
  growth in 42, 44–5
Letter of Common Intent 129
letters from members 199–203
Liberator Building Society 38
life assurance 103

limited company defined 63
Linklaters & Paines 64, 122
  conversion advisers 221–2
  Options A–E 111
Listing Particulars 197
Little, Arthur D see ADL
livery see uniforms
Lloyds
  Blackburn and 70–1
  and C & G 114, 115, 117, 121
Long Form report 197
Lourie, Serge
  against merger 34–5
  on conversion 242
  at SGM 149–50
loyalty cards 261–2

Maclean, Ian 51
mailing
  conversion documents 188
  error 207
  flotation documents 198–203
Manser, John 18
Marsh, Gary
  joins Halifax 59
  share allocations 216
  on Whitehouse 70
Martin, Paul
  comments about Day One 175–6
  coping after merger 169–70
  on television facility 164
meetings see under merger
membership records, clean up 189–90
Memorandum of Agreement 40
MENCAP 213
merger
  agreed 128–9
  benefits 92, 102
  disadvantages 92–4
  executed 155–64
  Halifax considers 88–96
  initial reactions 26–30
  key positions 124
  Leeds
    National Provincial 81–2

Southdown 80
legal issues 108–9
meetings 31, 32, 100, 105–6
  after merger decided 137
  with advisers 112
  board on merger 124
  with Warburg 108
membership records 189–90
Miller against 82
negotiations 108–13
opposition 103
overlap 103
points agreed with Leeds 124
staff position 102
thoughts on 73
workshop 99
Merger Dossier East and West 101
mergers commonplace 84–5
Merrill Lynch 226–7
  The Offering Process 248
Miller, John
  appointed to Halifax 77
  background 82
  conversation with Blackburn 97–8
  effects of conversion 264–5
  meeting with Halifax 100
  new position 161
  programme office chief 156–7
  stopping new accounts 22
  talks to Boyes 101–2
minors *see* children's share allocation
Mission Statement, Halifax 72, 89
  The Blue Book 98–9
Mitchell, Austin 33
MMC
  case against referral 131, 138
  not referred 139
  reasons for referral 113, 124
Monckton, Alan 66
Monopolies and Mergers Commission
  see MMC
Morgan Grenfell *see* Deutsche Morgan
  Grenfell
MORI poll 265–6
Morris, John 171

mortgage tax relief 45
mortgages from banks 44–6
MPs, letter to 33
Mulcahy, Sir Geoffrey 18
mutuality 118
  agreed to retain 74
  building societies remaining 263
  defined 63
  meeting 122–3

Nabarro, William 31, 128, 129, 130
National & Provincial 37, 54, 81–2
  merger prospect, Halifax 96
Nationwide
  and Anglia merger 27
  merger prospect, Halifax 95
negative equity 75
Negotiation Agreement 128, 129
Nelson, Anthony 33
newsletter *see* Converge
newspaper reports 18–20
  see also invidual names
Nicholls, Ged
  BBC interview 26
  staff association meetings 162
Northern Rock BS 115

O'Brien, David 81
Observer 113
Offering Process, The 248
Office of Fair Trading 33, 113, 131–3
Option E 122
Options A–E 111, 120–1
overseas members' shares 213–14

passbooks 160
payouts *see* shareholders; shares, free;
  windfalls
Peat Marwick McLintock 64
Peck, Andrew of Linklaters 122
PEP 247
PIBS 63–4
  free shares 140
plc *see* limited company defined;
  Halifax plc

PLDR 205–6
Portsea Island Building Society 38
Post Implementation Review 222, 228
postal strike 145
Potter, Sir Raymond 51
press
    interest 21, 22, 23, 25
        see also individual newspapers
    release 21, 24
Prices and Incomes Board 39, 42–3
Project Aviary 91–6
project office set up 168
property *see* house
public limited company *see* limited
    company defined

recession 40, 68
Recommended Rate system 42–4
redundancies 102, 124, 156, 157
    voluntary 159
Reeves, Christopher 226
relocations after merger 162
repossessions 68
resolutions 145–6
retail prices 1956–95 268–9
Right to Buy 42
RNIB on share allocations 209
roadshow 248
Rothschild, merchant bank 64, 65, 67
Royal Commission, friendly societies
    38

Salomon Brothers 260
Schedule 16 document 157
secondments after merger 172
SGM 148–52, 158, 240, 242
Shandwick 219–20
share
    advice 246
    certificates burned 198
    price 194–5, 245, 249–50, 251–2
    volatility, avoiding 248
    see also share allocation
share allocation 140ff, 191–2
    basic distribution 140, 240

children 208–9
deceased estates 208
disabled, allocation 209–13
divorcees 216–17
forms 217–18
    mailing 207
    to institutions 247–8, 249
    overseas members 213–14
    price 194–5, 245, 255
    queries 232–3
    sales 193, 247
    traded for cash 238–9
    variable distribution 140, 142, 146,
        240
    worth 240
Shareholder Account
shareholders 109
social events after merger 173
Southdown BS, merger with Leeds 80
Southwell, Philip 227
Spalding, John
    background 58
    BSA committee 61
    for conversion 66–7, 244
Special Resolutions *see* resolutions
speculation, preventing 22
Spelman, Dick 23–4
    makeshift office 24–5
    told about merger 135–6
    on Whitehouse 70
staff
    after merger 102, 168, 170–4, 177
    compensation 234
    Ellis praises 264
    enquiries to 165–6, 171
    key positions after merger 124, 161
    and merger 102
    newsletter 32, 155, 157–8
    numbers 131
    reaction to merger 170–1
    reassurance 22, 23, 31, 155, 156
    redundances see redundancies
    relocation after merger 162
    training 160, 168
    unprepared for Day One 172–3

views on merger 157
workshop after merger 173
Stewart, Ian, MP 63
strategic plan, Leeds 77–80
strategy of new Halifax 107
summonses against Halifax 201
Sun, The 251
Sunday Telegraph
  flotation suspicions 121
  Halifax position 250–1
Sunday Times, The 29–30
supermarket banking 261–2
Swiss Bank Corporation 224-5
Symons, John 65–6

Taylor, James Dearnley 47–8
television
  interviews 26
  network, in house 163–4
Thomas, Rob 230
Thornborrow, David 159
Times, The
  Halifax share price 252
  on merger 90–1, 135
timetable of conversion 179–85
training *see under* staff
Transfer Document 196
Tweddle, Sir William 54

uniforms 160
unions 34
  magazine 162
  see also Nicholls, Ged
Urwin, Robin 136
USA study 192

variable distribution 140, 142, 146, 240
  complaint from member 150
  all members eligible 189
Vesting Day 251–5
votes
  conversion 241–2, 244–5
  merger 151–2

Walkden, David
  blueprint for merger 168
  mailings error 207
  selecting registrar 192–3
Walker, Stanley, Leeds manager 53–4
Walkinshaw, Margaret 157
Walther, Robert
  demutualisation, Clerical Medical 256–7
  flotation 258
Warburg 223–6, 228
  meeting with 108, 125
  OFT decision 139
  on presenting merger case 133
What shares are about 246
Wheway, Richard 66
Whitaker, Clive 168
Whitaker, Sir James 65
Whitehouse, Mike
  bad debt problem 70
  on conversion 65
  left Leeds 72
Wilson
  Claire 233
  Kevin 232, 234
windfalls 114–116
  C & G 121
  survey of recipients 266
Wood, John
  on conversion doubts 66, 125
Woolwich
  and Leeds 52–3, 54, 87, 95
  tax refund 71
workshop on merger 99
workshops, new society 162
Wycks, Charles 248
Yorkshire BS 115
Your Share Allocation Guide 249

Ziff, Arnold 54, 81